of related interest

How to Understand Your Gender
A Practical Guide for Exploring Who You Are
Alex Iantaffi and Meg-John Barker
Foreword by S. Bear Bergman
ISBN 978 1 78592 746 1
eISBN 978 1 78450 517 2

**Everything You Ever Wanted to Know about
Trans (But Were Afraid to Ask)**
Brynn Tannehill
ISBN 978 1 78592 826 0
eISBN 978 1 78450 956 9

Queer Sex
A Trans and Non-Binary Guide to Intimacy,
Pleasure and Relationships
Juno Roche
ISBN 978 1 78592 406 4
eISBN 978 1 78450 770 1

To My Trans Sisters
Edited by Charlie Craggs
ISBN 978 1 78592 343 2
eISBN 978 1 78450 668 1

Trans Love
An Anthology of Transgender
and Non-Binary Voices
Edited by Freiya Benson
ISBN 978 1 78592 432 3
eISBN 978 1 78450 804 3

THEY/ THEM/ THEIR

A Guide to Nonbinary and Genderqueer Identities

Eris Young

Jessica Kingsley *Publishers*
London and Philadelphia

Contains public sector information licensed under the Open Government Licence v3.0.

First published in 2020
by Jessica Kingsley Publishers
73 Collier Street
London N1 9BE, UK
and
400 Market Street, Suite 400
Philadelphia, PA 19106, USA

www.jkp.com

Library of Congress Cataloging in Publication Data
A CIP catalog record for this book is available from the Library of Congress

British Library Cataloguing in Publication Data
A CIP catalogue record for this book is available from the British Library

ISBN 978 1 78592 483 5
eISBN 978 1 78450 872 2

Printed and bound in the United States

Contents

TRIGGER WARNINGS

Dear Reader,

Throughout this book you will find discussions of gender dysphoria and its effects, of non-consensual sex and gender assignment and occasional mention of coercive surgical interventions made against people with non-normative gender or sexual presentations. I make mention several times throughout the book of myths, misconceptions and bad-faith media portrayals of trans, genderqueer and nonbinary people that some readers may find difficult to read about.

Also discussed throughout is violence, a fact of life faced by trans people all over the world. This includes discussion of the statistics surrounding physical assault, murder and sexual violence towards trans people, and in-depth descriptions of institutional and non-physical violence: the non-consensual outing of people as trans, genderqueer or nonbinary, as well as misgendering, the erasure of our identities, systematic inequalities in spheres such as work and housing and gatekeeping of trans people's access to medical treatment.

Certain chapters and sections may be difficult to read for specific reasons. In Chapter 4, on community, there is an in-depth discussion of TERF (trans-exclusionary radical feminist) and 'radfem' ideologies, and there are discussions in chapters 4 and 5 of hostility faced by trans and nonbinary people from *within* the LGBT community. Chapter 5, on our experiences in wider society, includes some discussion of family and romantic partner rejection and domestic abuse, as well as of sex and relationships and the potential difficulties therein for genderqueer people.

Chapters 6 and 7 are devoted to discussions of nonbinary and genderqueer people's experiences of mental health and medicine, respectively. Both chapters discuss the pathologisation of trans and genderqueer identities, as well as the harm caused by conversion therapy and the historical institutionalisation of individuals with non-normative identities (this is also discussed briefly in the statistics and demographics sections of the first chapter).

Chapter 6 also discusses in some depth my own and my interviewees' specific experiences with mental illness like depression and anxiety, as well as statistics surrounding suicidality and substance abuse, linked to gender dysphoria and minority stress.

Anecdotes in Chapter 7 and to a lesser extent Chapter 6 discuss in detail specific instances of traumatic experiences with medical professionals, including a description of one of my own early traumatic experiences with a doctor, lasting for several paragraphs. Chapter 7 gives cursory descriptions of some surgical options for trans and nonbinary people.

Chapter 8 is devoted to discussion of our experiences with laws and the legal system, and as such includes discussion of experiences with the police, statistics and some specific anecdotes recounting domestic abuse.

I hope that those of you who need it find this warning helpful, and I urge you to skip over or approach in your own time sections or chapters which you might find difficult or traumatic to read.

Thank you for reading on,
Eris

CHAPTER 1

An Introduction to Nonbinary and Genderqueer Issues

Introduction

The purpose of this book is to introduce readers to the concepts, contexts and daily struggles of nonbinary-identified and genderqueer people – people whose gender identities lie outside the simple binary of male and female. We're a distinct social group existing within the larger transgender and LGBTQ communities, with our own set of vulnerabilities and privileges.

Nonbinary people are becoming more and more visible every day, in movies, TV shows, books (and no longer just science fiction!) and the news, on the runway, even in schools and workplaces. Several celebrities, including Jaden Smith, Amandla Stenberg and Miley Cyrus, have come out as trans or at least gender-nonconforming in some way; activist Maria Munir came out as nonbinary to President Barack Obama during a London town hall meeting in 2016.

Our sudden visibility has come with some backlash: genderqueer people have faced harassment, public ridicule and even violence from people who refuse to accept or try to understand us. But there have also been people willing to listen, to whom our gender identities are not unnatural or impossible but simply another one of the complexities which make us human.

This book is for those people: the people who want to understand but might not yet have the means to do so. Most nonbinary people find the community through the internet. I did, and I've found the vast majority of my interviewees through the internet as well. The terminology we use to describe ourselves, rooted conceptually in queer' theory and the work of Judith Butler and Michel Foucault, crystallised not in the classroom or in community meetings but on websites like LiveJournal and Tumblr. Most of it isn't standardised; self-applied terminology rarely is when it develops organically. Information about us – who we are, what the terms mean, how we differ from various other gender and sexual minorities – *can* be found on the internet by anyone with a mind to learn, but it is often contradictory or at least inconsistent. These websites can be hard to find, and while simply googling 'genderqueer' will get you some good sites written by actual genderqueer people, it will also get you a litany of shock-value, hate-mongering misery memoir articles, which are rarely written by the people they're about.

I don't claim to be master theorist, or even an expert on the subject of nonbinary and genderqueer identities: any authority vested in this book derives from statistics, extensive anecdotal evidence gathered from the community itself and a lifetime of personal experience. I will try to set out as clearly as possible the terminology you need to know to talk about and fully understand our gender identities, and illustrate some of the most common obstacles we face while navigating society at large.

These barriers take many forms; after all, we're trying to live our lives outside of, or in opposition to, one of the oldest, most ossified systems in human history: gender. Many domains – marriage, fashion, even language – are often rendered fully binarised, with no room left over for people who don't fit either label.

In addition, I believe that in today's culture of public shaming and virtue signalling there can be a fear associated with 'getting it wrong' which has perhaps hindered public willingness to learn and explore. I believe that every binary-gendered person should be given the chance to try and understand, and that it is inevitable that they should make mistakes. After all, we grow up in this system, it's like water to fish for us. It's a big job to get your head above water and break habits that have been drilled into us since birth; we of the nonbinary community should know this best of all.

On the other hand, being genderqueer *can* be exhausting. Because most people aren't readily equipped to understand our identities, we are constantly having to explain ourselves, our genders and our gender presentations. We get stares, invasive questions and even mockery daily, and this has led – quite reasonably – to the mentality among many of us that it is not our job to educate people outside our community. This is perfectly true, and it is why I feel privileged to have the energy and ability to explain on behalf of others.

Again, I don't claim to be an authority: I don't doubt I will get some things wrong (and I will happily correct any that are brought to my attention). My definitions are not the only ones; the identity terms I discuss are not the only valid ones. But I do believe that it is my duty to give what I can back to the community, and that begins with this book. As such, in addition to discussing my own experiences as a nonbinary person, I'll be making extensive use throughout this book of surveys and studies conducted by individuals and third-sector organisations like Stonewall and the Scottish Trans Alliance, as well as anecdotal evidence from a number of nonbinary and genderqueer people who have been so kind as to act as interviewees, and share their experiences with me. Throughout this book I will refer to these interviewees by their initials, or by a numbered 'XX' if they prefer to remain fully anonymous. The average age of my interviewees was 26, mode were 24 and 25 (three people each). My oldest interviewee was 45 (next oldest 32) and the youngest 20. I didn't ask my interviewees about ethnicity and race (as the questionnaire I used was meant to be more of a prompt for anecdotal evidence than an exhaustive demographic survey) but roughly speaking the majority of my interviewees were white British, or white American, Latino/a/x American and East or Southeast Asian American.

In this and in the chapter on language (Chapter 2), I will explain the most common terminology used in the nonbinary community, and discuss the ways English and a few other languages accommodate – or have adapted to accommodate – nonbinary identities. There have always been people who exist outside the binary of male and female. Many cultures extant today have an established third or 'other' gender category, and there have been documented cases throughout human history of people who consider themselves neither, both or multiple genders: these will be discussed in the chapter on the 'history' of nonbinarism (Chapter 3). The chapter on law (Chapter 8) will discuss the legal position of genderqueer people, mainly in terms of human rights, equality monitoring and official documentation, as well as in light of upcoming changes to the Gender Recognition Act – the UK's most pertinent piece of gender-related legislation.

In the chapters on relationships (Chapter 4), existing in wider society (Chapter 5), mental health (Chapter 6) and medicine (Chapter 7) I'll talk about what it's like to be genderqueer; the different ways we navigate the minefield of social interaction, the ways our identities can interact with our mental health, and the barriers and pitfalls we encounter when trying to obtain mental health and medical treatment. These chapters will also contain advice for binary-gendered people, doctors, counsellors and teachers, who want to know how best to support us in these environments. Chapter 9 will briefly discuss some of my hopes for the future of the nonbinary and genderqueer community. Finally, there will be a chapter (Chapter 10) listing the sources used in this book, and a list of resources: enlightening books, websites and authors for readers, binary-gendered and not, who want to go further.

Who are we?

The actual concept of *gender-queerness* and *gender nonbinarism*, the main, broad terms of identity with which this book is concerned and which I use largely interchangeably, are a bit abstract. They interact with and draw influence from a whole range of other identities and various areas of gender and social theory.

I always find that the more abstract a concept, the more I need to see its effect on the real world for it to make sense. This is probably why I'm not a philosopher. In that sense, perhaps the best way to start this chapter, and the book proper, is to try to sketch for you what my life, as person who identifies as nonbinary, looks like from day to day – ways in which it differs from the lives of people who aren't nonbinary and ways in which it doesn't. In this way throughout the book I hope to temper the abstract theoretical concepts and dry statistics with examples, from my life and from the lives of others I've known and spoken to.

I can't think of one single thing that fundamentally differentiates the way I live my life from someone who isn't nonbinary. I think we're all more similar than we are different. But there are a few things you might notice as you get to know me. My clothes, my voice and the structure of my face – after years of hormone replacement therapy – are such that I get called 'sir' and 'ma'am' in about equal measure.

I get tense when I sense a pronoun or gendered word coming up in a sentence – these words are the weathervane by which I gauge how I'm being perceived – but I try to react as little as possible. The receptionist at the dentist today, when explaining my question to her colleague, simply skipped over the 'her' or 'his', leaving the word out of her sentence. I don't like to encourage the use of either one (*they/them* is my preferred pronoun!), and I like to see what people do: will they decide on a pronoun, skip a word or even use the neutral pronoun I actually like to go by?

I still waver between answering to either pronoun, or to neither. I've got a floppy, hipstery haircut and a bit of a mustache that I'm trying to cultivate. I usually dress in clothes that the fashion industry deems 'unisex' – though they tend to come from the men's section. When I go out or if I'm not at work I try to play around a bit: I wear heels, suits, sack dresses, esoteric jewelry – though I think I'll always be rubbish at applying makeup. My new year's resolution for 2018 was to be *more femme*.

What I'm trying to say with all of this is that these are all ways by which I try to outwardly express an aspect of my personhood that I was never really given the tools to explore. When I say I'm nonbinary, that's a single word – like the visible part of an iceberg – being used to express a whole load of stuff underneath. It's complex and I'm still now trying to fully understand it. It has a palpable effect on my everyday life, on the way others perceive and treat me.

To put it very simply, my nonbinary gender identity means that I am neither a man nor a woman. Neither label describes me: I don't feel comfortable with the gender I was assigned at birth but neither am I simply *trans*gender, desiring to move from one end of a polarity to another. I'm not comfortable being called 'he' or 'she' in the third person – I like my friends and colleagues to refer to me as 'they' or simply by my name.

To dig a bit deeper, I feel that the idea of expressing myself *just* as a man or *just* as a woman would be to erase an essential part of who I am. I certainly don't begrudge anyone else their gender – contrary to some popular opinion, nonbinary people don't want to 'ban' gender, if such a thing were even possible – but I find that I'd much rather think of myself in terms of my writing ability, my love of cooking, the fears and ambitions I have for the future, than whether I'm male or female. If I could, I'd give up 'gender' entirely; I'd slough it off like an old skin and throw it away, and just be me.

But in order to leave gender behind – and I don't know if I'll ever entirely manage this – I've had to think about nothing *but* gender for a very long time. I've had to unlearn a lot of social conditioning, a lot of unspoken rules that were taught to me over the course of my life. I've had to endure a lot of scrutiny and felt more than a little anxiety and fear over the course of my transition.

Who am I?

I have a biography that reads like that of a lot of the gender-diverse people I know: I realised as a child that there was something *not quite right* about the way I was encouraged to act, to dress, to speak, to play, by the people around me. I could see that different people played different roles according to who they were. But the role it seemed I was being asked to play didn't match who I was. Did everyone feel this way sometimes? Would I grow out of it?

My parents, both fairly progressive, didn't try to force me into any traditionally gendered activities as a child; if I disliked wearing makeup it was because I don't like stuff on my face, if I didn't like sports it's because I was a bit lazy (though having to use gendered changing rooms certainly didn't help).

I think that somewhat ironically *because* of this childhood freedom, my transition began a bit later than it might have in a more conservative household. It was a long time before I realised that the discomfort I felt in department stores, restrooms, the doctor's office, filling out my passport application, at the DMV, was connected to my gender. It was even longer before I realised that there was anything I could do about it.

When I was a bit younger, still exploring the possibilities of alternative gender expression, the idea of having to use a gendered restroom, to *commit* myself in the view of others to gents or ladies and face scrutiny, ridicule or even violence in either one, was a constant source of stress. I'd try to steer my group of friends to places that had unisex toilets, or even to avoid using the restroom at all when I went out. This seems like a bit of a silly thing to worry about, but it had a palpable impact on my social life.

This is one of a million tiny daily trials that affect a majority of trans people: one study at UCLA's Williams Institute[2] found that of the 93 trans survey respondents, 54 per cent reported health problems due to avoiding public restrooms, including dehydration, UTIs and kidney problems. My discomfort in public gendered spaces, the threat of mockery and other sources of constant stress took their toll on me as they do on many of us: I grew up anxious, insomniac, depressed, and even now maintaining my mental health is a chore that takes daily, concerted effort.

These days I'm a little less stressed about what restroom to use, how I look and what people call me. I'm lucky enough to live in a place where hate crimes are relatively rare and I've learned to ignore stares, getting misgendered (called the wrong name or pronoun) or rude remarks – they reflect less on me than they do on the people that make them. No matter what I'm wearing or how I feel I generally keep my head high and try to project confidence, and usually no one questions me. I feel now – though I didn't always – that I have a right to exist.

But this confidence is borne of over a decade of self-doubt, anxiety and depression. It's taken years to build a thick enough skin, and become self-aware enough, to explore my gender publicly and without apology, and it often seems like there is very little standing between me and regression back into my wretched, pre-transition state.

As much as I want to say it's possible to exist as a happy, healthy genderqueer person in today's society, the reality is a bit more complex. It's true that now, today, this very minute, is better for us than the minute that came before it; we're more visible, we've got more explicit legal rights than we ever have before and we're gradually watching the world around us begin to think of gender in a more nuanced way. But just *living* is still quite often very difficult. We're still trans and as such we still face violence and rejection from our friends and families, and we still must navigate in public spaces not designed to accommodate us.

There is hope, however. It is visible genderqueer celebrities and public figures, social and legal acknowledgement of our existence, and, I hope, books like this one, that will make our day-to-day lives better.

Glossary

Before I go on I think it's time for a few definitions. There are a lot of words here with which the average cisgender person might not be familiar (including 'cisgender'). A lot of them are fairly clear from context but I want to make doubly sure we're all on the same page. At the same time, I don't want you (or me, for that matter) to get bogged down in academic terminology, so I'll be as clear, concise and jargon-free as possible.

Much of the terminology surrounding transgender people is quite new, and is often in flux. There is very little standardisation among much of nonbinary terminology past the relatively stable (though still occasionally contested) meanings of 'genderqueer' and 'nonbinary'. There are many terms to name and describe a nonbinary gender identity, most of which were developed, and are used by, the people to which they refer. The glossary below contains a few common useful terms for talking about gender variance and adjacent issues.

AMAB/AFAB: Assigned male at birth/assigned female at birth. These terms are often used to refer specifically to the sex that a trans or otherwise gender-nonconforming person was assigned when they were born (for example, a binary trans person who identifies as a woman could be described as AMAB). In most contexts it is disrespectful to talk about a trans person's assigned gender, especially without their consent, as this essentially constitutes outing them as trans. However in some cases birth sex must be discussed, for example in a medical context where a person's naturally-produced bodily hormones are relevant to treatment, and AFAB/AMAB represents a way to discuss this information while still acknowledging that the person in question is trans and doesn't identify with the gender they were assigned at birth.

cisgender: Someone who is not transgender and not nonbinary. The prefix 'cis' comes from Latin and means 'on the same side as', i.e. someone who has not crossed the boundary between the gender they were assigned at birth and a different gender (as is implied by the 'trans' in 'transgender'). Cisgender simply means someone who identifies, binarily, with the gender they were assigned at birth. Not in any way a slur or denigratory. Often abbreviated to 'cis'.

dysphoria: Gender dysphoria will be discussed further in Chapters 6 and 7 but generally refers to the discomfort a trans person feels due to the mismatch between the gender they were assigned at birth, and which people expect them to express, and the gender they identify with.

gender identity: The gender that a person considers themself to be.

gender-nonconforming: This is a catch-all term to refer to people whose gender identities and expressions don't match societal expectation. This term roughly includes transgender and genderqueer people, but also transvestites and crossdressers, and may include other, global categories of gender identity that don't have a Western analogue. A person can be cisgender and also gender-nonconforming.

gender presentation or expression: The physical manifestation (in appearance, dress, mannerisms and so on) of a person's gender identity. It's important to distinguish gender identity from gender expression, especially in contexts where being openly trans or gender-nonconforming is dangerous and gender identity must be hidden beneath a conventional presentation.

gender role: The social aspect of gender, for example the somewhat outdated expectation for men to be 'breadwinners' who work outside the home, and women to be 'homemakers'. 'Gender role' can also describe more subtle differences in social expectation, such as the expectation for women to perform various types of emotional labour: comforting, listening, caring, nurturing, etc.

gender-variant: Another catch-all term, often used in academic writing, which refers to any person whose gender presentation or identity is different from that which they were assigned at birth. Used similarly to transgender and gender-nonconforming but with different social and theoretical connotations. I use this term less than I use trans but it's still common in academic contexts.

genderfluid: A gender identity that changes from time to time. Genderfluid people can feel that they are female some of the time, male others, gender-neutral other times, and so on. A shifting identity. Genderfluid people can be accurately described using different gendered pronouns and labels at different times. Fluid identities will be discussed further in Chapter 4.

genderqueer: In the context of this book, unless otherwise specified, I'll be using 'genderqueer' to mean the same thing as 'nonbinary', though there are some important differences in the use and etymology of the term. Many people whose identities lie outside 'man' and 'woman' *don't* think of themselves as nonbinary, and I'll include a discussion of the reasoning behind this later in this chapter.

If I use the word 'genderqueer' slightly less frequently in this book than I use the word 'nonbinary' it's not intentional, it's only because I personally identify as nonbinary. This in turn is only because *nonbinary* is the term that was used by most people in the community where I first began exploring my gender identity. I include both terms because I want to remind the reader and myself that there's more than one valid way of describing these identities.

intersex: A person who, by a mismatch or unconventional formation of chromosomes and internal or external sex organs, is difficult to physically classify as male or female. An intersex condition can be accompanied by a genderqueer identity, but very often the intersex person is surgically 'sexed' by a doctor at birth, according to the wishes of the parents, and lives their life without thinking of themself differently from any other binary-gendered person. Further, an intersex person who is aware of their intersex status may not necessarily identify outside of the binary. Though intersex people *can* identify as nonbinary, and the gender identities of certain intersex people will be discussed in Chapter 3 in the discussion of 'nonbinary' historical figures, intersex conditions are not the focus of this book and an intersex condition neither necessitates nor increases the likelihood of a person identifying as genderqueer or nonbinary.[3]

misgender: A verb. To misgender someone is to refer to them as a gender other than that with which they identify, including by a gendered name. Cisgender people can be misgendered, but the social stigma associated with being trans and nonbinary, combined with the danger of 'coming out' and the lengths we must go to be recognised as our true gender identities, means that being misgendered can be harmful and upsetting. When you're trans, it can ruin your day, but it can also expose you to danger. To refer to a genderqueer or nonbinary person with *any* gendered label without their permission, unless they are genderfluid and currently identify as that label, would be to misgender them.

nonbinary: In this context *nonbinary* describes a gender identity which sits alongside many other identities, among which 'male' and 'female' are probably the most familiar. Generally speaking, and for the purposes of this book, 'nonbinary' broadly covers any gender identity which lies outside the one-or-the-other binary of 'man' and 'woman', 'he' and 'she', 'male' and 'female'. Nonbinary can also be spelled non-binary, but I'll be leaving out the hyphen in this text.

transgender: this is an umbrella term for someone who identifies as a gender which is different from the one they were assigned at birth. A trans person can identify as male, female, nonbinary, just 'transgender' or any number of other identities. Often abbreviated 'trans'. Many nonbinary and genderqueer people identify as trans, but some do not, and I'll discuss this fact further later on in this chapter. I use this word in this book in contexts where I specifically want to include both nonbinary/genderqueer people *and* binary transgender people, but acknowledge that these two groups may have different experiences, and that not all nonbinary and genderqueer people identify as trans. In this book I'll use 'trans' or 'transgender' when I'm talking about the experiences of the larger trans community, and 'nonbinary', 'genderqueer' and so on when I'm referring specifically to people who don't identify with a binary gender.

transition: The process a transgender, genderqueer or nonbinary person goes through in order to live fully as their true gender identity. Often associated with gender-affirming medical treatments such as surgery and hormones, but does not necessitate them.

transition (medical): Any medical treatment, including surgery and hormone replacement therapy, but also more 'cosmetically oriented' treatments such as hair removal, which a trans person goes through in order to alter their physical sex characteristics (i.e. body shape, genitalia, voice, even body hair, etc.) to aid their transition. These treatments make it easier for a trans person to 'pass', or be perceived as their actual gender. Medical options for nonbinary transitions will be discussed in the chapter on medicine (Chapter 7).

Thinking of gender

Some of the terms discussed above imply fundamentally different mental representations of gender, and of the relationship between the conventional labels of male and female. There are entire schools of thought devoted to studying the various ways in which gender can be conceptualised, but here I will limit myself to a few examples, so as to give an overview of the most common models of gender without veering too far into the theoretical.

The first and arguably most common model of gender is a binary one (see Figure 1.1). It can be thought of as a choice between two options, with no space to be occupied between. Under this model, a person can be only ever a woman or only ever a man, and never the twain shall meet.

Some people may conceptualise gender as binary but allow that not all people assigned female at birth are women, and not all people who were assigned male are men (see Figure 1.2). Under this system sex and gender are separate but the options are still only binary.

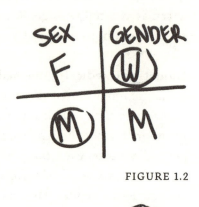

FIGURE 1.1

A slightly more nuanced view. Some people think of gender as a 'sliding scale', with M at one end and W at the other (see Figure 1.3). A person could conceivably exist at any point on the scale, with the ends of the scale being extremes of masculinity and femininity, 'man-ness' and 'woman-ness', though the definition of each of these is contentious and may change person to person. This is the first of this range of gender conceptions which allows for the existence of nonbinary and genderqueer people.

FIGURE 1.2

FIGURE 1.3

Yet another, more complex, model of gender may look like a graph with two or more axes, with binary extremes of gender identity on one axis and physical sex on the other, or even multiple diametrically opposed characteristics such as submissiveness/dominance, physical strength/weakness, butch/femme, etc. along the axes (see Figure 1.4).[4] This model is similar to the one described in Figure 1.2, but allows more variation in both gender and physical sex than Figure 1.2.

There are nearly infinite ways by which gender and sex can be measured, quantified or represented, and many people take a view of gender that is less rigid than even these flexible models (see Figure 1.5). Perhaps gender is a cloud of different social expectations and characteristics which interact, pushing and pulling and altering each other? Perhaps gender is measured on so many axes that it would look more like a porcupine than a graph?

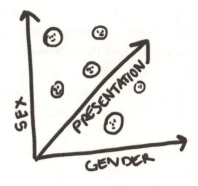

FIGURE 1.4

Perhaps gender is a linear journey beginning at birth and ending at death, which for some people is straight as an arrow, and for others is as twisted and tangled as a ball of string (see Figure 1.6). There are probably as many different possible mental representations of gender as there are gradations of male and female, or points on the graph, or even as there are people. Most of these, I imagine, are nuanced enough to accommodate the existence of both trans people and nonbinary people.

FIGURE 1.5

Sex versus gender

FIGURE 1.6

Over the course of this book I will occasionally discuss the idea of 'sex' as separate from 'gender'. It has occurred to me that some readers might not be familiar with this distinction. It isn't, after all, something most people are taught to think about. For the majority of people, the sex they are assigned at birth and the gender they identify with are the same, so it doesn't matter if sex and gender are different things. For trans people the physical sex of the person – their genitalia or chromosomes, which their doctor will have used to label them as 'female' or 'male' at or before birth – does not match up with the gendered behaviours and reactions they instinctually exhibit, which is often the opposite of the gender they were assigned at birth. This is known as being transgender.

Transgender children and young people often begin to feel a very deep sense of conflict as the way they are expected to behave clashes increasingly with the way they instinctively express themselves. They may also feel a strong sense of conflict or discomfort, that is to say dysphoria, with their bodies, especially genitalia and secondary sex characteristics like body hair and breasts. For a trans person, dysphoria can be remedied by being encouraged and supported to live as their preferred gender, and often by seeking transition-related medical treatment such as surgery or hormone therapy.

A genderqueer person will most likely have been raised as either male or female, and most likely will have either a penis or vagina and attendant chromosomes and hormones, but will not feel that either of these labels suits them wholly. They may feel that both or neither label applies, that they are 'male' and 'female' on different days or depending on their environment or emotional state. They may feel uncomfortable with the concept of gender at all, and wish to reject it categorically. For a genderqueer person, the idea of 'transition' doesn't necessarily represent a clear journey from point A (the gender one was assigned at birth) to point B (the 'opposite' gender). The process of 'coming out' as nonbinary can also have an extra layer of difficulty as many people still do not believe in the existence of genders outside male or female.

Transition, too, is difficult because most surgeries and courses of hormone treatment are designed – insofar as they are designed at all, which is a subject for a later chapter (Chapter 7) – to take the patient from one end of the gender/sex 'scale' to the other, or to move them between two fixed binary points. A nonbinary person may want to exist, physically, somewhere in the middle of the scale, or outside of it entirely, exhibiting no or many different sex characteristics.

A genderfluid person, also, may feel a need to alter their gendered appearance from day to day, and thus may not benefit from surgery or hormone treatment – and medical treatment is by no means the beginning and end of transition. It is my hope that this book will be as inclusive of and useful to genderfluid people, whose journey might not include transition-related medical treatment, as it is to any other variety of nonbinary-identified persons. Later chapters in this book will concern the mental health benefits of social transition and gender-affirming medical treatment in greater detail, and will discuss the experiences of transition for a variety of different people who identify outside the binary.

A theory of gender and gender variance

I'm not a gender theorist, but I'm increasingly aware that this book and its author have been influenced by a mode of thought known as queer theory, though my own ideas don't cleave perfectly to this model. To write this book without acknowledging the theoretical basis for my own gender politics would be disingenuous, and I think it will be helpful for readers of this book to know how I personally conceptualise gender.

Heavily influenced by the work of Judith Butler and Michel Foucault, among others, queer theory considers gender to be a flexible, performed identity which is subject to environment and context. This school of thought is called queer theory not because it applies only to members of the LGBT community but because it 'queers' or challenges the hegemonic idea of gender as a system, as a strict binary or as determined exclusively by biological sex. Thus, the identity label 'genderqueer' can be considered to challenge the existence of binary identities in a similar way to how queer theory challenges gender, sex and other 'systems' more generally.

The traditional binary model links bodily sex to gender in a causal relationship, claiming that one's gender is determined by *his or her* bodily conformation and, further, that this in turn determines who they are attracted to. This model is problematic for several reasons, not least of which being that gay, intersex and transgender people exist, and live lives which are in direct contradiction to this model. The theoretical basis for this book is one that accepts that gender and sex are two different things, and which, as per the work of Judith Butler, are *not* causally linked to each other.

Biological 'sex' is composed of several, sometimes contradictory, physical characteristics. On the other hand 'gender', conceptualised in different ways by different societies all over the world, is a set of social expectations, values and behaviours. These are performed by individuals raised in societies that uphold and perpetuate these social expectations. Gendered behaviour is taught, directly and indirectly, to each successive generation of people in a society, through observation, overt teaching in things like deportment and manners, and through positive and negative reinforcement; for example boys who play with dolls are often punished, girls who grow up to marry men and have children are often praised.

This joint social and generational transmission of behaviours explains why gender and its expression can differ between immediate relatives. This fact provides evidence for the idea that gender is *not* inextricably linked to biological sex. For example, a girl whose parents come from a more orthodox or restrictive society but who is raised in a more permissive one exhibits different gendered behaviours – performs femininity differently – than a girl who grows up in her parents' home community. If gender was *caused* by biological sex, which is determined for a child in utero, theoretically the girl should perform gender, should dress and speak and act, in the same way her mother does.

I'll admit this isn't an entirely plausible example; anyone can see that society teaches gendered behaviours and it's not my aim to set up biological essentialism (the idea of gender – and any number of other characteristics – as determined by biology alone) as some kind of straw man. But I think my example illustrates a weakness in the biological essentialist way of thinking, and opens the floor for the discussion of ways that gender is *learned* and *performed*, which are more useful for the purposes of this book and, I think, more true to life.

Sex has been used for millennia as a starting point by which previous generations (i.e. parents) shape the way individuals (i.e. their children) behave, and the way people are taught to perceive themselves and others. The bodily characteristics which comprise what we call 'sex' include chromosomes, internal and external sex organs, and naturally occurring hormones secreted by the body. In the majority of people these correspond to each other: generally people born with a penis and testes were influenced in utero by a testosterone hormone surge, and have bodies that produce testosterone and which have XY chromosomes.

Sex, especially hormones, does have an effect on behaviour and appearance. This, plus the shape of a person's genitals, which generally matches their hormonally influenced behaviours and aspects of appearance, perpetuate the human race as a loosely sexually dimorphic species though, again, by no means do the various axes of biological sex all always match each other. *Gender*, on the other hand, is the set of cultural values and behaviours that have been imposed on this loose dimorphism by *people*, over thousands of years and in countless different ways.

I've thought quite a bit about how to reconcile the school of thought that considers gendered behaviour to be entirely based on biology – the neater and more conventional view – and the one which considers gender to be a complete social construct, and which rejects any link between sex and gender whatsoever. There's considerable antagonism between both schools of thought and I see the argument between the two factions as counterproductive and extreme. Based on my own personal experience, and from countless conversations with trans, nonbinary and genderqueer people, I categorically disagree with the first view. I think the idea that gender is determined by sex alone is demonstrably false, simplistic and in many cases harmful. On the other hand I don't completely agree with the latter, either. I do think there's a link between biological sex and gender, but I think it's much more complex than a simple causal relationship.

I believe the most plausible explanation for that link lies in the field of cultural evolution. *Cultural evolution* is loosely defined as the way chronological cultural change, as happens over human generations, can be thought of like a Darwinian process, being influenced by the three processes of variation, selection and inheritance.[5] It is the study of the way specific aspects of human culture and behaviour perpetuate themselves.

In the field of cultural evolution it's an accepted fact that iteration – the generational repetition of any behaviour, from language learning to olympic sports – amplifies an original pattern or bias, strengthening patterns which may originally have been weak. I'm most familiar with these ideas as applied to the field of linguistics, to study how structure in human language might have emerged – how language may have gone from a loose collection of behaviours that vaguely signified meanings to a structured, learnable system that, importantly, *varies by geographic location and time* – but it was a bit of an epiphany for me to realise that the mechanisms of cultural evolution might be productively applied to sex and gender.

It seems plausible to me that a weak pattern created by sex hormones and genitals – such as the correlation between generally bigger body size, increased muscle mass and higher levels of aggression for people with penises, or the correlation between smaller, curvier bodies and higher body fat levels for people with vaginas and the ability to give birth – could become the basis for a global binary system.

A slight wrinkle occurs when you consider that there's an intermediate stage between hormones, which influence behaviour, and the social system of binary gender. Gender-based decisions, expectations and assumptions are assigned to a child as soon as doctors and parents discover the child's sex. Children grow up expected to behave a certain way based on how their parents name them, dress them, describe them to others and encourage them to behave – all because of the shape of the child's genitals and what the doctor tells the parents at or before the birth.

If the gendered behaviours expected to manifest were encouraged before they manifested, generation after generation, genitals could become a kind of shorthand for socialisation: people with penises are taught these things, people with vaginas are taught these things. This might have served an evolutionary purpose: the perpetuation of aggressive behaviour in children who were expected to grow up to be bigger and more muscular and more effective hunters, and the expectation of gathering and nurturing instincts in those who gave birth, might have been an efficient division of labour back when our ancestors were still scratching their living from the earth.

In order for children to learn gendered behaviours during their formative years, human sexual dimorphism must be visible before puberty, that is, visible before these hormone-influenced behaviours can manifest at puberty. But if human males and females had visibly indistinguishable genitals, for example, even if their bodies still produced either oestrogen or testosterone, it would have been impossible, for most of human history, for doctors and parents to assign gendered expectations to children before puberty. If this were the case I think it likely the gender binary would be weaker and there would be more flexibility in the gendered expectations placed on children – but that's a thought experiment for another day. As things are, the binary begins to be enforced in children, and children begin to absorb these gendered behaviours and expectations, long before hormones have a chance to do their work.

That the cultural evolution model allows for geographic variation is important as well, because it would also explain why the values associated with sex/gender vary from culture to culture, despite the sexual biology of the human species being consistent across racial or ethnic boundaries. This is important for trans people because we are the people for whom the distinction between sex and gender is most pertinent, and different cultures globally have come up with different categories for trans and gender-nonconforming people to occupy, with different expectations of behaviour.

For a cisgender person, the question of whether gender is determined by physical sex or by social expectations is largely moot: if they both match, what does it matter where gender comes from? But for a transgender person the origins of gender, and what they imply about the validity, longevity and innateness of gender as a system, are very important.

Analysing gender and biological sex through the lens of cultural evolution isn't new: scholars[6] have long been seeking to examine the way cultural transmission interacts with human biological evolution to create varying and changeable gender roles.[7] However, these papers generally begin with the assumption of innate differences between the genders, and focus more on the ways by which cultural evolution can be used to analyse and lessen gender inequality, that is to say, the oppression of people with vaginas by people with penises.

Since the true size of the trans population is only now beginning to be fully recognised, and our voices are only now beginning to be heard within academia, little work has been done as yet to explore how transgender people fit into this model. This is a difficult question to answer, and one which has given me lots of trouble: while the cultural/biological model allows for a flexible relationship between biological sex and culturally designated gender, it's not yet fully understood (and perhaps it never will be) exactly how the model allows for the highly demonstrable existence of people whose biological sexes don't match their genders.

But it's an incontrovertible fact that transgender people do exist: to ignore them in pursuit of a cleaner, more all-explanatory theory would be unscientific, and my goal here is to begin to create a theory of gender via cultural evolution which accounts for all the evidence. I believe that the difficulty here stems from the fact that the psychological, neurological and biological roots of gender variance are still not fully understood. Recent studies have indicated that biological sex assignment and the biological designation of a person's sexual orientation and gender identity – to the extent that they are biologically determined at all – may happen at different times in-utero,[8] as the foetus is influenced by gonadal steroids,[9] hormones and other epigenetic factors.

The psychological mechanics of the discomfort with and rejection of an assigned gender category has yet to be extensively studied. The studies that have been conducted on transgender psychology have been rife with unexamined prejudice and unconscious bias, and have often pathologised transgenderism, mistaking the rejection of a social role and attendant marginalisation stress for a psychological illness in and of itself. Our society has a preoccupation with equating any kind of variance to illness – a holdover from the Victorian pre-occupation with deriving scientific explanations for all phenomena. The logical progression of this mode of thinking is to try and find a cure. So-called gay and transgender 'conversion' therapies, which have their roots in psychoanalysis as practised at the turn of the twentieth century, have been proven to not only be ineffective at 'curing' sexual and gender variance, but also actively harmful to the health of the patient. The pathologisation of LGBT identities will be discussed further in the chapters on medicine and mental health.

Any psychological or neurological study which seeks to explore the 'root causes' of transgenderism is walking a very fine line: researchers must be aware, if they want to establish trust between themselves and the members of the community they want to study, of this long and painful history, and of the mistrust in medical and other institutional authorities it has created. Until this mistrust is addressed and institutions take steps to analyse gender variance on its own terms and in its own language, the biological and mental origins of the phenomenon may never be fully understood.

Presenting as nonbinary

After all that theory, I want to bring us back into the realm of the concrete and talk about how my nonbinary identity manifests in the real world, and how that affects the way people perceive me. My androgynous or 'queer' appearance is one of the first things people notice about me when they meet me, and it directly influences the way they treat me. Appearance and ambiguity of appearance, though it doesn't apply to everyone who identifies like I do, is at the heart of the issue for the majority of nonbinary and genderqueer-identified people, simply because humans in general are visual creatures: we draw conclusions and make judgments based on the appearance of the people we meet and we act accordingly.

So my appearance is something that I've cultivated over the many years since I first started questioning the nature of my gender, and the ability to *control* the way I look has long been the source of very much anxiety and the occasional feeling of powerful triumph.

Appearance, on the whole, affects the way we interface with the world. Using clothing, makeup, exercise and hairstyling, humans seek to control the way they appear to others. For some this is merely a matter of fashion, of social acceptance within a certain group, the assertion of a national or subcultural identity. But for some people the stakes are a bit higher. For binary transgender women, for example, especially trans women of colour, and especially trans women of colour in the United States, the ability to 'pass' as a (for absolute lack of a better term[10]) 'biological female' can be a matter of life and death. Trans women are far more likely to experience harassment, physical violence and sexual violence, and to be killed, than cisgender women.[11] For them, appearance is crucial. Presenting as conventionally female as possible is a way of, among other things, defending themselves against violence: conforming to a societally dictated idea of femininity ensures they are not marked out as aberrant, abnormal and targets for fear, intimidation and violence.

The situation is somewhat different for nonbinary people. While society dictates that transgender people be concerned with 'passing', that is, with looking like the conventional idea of what a man or a woman should look like, there is no idealised nonbinary person, no conventional 'look' that we can aim for or aspire to. This means that for many genderqueer people, we face scrutiny, mockery and yes, sometimes violence, no matter what we look like.

For this reason, though also sometimes because they consider outward appearance less important in transition than self-awareness or acceptance, some nonbinary people decide to not to present unconventionally. On the flip side, this scrutiny also means that people who present as openly genderqueer are often seen as transgressive, and therefore alluring, attractive or exotic. Over the years dozens of celebrities from David Bowie to Grace Jones to Tilda Swinton have played with gender, queerness and androgyny, and it can often be difficult to separate actual identity from public persona. In any case people, even public figures, often want to keep their identities – whatever they may be – private, and to speculate, especially publicly, may come off as intrusive.

The examples we see in public and in the media of nonbinary, genderqueer and genderfluid celebrities such as Ruby Rose, Miley Cyrus, Conchita Wurst and Andreja Pejić tend to be thin, wealthy, attractive, able-bodied and usually white, though Amandla Stenberg and Jaden Smith are notable exceptions. The phenomenon of the svelte, androgynous celebrity perpetuates the idea that there is only one way to express gender-queerness, and limits the perceived legitimacy of people who, whether by choice or not, present themselves differently. You can be nonbinary and wear dresses, even if you were assigned female at birth. You can have a beard, wear jewelry, even both at once! There is no one way to be genderqueer.

Nonbinary, genderqueer and 'othering'

As discussed in the glossary, I'll be using 'genderqueer' and 'nonbinary' largely interchangeably in this book. A number of the surveys and collections of demographic data I'll discuss below are phrased in terms of male, female and 'other', which raises an important issue that often affects nonbinary and genderqueer people: the aptly named phenomenon of 'othering'.

It's a fact that humans love to create binaries – right/wrong, black/white, female/male, yin/yang and so on – where perhaps a more nuanced and granular view would be more accurate and productive. It was pointed out to me by genderqueer scholar and activist CN Lester that to label one group of people 'non-binary' sets them in opposition to identities which are binary. It creates in itself a *new* binary between those who identify as binary-gendered and those who don't, the former being framed as normal and default, and the latter divergent, and implicitly aberrant in some way. This automatically (and often unintentionally) creates an *other* of the third, in this case nonbinary, group.

I think it's important to discuss this idea as a way to start moving our thinking beyond binaries in general, even if I continue to use both terms in the rest of the book. *Genderqueer* is a word I like very much. It's a bit older and in some ways more firmly established than *nonbinary*, and I think it's generally used by an, on average, slightly older subgroup within the trans community. Of the 14 people from whom I gathered anecdotal evidence for this book, nine said they identified as nonbinary (most interviewees listed more than one identity marker) and only two said they identified as genderqueer.

It also incorporates the word 'queer', a word with a long and rather fraught history behind it. The word queer is of foggy etymological origins. According to William Sayers in 'The Etymology of Queer',[12] it is traceable back to a reconstructed Indo-European root *terk-*, meaning simply 'turn'. It found its way to English through the Germanic subgroup, with Middle High German *twer*, 'oblique' or 'wrongheaded', changing to German *quer*, roughly 'crosswise'. Throughout its considerable lifetime the word has been associated with all sorts of meanings, most having to do with things being curved, bent, crooked or perverse, which facilitated its semantic narrowing and pejoration,[13] leading to an association with homosexuality which is first documented in the early twentieth century. The word was eventually reclaimed by the community it was used to oppress, and to this day it retains a subversive connotation which is especially apparent from its uses in critical theory: to 'queer' a text or idea is to re-evaluate it in light of sexual orientation and gender, as is the custom in queer theory, which will be discussed below.

When I use the word *queer* I think of it like a shorthand for all the transgressive and challenging expressions of gender and sexuality which allow us as a community to disrupt the status quo. It has a triumphant feel to it. 'Genderqueer', then, expresses this transgression within the specific context of gender; it stands in opposition to the conventions of gender itself and the rigid categories into which we've divided it. What I mean to say by this long explanation is that genderqueer is a complex way of talking about a complex identity, and one used by a great many people to describe their own identities. My use of the word will not be quite the same as anyone else's and, if I use genderqueer and nonbinary interchangeably, I do not mean to conflate them.

Demographics

It is probably obvious to anyone who has bothered to pick up this book that any marginalised group of people, however small, should be allowed to have their say, that they are worthy of understanding and support, regardless of numbers. However, I do think it is important to discuss how many people identify as nonbinary or genderqueer – in the UK, in the world, on college campuses, on the internet and so on. In this way we can get a feel for the size of the nonbinary population and its geographic distribution, become more aware of sectors and regions where nonbinary people are likely to live and work and better understand the unique challenges they face. Accurate population estimates are essential for policymaking, and the proper allocation of funds, resources and public services. This may be counting our chickens before they hatch, however, as the statistics on nonbinary demographics are severely lacking.

The United States Transgender Survey[14] (USTS), conducted in 2015, collected data on a number of different topics, from a rather astounding 27,715 people who identified themselves as transgender or otherwise gender-nonconforming. 'Non-binary' and 'genderqueer' were the fifth and sixth most frequently declared identity markers after 'Transgender', 'Trans', 'Trans woman (MtF, male to female)' and 'Trans man (FtM, female to male)'. Each broadly represented around a third of the sample (participants were allowed to pick more than one label to describe themselves). The USTS reported the following per-centages out of their participants who identified outside the binary:

Non-binary	31%	**Two-spirit**	7%
Genderqueer	29%	**Bi-gender**	6%
Genderfluid	20%	**Multigender**	4%
Androgynous	18%	**Third gender**	4%
Agender	14%	**A gender not listed above**	12%

Overall, 35 per cent of survey participants – around 9700 people – were grouped into the overarching category of non-binary/genderqueer (as opposed to 'man', 'woman' or 'crossdresser' – with only 3% placing themselves in this last category). Judging by this data, the United States nonbinary or genderqueer population might be estimated ex-tremely roughly at around 3 per cent of the overall population in 2015.

Compare this with the 2011 National Transgender Discrimination Survey[15] – which collected data from only around 6500 participants – to which the USTS is a follow-up. The total percentage of respond-ents who declared themselves genderqueer in the NTDS was only 22 per cent, followed closely by two-spirit at 15 per cent, androgynous at 14 per cent and third gender at 10 per cent. It's clear from these results, even if they were collected in the US, that nonbinary and genderqueer are rapidly growing demographics. Rising visibility goes hand in hand with increasing public acceptance and more and more people are comfortable declaring themselves outside the female/ male binary.

The situation becomes a bit more difficult when investigating how many people in the UK specifically identify outside the binary. Nat Titman's article[16] for Practical Androgyny, 'How Many People in the UK Are Nonbinary?', collates a number of demographic sources to try and get an estimate of the UK nonbinary and genderqueer population. Titman's study contains the most complete collection of data I can find on nonbinary and genderqueer identities within the United Kingdom, though it's important to point out that the article was written in 2014 and the numbers may be slightly different now.

I don't necessarily think that there are *more* of us now than Titman was able to discern in 2014; it seems more likely to me that, as nonbinary visibility has increased considerably even in the last few years, and given terminology they didn't have access to until recently, more people are coming to grips with a term that they may feel has always described them. In 2017 Jennie Kermode, chair of Trans Media Watch, said in a comment on Titman's article that, were Trans Media Watch to re-run their 2009/10 survey (*How Transgender People Experience the Media*), she thought a higher percentage of respondents would self-identify outside the binary. Kermode also estimated that roughly a third of the trans people she dealt with on a daily basis identified outside the binary, a figure roughly in line with the findings of the USTS in 2016.

The national census questions which Titman analysed, collected in 2011, included only 'male' and 'female' gender options. In this case, the existence of genderqueer respondents was surmised by the number (0.4% of 224,632 people) who either skipped the gender question, ticked both boxes or wrote something else on the form. It's important to note that in recent years the UK census has strongly encouraged respondents to use the online form rather than the paper one, which only allows a binary response to the gender question, and does not allow the participant to continue with the form without picking either 'male' or 'female'.

In 2011 the Equality and Human Rights Commission (EHRC) set about creating some questions that were as inclusive as possible of transgender people. This was in response to the revelation that the Equality Act 2010, intended to legally protect people from discrimination in the workplace and wider society, was not equipped to accurately reflect the size and diversity of the transgender population. This population was defined in the original act as the number of people who would now be protected under the section of the act devoted to 'gender reassignment', but it has been acknowledged that not all trans people have undergone or even *want* to undergo gender-affirming medical treatment, and so would not be protected. The Equality Act also uses exclusively binary language and makes no explicit acknowledgement of genders lying outside the binary.

The questions the EHRC ultimately derived separated 'sex assigned at birth' from 'gender' (a practice which is helpful to organisations trying to collect data on the transgender population, but less helpful to trans people who don't wish to reveal their trans status), included more options than simply 'male' and 'female' in both sections and asked participants about their 'gender reassignment' status. There has been discussion of the possibility of including questions on gender, sex and gender identity on the 2021 census, and the EHRC questions were presented in a self-reported online survey which was completed by 10,039 people, 38 of which said they think of themselves 'in another way' than male or female. The respondents were randomly sampled from the general population, and this result can be taken as an indication that around 0.3 to 0.4 per cent of people in the UK identify outside the gender binary.

Some of the best and most far-reaching data on this subject comes from the Scottish Trans Alliance (STA) survey on trans mental health," conducted in 2012. Of a sample of 889 trans people, roughly 27 per cent identify in some way outside the gender binary. The questions included in the STA survey are very inclusive, and are highly instructive if you are trying to put together a sensitive questionnaire about gender identity.

Several trans organisations have conducted surveys asking gender identity clinics (GICs)[18] – theoretically a great place to gather demographic information within the trans community – about the size of their nonbinary patient population. Unfortunately the results were limited as a great many GICs, despite professing to espouse a more complex model of gender than binary male and female, do not allow patients the option of marking their gender as anything but female or male. Some clinics, bafflingly, record only the 'legal' sex of their patients, or the sex that they were assigned at birth. This practice may seem intuitive if your concept of transgender identity allows for only male-to-female and female-to-male transitions, but it denies the existence of nonbinary people and limits patients, many of whom identify in some way outside the binary to a simplistic or even downright incorrect representation of themselves. This, in turn, perpetuates not only the erasure of nonbinary identities but also the fear, within the nonbinary community, that disclosure of a nonbinary identity opens one up to the risk of treatment being withheld.

Unfortunately, this binary mentality can occur even in trans rights organisations themselves: as recently as 2011, GIRES (the Gender Identity Research and Education Society), one of the biggest trans advocacy groups in the UK, had stated in a research report that all people who've undergone a medical transition were either trans women or trans men. Speaking exclusively from personal experience and from the experience of several acquaintances, I can state categorically that this is nonsense, and the participant figures in the USTS and Titman's article furnish solid evidence against this claim.

It's clear that these numbers vary wildly depending on the location, methodology and organisation conducting the study. What I want the reader to take away from this section is not necessarily a clear and accurate idea of the size of the nonbinary population but rather an idea of the complexities that we, and organisations wishing to study us, must navigate if we wish to represent ourselves accurately.

There is an additional difficulty here, which I think is important to discuss further, with the way that statistics are collected.

Titman addresses this in their paper, and I've spent a great deal of time already explaining how gender identities can exist outside the existing framework of female/male. The fact that I've had to spend so much time discussing it is itself a pretty good indication of the difficulty in articulating nonbinarism within our existing system. It follows, then, that it should be difficult to frame these subtleties as a question on something as rigid as a census form, and so it has proved.

There have been a few advances in survey methodology, spear-headed especially in the UK by the EHRC. In 2011 the EHRC found that the Office for National Statistics was not adequately prepared to capture data on people in the UK whose gender did not match the sex they were assigned at birth (largely defined as transgender people). For example, the 2011 UK census allowed participants to respond to the sex/gender question with only 'male' or 'female', which necessarily limited the ability of nonbinary people to accurately convey their identities.

The EHRC research report recommended a more inclusive version of the 'sex' question, one that is reworded and split into several separate questions that, at the very least, differentiate 'sex' from 'gender' and allow for a nonbinary option. It begins by asking what sex a person was designated at birth, with possible answers including two extra options besides 'female' and 'male': 'intersex' and 'prefer not to say'. The report also recommends including a gender identity question which allows respondents to say how they identify currently, with options 'male', 'female' and 'in another way', with an accompanying blank. This question would allow the data collector to find out how many respondents identify, broadly, as a gender outside the binary of female and male.

They stressed the need for the development of survey questions that had been reviewed and tested by both cisgender and transgender people, to ensure that all felt that the questions allowed them to accurately represent their gender identities, in the same way that racial and ethnic, religious and sexual identity are represented. While gender identity is being increasingly acknowledged as granular, in such a way that people are often reluctant to approach it in all its variation, it's no different from any other type of identity, and trans people deserve the right to represent themselves accurately.

Speaking generally, things are looking brighter than they were even just a few years ago. Nonetheless, an accurate survey of the nonbinary and genderqueer population in any country is still a long way off. The main difficulty with collecting demographic data on us is the fact that, unless the survey or study in question is specifically intended for use within the LGBT community, it is unlikely to even include gender options outside 'female' and 'male'. The United States Transgender Survey is a notable exception; conducted by the National Center for Transgender Equality, it has the backing of a large organisation and several grants, and institutional and corporate funding bodies. Nat Titman's data, collated as far as I can tell on their own initiative, was drawn from a range of sources, none of them approaching the size and specificity of the USTS. The results of these two surveys vary quite a bit, but it is possible to draw some very general conclusions from them. At the very least the (lack of) data makes it clear that far more, and more specific, study is necessary. Increased visibility, brought about by surveys such as these and, hopefully, books such as this one, is a step towards the collection of this data.

The UK versus elsewhere

This book is being written in the United Kingdom for a UK publisher. Most of the interviewees whose anecdotal evidence I include in the text live in the UK – though a notable few are American as well. My results are heavily skewed in favour of anglophone countries. As such, this book will be most representative of the experience of genderqueer and nonbinary people living in the UK. However, where possible, I'll be including real life anecdotes, policies and practices from countries outside the UK. Where relevant, I'll say where a interviewee comes from or in what country a certain policy is enforced.

Please keep in mind while reading that no single demographic from any country is representative of the world genderqueer experience, anglophone and Western or not. It's also important to remember that for all that a binary model seems like an organic or natural one, there are a number of models that include genders existing outside or alongside the binary, and many of these alternative or non-binary conceptions are culturally established and historically documented. A few of these models will be discussed in the chapter on the history of genderqueer identities (Chapter 3).

Why demographic information is important

While the statistics on the size of the nonbinary population are extremely limited, there is extensive data available on the transgender population more generally. To give you an idea of what trans people face in everyday life, I'll discuss some of the findings of a study[19] conducted by Stonewall, an LGBT rights organisation, in 2017. The survey recorded the responses of 5000 LGBT people, including 871 transgender people. Of these transgender people, 41 per cent had experienced a hate crime connected to their gender identity in the year leading up to the study. Almost half of all transgender respondents said they were uncomfortable using public toilets. A quarter of trans respondents had experienced homelessness, and more than a quarter had been subject to domestic abuse from a partner.

A few of these figures were nonbinary-specific: over half of nonbinary survey respondents said that they actively adjusted the way they dress out of fear of discrimination or harassment, and one fifth of nonbinary people experienced discrimination while looking for a house or flat to rent or buy. One in four nonbinary people aren't open to their family about their gender identity.

For the reasons discussed above I doubt these numbers are exactly accurate, but they are some of the most recent and, considering the sample size, likely the most accurate numbers we have concerning the trans lived experience in the UK. While the genderqueer experience is not the same as the binary trans experience – we struggle more than binary trans people in some respects and less in others – the numbers are chilling nonetheless. Nonbinary, genderqueer and genderfluid people exist in society and they're not just limited to the cities or universities, though this is often where they find the most support. We may be your children, your neighbours, your students and your patients; we might even be you. And we dearly need more visibility, respect and support.

Exercises and discussion questions

In this section I want to propose some exercises to help the reader start moving away from binaristic thinking, and to start thinking about gender as something constructed, mutable and more complex than simply 'male' and 'female'. I've written each exercise as a thought experiment that can be applied in a classroom or workshop setting.

There is a lot of discussion of 'binaries' in this chapter, and in the rest of the book. We're not usually given, as children or even as students, the tools to think about binaries as something to be questioned and deconstructed. We engage in debates in which one side is pitted against another, with the goal of determining a 'winner', and these discussions rarely leave room for compromise. Binaries are a simple and, admittedly, efficient way to frame social, moral and philosophical questions, but I think they can also be quite insidious, especially when moral or identity issues are framed this way. A healthy debate can very easily slide into one side being 'right' or 'good' and the other 'wrong' or 'bad', at which point any further debate is useless: both sides have made up their minds and will not be swayed by argument.

1. Name some of the binaries that your community teaches you. This can be something as complex and contentious as 'vegan' vs 'carnivore' or something as innocuous as 'ketchup' vs 'mayonnaise', as abstract as 'dreamer' vs 'realist' or as concrete as 'tall' vs 'short'. Think about how these binaries can be made more granular; what

about vegetarians, or people who don't eat red meat? What about mustard? Try discussing the ways that morals may be tied up in these binaries and, if the shades in between are discussed, ways that the two sides might find some common ground.

2. How do you personally conceptualise gender? Try coming up with a visual representation for how you represent the concept of 'gender' in your mind. Is it a simple binary of only 'male' and 'female'? Is it a spectrum with 'male' on one end and 'female' on the other? Or is it more complex, flexible or fluid? How granular is it? You can refer to the 'Thinking of gender' section, but don't worry if your conception is quite binaristic or if it doesn't fit with one of the diagrammes above. This book isn't meant to dictate how anyone thinks of as complex and abstract a concept as gender, and each person's mental representation will be different.

3. Where does *your* gender identity fit into the conceptualisation from Exercise 2? Even if you are cisgender – *especially* if you are cisgender – I encourage you to give this active thought. For example, if you consider yourself a man, and conceptualise gender as a sliding scale, you might still not identify with the very farthest reaches of 'man-ness'. Think about how your own masculinity sits in the wider society, among your friends and colleagues. Think, also, about how this colours your behaviour and your interactions with other people.

It's important to think actively about gender, especially if you are, for example, a medical practitioner with trans or genderqueer patients. Gender-diverse people have to devote a lot more active thought to their own gender identities than the average person does, and this influences how they are perceived by others, and how they want to be perceived. Thinking about this yourself, even if you are cisgender, will help foster empathy between you and your trans friends, colleagues, patients, students, etc. Empathy is absolutely essential to treating others with respect and humanity, and is often lacking in the way gender-diverse people are treated by the world at large.

CHAPTER 2

Language

Introduction

Language was one of the topics I knew I wanted to include as soon as I started writing this book. I'm a linguist by training and hold two linguistics degrees of nebulous utility, so any chance I get to hold forth on the subject, I take. A discussion of language isn't just a chance for me to show off, though: the gendered (and often binary) uses of language throughout the world present one of the biggest obstacles to the social and legal acceptance, and perceived legitimacy, of nonbinary and genderqueer identities. Language, which often only allows the speaker to express ideas in terms of male and female, presents an easy excuse to exclude nonbinary people, with the justification that the pronouns they use to identify themselves and assert their identities are ungrammatical and therefore illegitimate.

Language is important precisely because it's so everyday: it's a human milieu, it's an institution. It's the only way I can convey my ideas to you, and it's nearly impossible to avoid engaging with it on a daily basis. Unfortunately for nonbinary and genderqueer speakers of English, and a great many other languages, it's nearly impossible to speak conventionally without assigning yourself or others one or the other binary gender.

Like the medical system which will be discussed in Chapter 7, language is an institution nonbinary and genderqueer people are forced to engage with regularly, and which has historically been built and maintained by a cisgender, binary-thinking majority. This isn't because of any malicious intent on the part of our forebears, and I'm certainly not suggesting we tear the whole thing down and start from scratch; it's just an artifact of how entrenched binary gender is in society as a whole. Nonetheless, in consequence, when we are faced with people who want to delegitimise our identities and call our place in society into question, language is often used as a tool to that end.

On the other hand, public and official acceptance of gender-neutral language – in the same way that any new word or phrase is introduced into the language – would represent at the very least a huge symbolic milestone for the genderqueer community, and contribute tangibly to our visibility. This has been demonstrated in countries like Sweden, which has adopted the use of a neutral pronoun, at first in editorial contexts but lately in more common usage.

This chapter is intended to illustrate how language both enforces gender norms and allows for the subversion of the same. I'll talk a little bit about the ways different languages express gender and how that might affect the ways genderqueer and nonbinary speakers of those languages communicate and express themselves, and I'll discuss some of the less intuitive ways language works, which have bearing on mainstream perception of unconventional language use.

In this chapter I'll also discuss the debate surrounding the gender-neutral 'they', and alternative pronouns such as 'ze' and 'ey'. I'll give historical and sociolinguistic evidence arguing for the grammaticality of singular neutral 'they', and explain some of the reasoning behind the alternative or invented pronouns. Finally, I'll end the chapter with a few questions and exercises to get the reader thinking more deeply about gender in language.

The majority of the anecdotal evidence discussed in this book is from speakers of English, and the policies and social trends of anglophone countries are the primary focus of this book. But I've decided to discuss other languages in this chapter for much the same reason I include global examples in the next chapter: even if we're not precisely comparing like-for-like, knowing how other languages and cultures do things can only deepen our understanding of how gender works, and give us new ways to conceptualise and challenge the rigid binary structure we've imposed upon gender in the West. Other languages and cultures offer alternative models we can use in our everyday lives.

Gender in language

Languages may be thought to have gender[20] in two ways: grammatical and natural. *Natural gender* is gender reflected in the *meaning* of a noun, that is, natural gender describes a thing that has gender in real life. 'Woman' and 'man', Spanish 'mujer' and 'hombre', 'sow' and 'boar', 'actress' and 'actor' all have natural gender; the gender of 'woman' is expressed even if the language in question (English) has only minimal instances of grammatical gender.

Grammatical gender is all the ways that gender is embedded into a language 'arbitrarily'. Generally, a speaker of a language with grammatical gender has no choice but to use the gendered forms. Grammatical gender is especially popular within the Indo-European language family, which is thought to have originated in Anatolia around 9000 years ago.[21] Indo-European languages are now spoken all over the world, including English, Spanish, German, Hindi, Irish Gaelic, Afrikaans, Icelandic and many others – basically, all the languages spoken in Europe (excepting Finnish, Estonian and Hungarian, which are Uralic languages), and several of the world's most populous diasporic languages.

Italian is a good example of a grammatically-gendered language: all nouns in the language have a gender which is expressed with a suffix that you cannot leave off of the word. These nouns are accompanied by articles like 'a' or 'the', and adjectives, which also must be gendered. Most importantly for our purposes, when a person talks about themself or another person in Italian, they must say whether they are, for example, *uno* (male) *studente*, or *una* (female) *studentessa*. There is no neutral version, and creating a more inclusive alternative may be more complex than simply inventing a new word to swap for a pronoun. Making the Italian language more inclusive of nonbinary and genderqueer people might have implications for the entire structure of the language. This is why grammatical gender can represent some difficulty when it comes to talking about nonbinary people in these languages, and it is especially interesting to see where some speakers of languages that have a degree of grammatical gender have created workarounds, such as in Spanish and Swedish.

Noun classes

Gender is firmly embedded in the forms that words take in a great many languages. This can make gender seem like an essential criteria on which to differentiate people and things, and can make it difficult for speakers of these languages to conceive of anything as important or fundamental as gender.

But not every language has grammatical gender. There are plenty of languages, especially outside of Europe, which don't distinguish between 'he' and 'she', for example, when speaking about someone in third person. These languages may certainly still have *natural* gender, words like 'cow' and 'bull' and 'girl' and 'boy' may be different – just because gender isn't embedded in the fabric of the language doesn't mean they don't perceive it. But looking at how many of these languages differentiate *types* of nouns on axes other than male and female may offer insight to readers who only speak languages that do have grammatical gender.

Just as gender affects the way a noun is inflected in Italian, or affects the pronoun used to refer to it in third person in English, so too can other aspects of a noun affect the way it is expressed in other languages. Many languages use different prefixes or suffixes to distinguish things that are *animate* from things that are *inanimate*, such as in Basque, an indigenous language of Spain, and Ojibwe, an indigenous language spoken in North America. Other languages make a distinction between things that are human versus things that are not human. And this distinction doesn't need to be binary either: languages such as Navajo (spoken in North America) distinguish grammatically between things which are, for example, flat, or thin and flexible, or mushy in consistency rather than solid – the texture of the thing in question determines the way the verb is conjugated. Some languages have a myriad of noun classes: in Swahili different prefixes are used to talk about people, plants, fruits, animals and 'miscellaneous' others.

I include all this to suggest that gender might not be the most important, or marked, quality a thing can have. Many languages, for example Turkish, do not use a different pronoun when speaking about a man or a woman, and context or 'natural' gendered qualities are sufficient to understand whether the person in question is male or female – if the distinction is even relevant.

It occurs to me that, with a few exceptions (for example Swahili), in many places throughout the world a native language that doesn't have grammatical gender may be in the process of being forced out or overtaken by a language which does. The rapid and continuing expansion of the grammatical-gender-loving Indo-European language family means that, statistically speaking, the proportion of the world's languages is changing such that more and more speakers throughout the world regularly use – and therefore regularly distinguish mentally – grammatical binary gender.

This has nothing to do with any inherent quality of the languages in question; there's nothing about speakers of languages with grammatical gender to make them more 'aggressive' or their languages more 'hardy' than languages or speakers without grammatical gender. It's simply a fact that many of the world's rapidly growing languages, whether due to colonialism, imperialism or diaspora, are mostly descended from the same ancient mother tongue. In fact, it's been theorised that the original binary distinction in Proto-Indo-European was actually one of animate/inanimate or active/inactive rather than gender,[22] and that a masculine/feminine distinction developed later. So, had early Indo-European languages not developed grammatical gender, be it binary male/female or ternary male/female/neuter, and had the speakers of languages in this family not turned out to be especially good at expanding and moving into the territory of other speakers, grammatical gender might not be so pervasive, and might not seem today to be so fundamental, so eternal and so global.

How various languages use gender

For languages that oblige the speaker to express gender in various contexts, languages that nonbinary and genderqueer people today must speak, daily use can present unique challenges to navigate. The way a language treats gender reflects and, to an extent, affects the gendered values of the society in which it is spoken. This topic could probably fill a book in and of itself, so I'll stick to just a few examples here and focus on the ways nonbinary speakers of these languages navigate each one. Of course, much more study is needed before we can draw any firm conclusions about the lived experiences of the genderqueer people who speak these languages, especially since differences in language often exist alongside parallel differences in culture, but the languages here are still useful as illustrative examples.

In spoken Japanese there is very little in the way of *grammatical* gender, however there are certain phrases, words and speech patterns which are broadly associated with women and others broadly associated with men, in the same way that certain occupations and behaviours are associated with different genders.[23] Unlike using 'he' or 'she' in English, however, the use of these modes of speech is governed by social convention, and while a person assigned one gender using a mode of speech associated with a different gender may come off as weird, impolite or improper, it's not considered ungrammatical. In addition, there is no gendered third-person pronoun in spoken Japanese: generally another person is referred to by a word *other* than a pronoun, i.e. their name or occupation.

The personal pronoun *I* is a good example of the gendered conventions in spoken Japanese: my interviewee LE, for example, is a bilingual speaker of English and Japanese, and chooses to use *boku*, a pronoun generally used by young boys, to refer to themself. In this way, LE has the freedom to signal to other Japanese speakers how they perceive their own gender. Regardless of how they fare socially in Japan, this socially coded aspect of language may afford nonbinary speakers some level of self-determination.

In Spanish, like in Italian, personal pronouns and nouns generally have one of two binary genders, which also affects surrounding articles, numerals and adjectives. One must gender another person in order to speak about them – even words that are genderless in English like 'student' and 'partner' must have a grammatical gender in Spanish – and one must submit to being gendered oneself in the same way. Genderqueer speakers of languages like Spanish have to contend with this lack of a neutral alternative every day, and as of yet I've not come across a neutral pronoun in popular use, though in time one may come about in the same way that English *they/them* has become popular.[24] My interviewee XX3, who identifies as genderfluid and is a bilingual speaker of English and Spanish, is comfortable with male, female and neutral pronouns, though in Spanish they use male pronouns.

As the Spanish-speaking genderqueer community has grown, especially in text-based mediums like the internet, workarounds are being developed. For example, in order to avoid using a gendered '-o' or '-a' suffix to describe their community, many people have turned to using the word *Latinx* (pronounced 'latin-eks') to refer to themselves and their community.[25] Not all Spanish speakers approve of the use of Latinx, I suspect for many of the same reasons some English speakers disapprove of the use of neutral they/them.

Some languages, like Russian, have a neutral singular pronoun that is generally only used for inanimate objects. While some people, such as my interviewee SG, and Russian transgender artist and activist Seroe Fioletovoe, use the neutral inanimate pronoun *оно* (it) to describe themselves, others feel *it* dehumanises them and prefer to use masculine pronouns which are considered akin to a neutral or 'default' option, in much the same way that English 'he' was often used as a generic up until late last century. This default-to-male usage doesn't work for everyone, however; for a genderqueer person who was assigned male at birth, for example, usage of the default 'he' may reinforce the perception that they are cisgender and identify as male, and contribute to dysphoria. In these cases female pronouns may be preferable, to imply at least some flexibility or crossing of gender boundaries. Again, though, it would be necessary to speak to many more gender-neutral speakers of Russian to see whether a clear trend is emerging.

Some languages such as Estonian and Finnish (tellingly, two of the very few non-Indo-European languages spoken in Europe) have a gender-neutral pronoun which genderqueer and genderless speakers can and do happily use.[26]

Swedish (which is Indo-European) has a gender-neutral personal pronoun *hen*, which was officially added to the dictionary in 2015, though it had been coined in the 1960s to move away from the use of masculine-as-neutral. In the last few years a few gender-neutral schools have opened, which, along with encouraging students to cross conventional gender boundaries in activities and play, also exclusively use the gender-neutral pronoun *hen* to refer to students. Studies suggest that children in these schools are more likely to pursue activities they prefer, without being restricted by gender norms.[27] Its official recognition makes *hen* a very good example of a neutral pronoun that is on its way to being accepted by the mainstream and that, hopefully, will continue to enter common use. Indeed research[28] has shown that, despite initial reactions of hostility towards the use of *hen*, popular attitudes towards the use of the neutral pronoun seem to be becoming more and more positive with time. The case in Sweden is unique and, I think, suggests that minor changes towards more inclusive language are a real possibility.

Language change and pronouns

Be they cis, binary trans or genderqueer, the pronouns a person uses to refer to themself, at least in English, are a signal of their gender identity. For a trans person to use a certain set of pronouns that are divergent from those they were assigned at birth is an uncategorical, public statement of their gender identity, and is therefore important. Any discussion in English of nonbinary identities would be incomplete without an accompanying discussion of pronouns, specifically of the neutral, singular use of the word 'they', 'them' and 'their', and the range of alternative pronouns, including xe/xem, ze/hir, and ey/em, which have been created specifically for use by, and to refer to, people with genders other than woman or man. Throughout this section I'll broadly refer to all of these neutral pronouns as 'inclusive pronouns'.

But it's also important to point out that although binary-gendered language is a barrier to full genderqueer equality, not every genderqueer, nonbinary or genderfluid person uses the same pronouns, and not all of us like to use pronouns other than 'he' or 'she'. For some people, the pronoun they use has nothing to do with their gender identity; pronouns and what they signal to other people might simply be unimportant to them. Some people, for example people who identify as genderfluid, might use 'he', 'she', 'they' or another pronoun at different times, depending on fluctuations in their identity.

Some genderqueer and nonbinary people ask that others just use their name to refer to them. In some contexts this can act as a 'more acceptable' compromise where the use of the neutral pronoun has been rejected – for example I've had a university professor insist on this because he didn't think they/them/their was grammatical. But just as often the use of just a name is a conscious choice by the nonbinary person, who would rather not declare an alignment with any category by attaching a pronoun to themself.

On the other hand, quite a few people who think of themselves as something other than exclusively male or female don't mind what pronouns people use for them, for example interviewee EB1 has 'no pronoun preference whatsoever', and presents as a cisgender woman most of the time. Interviewee SG prefers whichever pronoun the person they're speaking to wants to use for them.

There are also people who *present*, broadly, as a binary gender opposite the one they were assigned at birth, and who use a pronoun that suggests they're binary trans (i.e. 'he' and 'she'), but whose gender identity is more complex than a simple male or female. Many people who I've met who I first read as binary trans, and who I later found out identify outside the binary, give their pronoun preference as something like 'he or they' or 'she/they'.

As I've said before, there are multiple separate identities encompassed within the larger category of 'nonbinary' and no single way to be nonbinary, either. Generally speaking, the language used in the genderqueer and nonbinary community is flexible, determined by trends within that community and highly individualised.

Even though not all genderqueer people use the neutral singular 'they', these pronouns are where the gender issue in anglophone countries usually centres, the anchor to which the whole debate is attached. As this is a book in English, I'll give as full an explanation of the issues surrounding these pronouns as possible.

Before I get into the nitty gritty of the various neutral pronouns currently in use in English, I want to briefly discuss the controversy behind them, and what this debate implies about both the users of these pronouns and about their detractors. Gendered pronouns such as 'he' and 'she' have gender in both the grammatical and natural sense: in many languages the speaker has no choice but to use one or the other to refer to themself and others, and the two forms of these words are directly tied to a real characteristic of the thing they're referring to: its sex or gender.

The fact that these pronouns are the only instances of grammatical gender in English means that there is a little bit of leeway for flexibility; altering the pronouns themselves to make them more inclusive doesn't have larger knock-on effects for the rest of the language: there are no suffixes that need changing, new declensions don't need to be invented.

Despite the relatively small effect that inclusive pronouns have on the rest of the language, the increasingly widespread use of these pronouns is one of the things people tend to get the most upset about in the discussion of nonbinary equality. When I started writing this book, I knew this was the case, but I hadn't yet thought deeply about why.

The question at the heart of the pronoun debate is fundamentally one of autonymy – the ability of a demographic, especially a marginalised one, to name itself and thus claim agency or control over how it is referred to, and by extension, treated. Reluctance on the part of the cisgender majority to acknowledge and use nonbinary people's preferred pronouns, regardless of their grammaticality, has deeper roots than a simple unwillingness to learn a new word.

Language is often used as a synecdoche for society as a whole, and therefore any perceived 'breakdown' in language, or change in its conventional use, is often taken to indicate a corresponding breakdown in society. Any kind of alternative usage, especially by younger people in more informal settings, is often considered by older generations – the people who benefit from elevated or standardised language as a key to education and privilege – to be sloppy or demonstrating ignorance in the user. The spread of new or unconventional forms doesn't necessarily need to correspond to an actual change in the status quo (people got upset when words like 'net neutrality' and 'jeggings' were added to the Oxford English Dictionary, for example) but when it does, things can get heated.

Gender, and its binary, is one of the oldest and most entrenched systems in human society. The proportion of words that are gendered in the English language has remained relatively stable for almost a thousand years. So the incorporation of inclusive pronouns into common use represents a change to a longstanding tradition, a change which is often seen, sometimes unconsciously, as a threat to the very fabric of anglophone society.

The water surrounding debates like this is muddied further by the fact that judgments about 'improper' language use often carry with them unconscious undercurrents of prejudice: what I mean by this is that the people who are most likely to use English in an unconventional way, to make mistakes, and to need new, different or unconventional words, are the people who are new to the language, who haven't had the benefit of a formal education and who are not in a position to determine what is considered 'standard' use. This group will include, very generally speaking, immigrants and working- or lower-class people, and members of minority groups. Again, the unconscious perceptions that members of the majority have of these groups – in the case of this book of 'other' or 'outsider' groups like trans people – will show strongly in a condemnation of their unconventional language use.

But the truth is, all languages change, all the time. Because individual humans exist on a short time scale relative to the rate at which languages (and geology, ecology, genes...) change, we only get to glimpse a static version or a snapshot of the language we speak.[29] At most each of us has only an inkling of the way our language differs from how it was spoken in our grandparents' time.

It's therefore very easy to see language as stable and permanent. New or different usages can be jarring to our sensibilities. But for the most part, rules that seem unbreakable, words that seem to have a fossilised meaning, are the result of long periods of flux, uncertainty, change and 'misuse'. Words that seem old-fashioned to us may once have been innovations decried by an older generation. The 'you' we use in standard English to refer to a person or group of people in second person was in Early Modern English[30] only used to refer to a *group* of people as the *object* of a sentence, with 'thou' and 'ye' being used for subjects and 'thee' for singular second person objects.

Older speakers in the Early Modern period may have heard 'you' used for all four meanings by younger speakers, and probably considered it sloppy or rude.[31]

Language change happens through both conscious and unconscious efforts on the part of its speakers: new inventions or changes in social structure, use by second-language speakers and, indeed, newly visible social demographics can all be sources of linguistic change. At the same time, terms that are no longer relevant, or are perceived as redundant or implying prejudice on the part of the user, fall out of favour. For example, in the United States, the word 'phone' is increasingly used by default to refer to a wireless or mobile phone, with the word 'cellphone' falling out of use. In turn, 'landline' rather than 'phone' is often used for the increasingly rare occasions in which someone specifically uses a corded phone attached to a wall. The word 'oriental', used for many years to describe a person of East Asian descent, is now largely considered reductive, outdated and racist by most Americans, and is also starting to fall out of use in the UK. Language change, then, implies nothing more about society than that the contexts in which we use certain words is also changing. This no more represents social deterioration than does the advancement of technology or human rights.

They/them/their

In my experience, though I've been unable to find hard statistics, they/them/their is the most common pronoun set used by the genderqueer and nonbinary community. I personally use this set for a range of reasons: they're neutral, they're used quite commonly, they exist already in English in other contexts and I've found they're fairly easy for people to remember. They're also the standard set of pronouns used by the nonbinary people I 'grew up with' when I was first discovering my identity.

And gender-neutral use of the word 'they' is by no means a new phenomenon, though it did not always refer specifically to people who thought of themselves as neither male nor female. The neutral 'they' has been in use continuously since at least the Middle Ages. In Chaucer's day, 'they' could be used to refer to a hypothetical single person of indeterminate gender, such as in the following lines of the passage 'Prologue of the Pardoner's Tale' in *The Canterbury Tales*:

> *And whoso fyndeth hym out of swich blame, / They wol come up and offre a Goddés name*
> (And whoso findeth him out of such blame, / They will come up and offer in God's name)[32]

In act IV, scene 3 of Shakespeare's *A Comedy of Errors*, Antipholus of Syracuse says, 'There's not a man I meet but doth salute me / As if I were their well-acquainted friend.' In *Pride and Prejudice* (and many other of Austen's works), Elizabeth Bennett says 'I always delight in overthrowing those kind of schemes, and cheating a person of their premeditated contempt.'

There is also historical evidence of various other 'epicene' or gender-neutral pronouns in use in different regions and at various periods in history.[33] For example in discussing the Gloucester dialect of English spoken in the late eighteenth century, William Marshall wrote:[34]

> Beside these and various other misapplications (as they for them – I for me, &c.), an extra pronoun is here in use; – ou : a pronoun of the singular number; – analogous with the plural they; – being applied either in a masculine, a feminine, or a neuter sense. Thus 'ou will' expresses either *he* will, *she* will, or *it* will.

Writers (and presumably speakers) have seen fit to use or improvise a neutral pronoun for centuries, and while this was likely not due to the presence of gender-neutral people in their lives, it does give us an interesting look at the flexibility of language and the creativity of its users. It suggests that the gender system which seems to be so ingrained in our usage might not be so essential after all, and it presents some fairly strong evidence against the 'grammaticality' argument.

Neopronouns

The other type of neutral pronoun commonly used in the genderqueer community are invented, created or 'neopronouns', such as ze or ey (also called Spivak pronouns[35]). These neutral pronouns are a perfect example of the way that genderqueer and nonbinary terminology is still growing and changing over time. There are dozens of invented pronouns currently in use by different people all over the world and only recently has the list begun to stabilise, settling on a handful of more common sets. In addition, since many of these pronoun sets are derived from existing gendered pronouns, a delicate balance must be struck such that pronunciation doesn't evoke one gender more than the other. The following table includes some (but by no means all) of the more common invented pronouns I've encountered. They're inflected in much the same way that he, she and they are, for example:[36]

subject 'she/he/they'	object 'her/him/them'	possessive determiner 'her/his/their'	possessive pronoun 'hers/his/theirs'	reflexive 'herself/himself/themself'
ey pronouns	em	eir	eirs	emself
ze	hir	hir	hirs	hirself
xe	xem	xyr	xyrs	xemself
ve	ver	vis	vis	verself
per	per	per	pers	perself

Each of these pronoun sets aren't necessarily associated with *specific* nonbinary or genderqueer subcategories; preference as to which one to use varies from person to person. Use of these pronouns can also be heavily dependent on social context. One of my interviewees, XX1, prefers that their close friends refer to them with shme (like 'he')/shmer (like 'her')/shmis (like 'his'). Considering how much backlash there's been against trans people trying to publicly use invented pronouns (or express themselves generally), it's not surprising that many people aren't comfortable using their preferred pronouns in all social circles.

I've not been able to find a real consensus as to *why* some people prefer invented pronouns over they/them/their or just a name – this is a question I intend to look into more in future research. As far as I can tell, each person will have their own reasons for their own pronoun use, connected to their personal history, linguistic preferences, the nuances of their identity and the way they relate to their community. And just as no one alternative pronoun is tied to any specific nonbinary-umbrella identity, there's no standard or guide which tells a person what pronoun they should be using. Faced with a system that is inherently inhospitable to our identities, we choose pronouns that feel right to us.

I've periodically encountered people, like my university professor, who were willing to accept some, but not all, gender-neutral ways of referring to a nonbinary person. Again, the question is fundamentally one of autonomy, not of grammaticality. Language and pronouns, as tools which can be used to both signal and invalidate a person's gender identity, are very important to the nonbinary equality movement. The willingness to make a minor change to one's own language use in order extend to a genderqueer person the courtesy of using their preferred pronouns, and validation of their identity, is one of respect. So I've become sceptical of people who say they're willing to use they/them/their but *not* invented pronouns, or just the person's name but *not* they/them/their, because of perceived notions of correctness or acceptability. When person A denies person B the right to be referred to as they wish, person A is telling person B that they don't deserve to control how others refer to them. To me, when someone refuses to use my preferred pronouns because of questions of their grammaticality, it feels like my identity is being held hostage, a guarantee for my good linguistic behaviour. So, while I'm not necessarily suggesting that a person unquestioningly change the way they think and begin to accept all forms of gender-neutral address, I am suggesting they think hard about why they consider some forms more or less acceptable, and weigh their own grammaticality judgments against a genderqueer person's right to exist.

Conclusion

Language is big. It's a massive entity that connects us to some people and isolates us from others. The way we use it is a signal to others of our identity, be that identity gender, cultural or subcultural. I could write an entire book about how gender in language affects our daily lives, and in a few years that book would most likely be obsolete! I've done my best in this chapter to give a balanced view of the 'debate' surrounding gender-neutral language, but I hope I've made it clear that the question here is bigger even than language. Language is a symbol for society, and using it in a certain way is for many people an act both political and personal.

In debates over gender-neutral language, a cisgender person's ideas about what is 'correct' or 'proper' are often pitted against the very nature of a trans person's identity, that person's right to exist. These two things are not equivalent. It's difficult to change the way you use language, especially when you have to refer to one person with a pronoun you don't use for anyone else. Tied as they are to self-actualisation, agency and identity, pronouns are a touchy subject for many trans people. Being misgendered can be hurtful and upsetting because it invalidates a person's efforts to present, and to be perceived, as they actually are. But all of us, even genderqueer people ourselves, are bound to make mistakes sometimes. If you approach the question of pronouns in good faith and are respectful of individuals' preferences in terms of language use, you'll be fine.

A question I see cisgender people often ask is 'If I'm not sure of someone's gender and don't want to misgender them, how do I find out their pronouns?' This is a reasonable question: asking about and specifying pronouns is a relatively new practice that's just now gaining currency. It's reasonable to want to know how a person identifies in order to respect that identity, but I'd suggest first and foremost stopping to consider *why* you want to know. Maybe in that context it's not actually necessary for everyone's gender to be clearly established. If you're just curious, rather than approaching the person and putting them on the spot, consider being satisfied not knowing. The person may tell you themself how they prefer to be addressed, but if they don't bring it up they may be uncomfortable discussing it for any number of reasons.

If you're in a position where you *must* refer to someone by a pronoun, then it's perfectly acceptable to ask them what pronoun they prefer. When asking a person their pronouns, keep in mind that gender identity can be very personal, and not everyone is out as trans. If not everyone in the immediate vicinity is specifying their pronouns, but you want to refer to a new acquaintance correctly, be discreet and ask for pronouns privately if possible after you've been introduced. Consider stating your own pronoun preference when introducing yourself to other people, to create an environment in which trans people can specify their preference without being put on the spot. If you're running or are involved in an event in which nametags are used, consider having everyone in attendance specify their preferred gender pronoun (often abbreviated PGP) on their nametag. The practice of everyone stating their preference shouldn't necessarily be limited to queer spaces, either! The more environments in which pronoun preference is expected to be specified, the less pushback there will be against it generally.

Admittedly, the way pronoun preference has been – and sometimes still is – enforced, especially on the internet, can create an element of fear or trepidation among cis people about 'getting it wrong'. In these cases I encourage cisgender people who feel reluctance about using alternative pronouns to compare their own discomfort to the difficulty nonbinary people must face trying to exist in a world that has been built to accommodate binary people. For this very reason, we've all had to grow thick skins, and most of us are used to people getting it wrong. What really stings is when people get our pronouns wrong on purpose, or don't care enough to try to get them right. So, we're not asking you to get it perfect every time. If you're discreet, and respectfully ask us about our pronoun preference, we generally won't get offended. For the most part, nonbinary and genderqueer people will be pleased when someone cares enough to ask them how they identify. Asking for pronouns shows that you respect a person's identity and want to refer to them correctly. I've had a coworker apologise for using the wrong pronoun to refer to me, when I hadn't even heard or noticed him do it. The fact that he owned up and apologised showed me that he was willing to put his respect for me over his own comfort, and I all I did was smile and thank him for making the effort.

As a rule of thumb, if you're respectful and polite and approach us as normal people rather than some kind of exotic beast, we'll probably be happy to explain. There's a public image of the nonbinary person as a 'special snowflake' or 'delicate flower': we're portrayed as touchy, fussy or prone to react badly when questioned. Trans people often have to deal with harassment, abuse and physical violence. Sometimes, being misgendered is enough to ruin your day. But more often than not it's the implication of disrespect behind it that is the most hurtful. The idea that someone has misgendered you because they don't *care* about your identity – and by extension, you – is dehumanising, alienating and depressing. A simple mistake isn't going to hurt us. Aside from this being a reasonable reaction to years of marginalisation and ridicule, it simply isn't true of most of us. We're becoming more and more visible and while it can be exhausting to constantly have to justify and explain ourselves to others, most genderqueer people are pretty tolerant of questions. Own up to your mistakes and try not to get defensive when you get it wrong, and you'll do fine. We're all human.

Exercises and discussion questions

1. Think about the different ways English conveys gender, explicitly and implicitly, through pronouns, titles (i.e. Mr and Mrs but also Sir and Ma'am) and descriptive nouns like 'man', 'actress', 'police-man'. What are some ways that we, especially people working in institutions who use titles and honorifics to refer to each other, could be more linguistically accommodating of nonbinary and genderqueer people?

2. Are you a speaker of a language other than English? How does that language deal with gender? Are there gendered pronouns? Which person are they in (i.e. first, second, third, etc.)? What about gendered nouns, for example the Italian 'professore/professoressa'? Do people use gendered terms to refer to themselves?

3. Do you know any genderqueer or nonbinary people who are speakers of this language? How do you think they could use language to reflect their nonbinary identity? If you can do so politely and respectfully, ask them about what they do.

4. If you don't know any genderqueer speakers of other languages, think about the way the non-English languages you speak use gender, and think about ways a nonbinary person could use that language to reflect their identity. Remember, language is always changing to suit the needs of its speakers, altering it to accommodate new meanings and perspectives is natural.

CHAPTER 3

A Global and Historical Perspective

Introduction

In the strictest sense, there is no 'history' of nonbinary gender. The term itself, and the specific way modern genderqueer and nonbinary people understand their genders, is relatively new. It's a product of a post-structuralist, queer mode of thought that is a result of, and reaction to, ways of thinking of gender that came about in the last couple of centuries.

This is not to say, however, that we – or people like us – never existed before the twenty-first century. In fact, since ancient times and throughout the world, there have always been people, and sometimes established cultural categories for those people, outside of the strict binary of man and woman. And it is through the study, however amateur, of the ways in which the rigid structure of binary gender is subverted and bent throughout the world and throughout history, that I feel most sure that my own community, however different it is from the disparate social categories I'll explore in this chapter, is indeed a community. It is through my feeling of connection to these people – like the adventurous genderfluid seventeenth-century servant Thomas(ine) Hall – and these cultural groups – like the Bissu priests of modern Indonesia or the Byzantine eunuchs who were considered a 'third sex' by their ancient contemporaries – that I begin, as a nonbinary person, to feel the distant roots of something like *tradition*.

For a history to be written on a group of people they must first be recognised as a distinct group. For most people who have thought of themselves as neither man nor woman, there has been no place to seek shelter or guidance. As yet, we don't have a 'history', so to speak, and no canon, collected writings or a literary tradition. But we are beginning to create community spaces, both virtual and physical, and a vocabulary to describe ourselves.

This is the natural result of the proliferation of knowledge that has come with the information age, a proliferation which has led many people (myself included) to realise for the first time that they're not alone, that they could be part of a larger, even a global and historical, community. It's no coincidence that only in the last ten years or so have terms like genderqueer and nonbinary come into mainstream use. With the internet came the possibility of interaction between us in larger numbers, and with its potential for anonymity came the safety to begin to fully explore the possibilities of our identities.

Mine was the first generation to grow up with the internet and, I think, one of the first to actively, collectively and publicly begin to question the rules of binary gender we were taught as children. However, most of us came to this newfound awareness in our late teens or university years, and had to choose to do a lot of unlearning before we could begin to explore new frontiers of gender.

Even as recently as the nineties and early noughties there were people we would call nonbinary, who had to figure out their own identities without the support of a community or role models. One of my interviewees, CP, describes growing up in small-town Essex in the 1960s, before the internet and before even gay (let alone LGBT) culture was widely acknowledged or understood. CP says:

I first heard the term genderqueer in the late 90s and remember thinking that it was a good description of me, but all the people who used it seemed to be young, trendy and mostly US-American, so I felt uncomfortable about applying it to myself… I usually use the term nonbinary when coming out to people as it is better understood than genderqueer. But I do get frustrated when people talk about nonbinary identities being a 'generational' thing and I feel it's important for those of us who are older to emphasise that it is not some kind of trendy teenage fad, it is simply that there is now a word to describe our identity.

The generation after millennials, sometimes called 'Generation Z', now has access to alternative ways of thinking about gender during their formative years, and I confess I envy them this a little. I am constantly astounded, when I speak to younger people or see them on social media, by the subtlety with which they engage with topics it took me years to get a handle on. I admire the ease with which my young genderqueer peers demonstrate theoretical knowledge and articulate a nuanced understanding of gender. So while my generation might be the first to have claimed nonbinary as an *identity*, it is this next generation that is making it possible for these identities to truly enter the mainstream.

Indeed, the claim that millennials and genderqueer people belonging to Generation Z have to contend with, that gender-queerness is somehow 'new', a fad created by a generation of special snowflakes desperate for attention, is not only false but also contributes directly to the invalidation and erasure of our identities and the growth of our nascent community. Because just as we need space to exist and interact with each other, we also need to believe that we, as individuals and as a group, are not so alone in the vast stretch of human history. The idea of our community as something synthetic or reactionary, with no basis in 'nature' or 'history' and no access to the legitimacy that 'nature' and 'history' confer, is a weapon used against us by people who feel that, by bending the rules, we are threatening

the system that made them. And just as language is used as synecdoche for society as a whole when popular use defies convention, the
fear associated with gender-queerness is actually about power and
the status quo.

But this way of thinking about gender – as fluid and flexible, as
only loosely tied to biological sex, and even of biological sex as not as
discrete or unequivocal as commonly thought – is not unique to this
century. The so-called 'mainstream' idea of gender as rigid, categorical
and inborn is actually relatively new – and not the inevitable result
of 'nature'.

A shift in understanding

As beings with lifespans of generally only up to 100 years, it can be
difficult for us to really comprehend how different various aspects of
the past were to today. Binary gender is ingrained in our society and
taught to us by previous generations; it's a social convention that to
most of us seems immutable and eternal. I myself was surprised to
learn that the way that we think about gender – as binary, determined
in utero and tied irrevocably to genitals and chromosomes – seems
actually to be a result of changes in scientific and social thinking of
just the last couple centuries.

A useful[37] theory for thinking about an evolving model of gender
is the one posited in Thomas Laqueur's book,[38] *Making Sex: Body and
Gender from the Greeks to Freud*. In *Making Sex*, Laqueur proposes that
before the Enlightenment the way people conceptualised gender
(though this was probably not something the common person consciously thought about very often) was very different from the way
people today do.

Gender, it seems, has gone through a series of conceptual changes from ancient times up to the Victorian era, at which point our
current model of 'biology=gender' was solidified. Most importantly,
Laqueur's theory suggests that as massive social and economic changes irrevocably changed the relationship between the social categories,

especially men and women, each different model of gender has been informed by the social context of the day, the goals of the people in power and the human attributes that were considered important or relevant at the time.

In the time of Galen, an ancient Greek physician and medical researcher, gender was thought of as a hierarchy, with women at the bottom and men at the top. Rather than a binary system of opposition, this model was more akin to a ladder: it placed masculinity and male sex at the apex, women at the bottom and sexually immature boys and eunuchs at varying levels in between, as each approached (or failed to approach) the privileged masculine ideal. Young boys, whose genitalia developed and 'dropped' as they matured, were thought of as mobile on this scale. Castrated eunuchs, who could never attain the sexual maturity of 'uncut' men, with all its attendant hairiness, virility and muscularity, were placed higher than boys on this scale but considered stationary on it.[39]

This model, in which every person lies somewhere along a scale approaching a masculine ideal, Laqueur calls the one-sex model. This, Laqueur suggests, was the underlying theoretical model of gender up until the Enlightenment, at which point gender began to be thought of differently. Under the 'Galenic' model of gender, women were seen simply as a less perfect version of men. This idea is backed up by historical sources which describe, for example, the ovaries as internal testes, the vagina as a kind of 'reversed' penis and so on. Many ancient languages, Laqueur argues, had no separate word for the female genitalia as contrasted to the male, which suggests that the speakers (or at least the writers and intellectuals) of the time did not see the two as different in kind, only in degree.

Under the one-sex model, it is social *gender* that is considered the innate, relevant and unchanging category. The fact that women's bodies were (by the skewed standards of the time) considered 'less perfect' than men's was taken as an outward representation of the fact that women *themselves* were less perfect than men.

Tellingly, these bodies, it was thought, were also capable of change.

Before the Enlightenment, it was widely thought that a person's behaviour, manner and personality determined their gender – and by
extension their sex. It was commonly accepted that feminine men
could lactate, and that the bodily fluids of men and women were
as analogous to each other as their genitals. There are medical texts
dating from the fifteenth and sixteenth centuries documenting 'case
studies' in which people with vaginas (milkmaids, shepherdesses and
so on) spontaneously transformed into men, usually in a context of
the application of heat and physical activity.[40] After undergoing some
kind of 'transformation', these people with vaginas-turned-penises
might live their lives as men and be accepted as such. In *Making
Sex*,[41] Laqueur cites a story recounted by several different Renaissance
writers, including Michel de Montaigne, in which a French shepherd-
ess named Marie, in the process of running after a flock of sheep in
the midst of a hot summer, leaps over a stream with such force that
'the genitalia and the male rod' literally fall out of her: her vagina
becomes a penis, she changes her name to Germain and lives the rest
of her life as a man.

What stories like Marie/Germain's suggest is a popular model in
which sex and gender were seen not only as fluid and gradient but
also socially and behaviourally determined. Renaissance and classical
people apparently saw nothing inherently wrong or strange about
the idea that a person's socially gendered role could change within
their lifetime, and further that this could occur concurrently with a
change in the shape of their genitals.

Human sexual anatomy has, presumably, remained the same
since we first evolved. Barring the 'invisible' sex characteristics like
chromosomes and hormones, it's fairly easy to see with the naked
eye what we now call the anatomical 'differences' between the sexes.
What Laqueur is interested in in *Making Sex* is a shift in mindset, in
the context of vast socioeconomic changes, that changed popular
thinking of sex from gradient, fluid and socially determined to
discrete, rigidly binary and innate. What changed, then, during the
Enlightenment to give us our current model? Why the switch from

the hierarchical 'one-sex' system to the binary 'two-sex' system that we're familiar with today?

In the Enlightenment era, Laqueur points out, female and male anatomy began to be more widely given differentiating names, and 'woman' began to be posited as different in kind from 'man' in both physical and moral senses. Rather than implying a hierarchy, this new understanding was able to be used to advance various ideologies, for example to frame women as morally superior or inherently 'passionless' or physically inferior to men. Those in power at this time would then have been able to use a new, more detailed understanding of human sexual anatomy and development as evidence to support the social, economic and political system which benefited them.

The roles of women and men became increasingly differentiated and oppositional in the late eighteenth and nineteenth centuries, as the loci of trade and economy moved away from the home and towards factories and offices. During this time women became increasingly relegated to the home and the realm of domesticity. It behoved men, as mobile agents and, potentially, sole participants in the economy, to reinforce this system. Anatomical differences could be used to do this.

So, until it became necessary for the maintenance of the status quo, sexual difference was not considered an important topic or a potential determiner of social status or role. Our conventional view of gender as immutable and innately linked to sex, and thus prohibiting the transgression of the boundary between the sexes, is grounded in a medical and biological essentialist school of thought that wasn't prevalent until the eighteenth and nineteenth centuries.

It's tempting to call our modern two-sex model enlightened, even 'factual', because it comes chronologically most recently, during a scientific revolution, and because it is often couched in scientific terminology. And I'm not saying that our current understanding of the human developmental, sexual and reproductive system isn't more detailed and complete than it was 400 years ago – of course it is. But increases in our understanding of human sexual anatomy have been continuous since the Victorian era, and have if anything complicated the supposed 'differences' rather than clarifying them. Why are some scientific advances taken as incontrovertible proof to support the two-sex model, while other discoveries, such as the notion that intersex conditions are much more common than once thought,[42] the existence of the perineal raphe[43] or the fact that many apparently cisgender women are born with a Y chromosome,[44] aren't immediately taken up as evidence against the gender binary?

This is because even though it may seem essential, organic and incontrovertible, scientific fact has always been subordinate to the system it serves. It can be framed and reframed to fit an ideology, and the ideology currently in power is one which advocates the separation and differentiation of women and men, and the conflation of gender and sex. There are still people who think that men and women are fundamentally different: these people tend to use these supposed differences to justify placing men and women into differing roles, such as men in leadership roles and women in roles involving emotional labour and nurturing.

But this ideological landscape is changing. Women and men are now largely considered to be the same in neurological terms, and our understanding of natal development is increasingly one of degrees of hormonal influence on the same basic template. By discussing all of this I'm suggesting that we shouldn't see the rigid, discrete categories of male and female as the only conclusion to be drawn from our understanding of biological sex, and that we should take into account social context, politics and power when we think about gender, and consider instead who our model of gender serves.

And I have to wonder what will happen to the binary model of gender once the evidence discussed above becomes common knowledge, and is no longer suppressed. What will happen to binary gender if intersex babies are allowed to develop without coercive surgery? If we stop suppressing, shaming and marginalising people whose gender presentations are unconventional, variable or ambiguous?

Genderqueer through time

There have always been people who think of themselves as neither man nor woman.

In some rare instances these individuals – who just by being themselves could not help but attract attention – were considered so notable that writers of the time preserved written accounts of their behaviour and appearance. There are a handful of documents that record the cases of people who, due to their actions or modes of dress that mix or alternate between male and female, or because of irregularities in their anatomy that became publicly acknowledged, became controversial figures at the time.

Thomas(ine) Hall was an English servant living in the seventeenth century. Witnessing the way that members of the nobility at the time experimented with gender presentation and expression, Thomas(ine), who was intersex and evidently saw in themselves aspects of both the male and female, was raised doing feminine activities like needlework but followed their brother into military service. When they returned from the military they again took up needlework, but when they relocated to Virginia, where men were often hired to work tobacco plantations, they again took on the guise of a man. When Hall was found to have a 'liaison' with a maid, they were charged with sexual misconduct with a servant and eventually taken to court, where it was discovered they were intersex. Hall's case is unique in that rather than being required, as was customary, to choose either a permanent masculine or feminine identity, they were ordered by the judge to dress in both men's and women's clothing from then on.

Overall it seems that Hall approached gender with a fluid and casual attitude that depended on their economic needs and social context. They seemed to also be bisexual, as there is evidence that they had sexual relationships with both men and women, and dressed as the opposite sex in each case. In this sense, too, their environment (i.e. the sex of their partner) determined their presentation and conduct.

Elena/o de Céspedes[45] was a sixteenth-century tailor-turned-surgeon whose gender fluidity eventually landed them in an interrogation before the Spanish Inquisition on a charge of sodomy. Elena/o had been married to a man and borne a child, then left to become a soldier and later a (male) tailor, and had numerous relationships with women. It's now thought that Elena/o was a 'hermaphrodite',[46] or intersex person, though as the evidence we have relies heavily on Elena/o's own testimony in their defence, in a context in which sodomy was punishable by burning at the stake. It may be the case that Elena/o, feeling their gender to be fluid and acting according to their identity throughout their life, then later claimed hermaphroditism – that they had been a woman when they were first married, and a man during their relationships with women – in order to avoid a much more serious charge of homosexuality, which did not take identity into account. As it was, Elena/o was charged with 'sorcery and disrespect for the marriage sacrament' and, somewhat ironically, sentenced to serve the poor as a surgeon (a male profession), while wearing women's clothing.

The people I discuss above didn't write about themselves, and as such it's difficult to know how, exactly, they thought of their own genders. Both Thomas(ine) and Elena/o may have also been intersex, that is, born with unconventional or ambiguous external genitalia, or genitalia which developed differently from how it would be expected to based on the gender they were assigned at birth. Intersex conditions and nonbinary gender are *not* the same thing, and by no means do I consider being intersex to be the only way that people in the past could exist outside the male/female binary. But it would be disingenuous to avoid mentioning this commonality which may have existed between them, and I think that in many cases being intersex may have been only the most public way by which people could transgress or straddle the male/female binary without being forced by outside observers or authority figures into one or the other category.

I think it likely (though I'll admit completely unprovable) that in many cases, people who didn't think of themselves as men or women, and who presented publicly in an ambiguous or inconsistent way, would likely have been 'gendered' by outside observers. Intersex people like Thomas(ine) Hall would probably have been peripherally aware of stories like that of Marie/Germain and indeed some of them would probably have envisioned their own 'transformations' or 'abnormal' development in that light,[47] as influenced by external factors, such as Elena/o's possible development of a penis after the trauma of childbirth, or their loss of it from an injury while horseback riding.[48]

In societies that conceptualised men and women as (for the most part) discrete categories, which didn't have established social roles for 'third gender' people such as eunuchs or inverts (and didn't have access to knowledge of these categories), and in which transgressing social boundaries was frowned upon, it might have been extremely difficult for most people to conceive of a way of being that was neither male or female. Even people who might have thought of themselves as neither man nor woman may have simply ignored these feelings due to outside pressure to be one or the other. Because there are very few surviving documents in which people describe their *own* concept of gender, it's very difficult to say.

Indeed a number of the accounts of historical figures who transgressed gender roles were made in a context of legal proceedings and public investigations, such as of the trial in which Thomas(ine) was made to wear both men's and women's clothing, and Elena/o's testimony on their own genitals before the Spanish Inquisition. These accounts were created by members of the cisgender majority and only survived because there was physical 'evidence' – i.e. an intersex condition – to back up the ambiguity of social role.

In other cases, for example where people with vaginas have taken on male roles and lived as men, such as the accomplished physician Dr James Barry who by his own admission thought of himself as a man, we see accounts of their lives generally framed as a 'revelation', rather, a person who was thought to be a man is 'revealed' to be a woman, no matter how the person in question thinks of themself.

So I suggest that being intersex, while it didn't necessarily *predispose* someone to think of or present themself as neither a man nor a woman, it would have allowed them the freedom to do so, without a binary role forced upon them by a cisgender observer.

Even as they've drawn boundaries between man and woman, human societies have long been at least peripherally aware of people who defied these categories. In some cases these societies have carved out an established, if stigmatised, place for them. The nature of these 'established' third (or fourth or fifth) genders depended heavily on how 'woman' and 'man' were conceptualised in the first place, and their origins are not always certain. Perhaps the level of frequency or visibility of a few early trans people had to reach a threshold before they could be given space.

Membership in these categories was often associated with certain external characteristics, from genital shape to sexual behaviour, and sometimes the categories were associated with certain occupations and professions. Members of these 'socially sanctioned' – and also often heavily marginalised – gender categories might even have understood themselves as part of a larger community – though whether this entailed the full meaning of the word in today's sense, implying a kind of shared 'history' and mutual support networks, is uncertain and varies from context to context.

In Europe and anglophone countries, for the most part, the criteria by which people were considered to occupy these third gender categories were strongly informed by whichever conceptualisation of gender was prevalent at the time. As Western ideas on gender changed, so too did the way we labelled people who transgressed the boundaries we set. For most of Western history, ideas about sexual or gender 'identity' were very different from those of today. Because most Western societies have marginalised, vilified or criminalised any kind of sexual or gender diversity for most of their history, there has been no question of openly declaring one's membership in a certain group. For most trans people, then, there has been no such thing as community.

Before biological sex and social gender were unlinked in popular and academic thought, there was considered to be a direct causal link between sex, gender and sexuality– though the order in which these characteristics informed each other changed over the centuries. In the nineteenth and twentieth centuries, a phenomenon known as 'sexual inversion' was supposed to account for homosexual behaviour among men and women. It was thought, somewhat like modern mainstream ideas about transgender people, that a homosexual woman, for example, had the personality, soul or 'spirit' of a man, inside a body that was female. Rather than just thinking of them as men and women as we generally do trans men and trans women nowadays, though, inverts were considered to occupy a 'third' sex or state of 'hermaphrodism'.

And unlike our modern understanding that the sexualities of transgender people don't necessarily correlate with their gender identities, the 'inversion' theory drew a direct link between sexual behaviour (rather than social role or gender presentation) and the nature of their inner self. 'Sexual inverts' didn't always dress or be- have as the 'opposite' gender to the one they were assigned at birth – though in some contexts they could and did – and they did not seem concerned with passing as the 'opposite sex' in most cases. In his essay, 'A Female Soul in a Male Body',[49] Gert Hekla argues that, while they were often considered by outsiders to be neither male nor female, they didn't necessarily think of *themself* as a third gender or sex. And while many male 'inverts' sought out each others' company, forming a community of sorts for purposes of socialisation and to ensure relative safety when engaging in sexual relationships, it was *sexual preference* which united them rather than any commonality in terms of gender identity.

In other cases, membership in these historical trans categories was based on coercion: in the Byzantine era, for example, eunuchs constituted one such group. Usually prisoners of war, but in later centuries sometimes illegitimate children of the imperial house who were forbidden to procreate, eunuchs were men and boys who had been castrated before puberty, sold as slaves and trained to be anything from servants to advisors to the emperor. Because of their unique position – that is, lacking the potential to sire heirs or found dynasties – eunuchs were thought of as 'safe' to have as imperial attendants, and to employ in the harem, where the 'purity' of the women must be preserved.

Because of their proximity to power, eunuchs could sometimes attain incredible socioeconomic mobility, and increased the prestige of their community, as it were, over the years, though their origins were usually humble and their position always tenuous as they were liable to fall in and out of favour with a changing roster of monarchs. They were a common fixture in the imperial palace and in daily life for much of the reign of the Byzantine empire, and as such they were well-integrated into daily life for most people who lived in Constantinople.

The very obvious signals which distinguished eunuchs perceptibly from their 'uncut' peers, combined with their association with specific professions, contributed directly to the eunuch being seen as a discrete social category, a 'third sex'. In her essay, 'Living in the Shadows',[50] which discusses the popular perception of eunuchs in Constantinople, Kathryn M Ringrose discusses a number of misconceptions, myths and stereotypes associated with eunuchs in contemporary popular imagination; they were considered changeable and capricious, quick to anger, 'fainthearted', even sinister and frightening. They were generally considered to be pale, cool, soft, damp and impotent, in opposition to the male ideals, under the two-sex model that held sway in those days, of tanned, hot, hard, dry and virile. Ringrose says that, within the strictly gendered context of the imperial court, eunuchs 'were believed to be able to change their psychological affect and share attributes of two genders'.[51]

In this way, seen as distinct from men and women *by* men and women, with their social role (possibly more than their actual anatomy) causing their contemporaries to regard them in light of an established popular understanding of their group as a whole, eunuchs could be considered to occupy a distinct category, and *potentially* a community of their own. They were subject to marginalisation and stigma but, rather than trying to assimilate, they could use their eunuch status to occupy specific, prestigious roles.

It's difficult to say how eunuchs thought of themselves. The primary sources Ringrose cites suggest that the masculine ideals of strength and virility were extremely privileged. Eunuchs would doubtless have suffered from their inability to conform to this narrow definition, and perhaps that was part of the reason why they were considered so distinct from 'uncut' men. Perhaps, being raised in a society with such a rigid category for man, they would indeed consider themselves as belonging to a third sex.

These historic, alternative gender categories developed in many different historical contexts, and under many different ways of thinking about gender. Gender and sexual identity, as well as the social roles associated with gender in any form, are inextricably tied to place and period. In nearly all historical cases, it is very difficult to tell how these people thought of themselves in terms of the gender structure of their day, and I by no means want to assert that the people discussed considered themselves specifically genderqueer or nonbinary. Most of these people likely didn't conceptualise gender the way we do, and the importance that their cultures placed on body, sexuality and performative social role would have been differently configured to our modern, Western one.

Generally speaking, the criteria on which these historical 'third' categories are based take into account personal identity less, and appearance, anatomy and sexual behaviour more. I do think there were people of all and any sex who thought of themselves as neither male nor female, regardless of sexuality or anatomy. But the boundaries of the 'third sex' categories were set by outsiders, and membership in them could expose a person to social stigma and even danger. Indeed, when 'sodomites' (as homosexuals were called in the eighteenth century) began to establish social networks, shared signals and meeting places, the discovery of these networks led to extreme levels of persecution lasting for more than two centuries.[52]

These categories differed from modern transgender and nonbinary identities, then, in that members were largely unable to self-define, to set the boundaries of their own communities and actively seek each other out. The labels applied to these groups tend to be, at least at the start, exonyms or even slurs, and most of the historical accounts of individuals were likewise written by members of the cisgender majority of the day, who had no way of distinguishing between the identity of self-image and that of group membership.

I inventory these people and categories here because I want to demonstrate that, despite our terminology being new, the genderqueer and nonbinary identities of today can be considered merely the most recent iteration of a state of being that has always existed in various forms. It's only now that we have the theoretical tools to understand gender as separate from sex – and as fluid and blurry – and the safety to exist without being forced into the confines of a category that doesn't suit us, that contemporary genderqueer people are able equipped to articulate the subtleties of their own gender identities.

Elena/o de Céspedes and Thomas(ine) Hall, and even genderqueer people at the beginning of this century, have made do without any possibility of a community. I include their stories here not only to lend historical continuity to my writing about contemporary nonbinary people, but to honour them. Asserting their identities – whatever those identities may have been – was an act of bravery as much as it is for us today.

Global alternative gender categories

At the same time as gender hasn't always been conceptualised in the same way, neither do all cultures conceptualise gender as both binary and immutable. There are a number of cultures throughout the world that conceptualise gender as more complex than just woman and man, and who acknowledge the existence of one or more alternate or 'third' gender categories, to be variously celebrated or stigmatised.

The cultures and culturally-tied gender categories I discuss in this section are separate from Western categories of transgender or genderqueer identity.

Before I go on I think it's important to discuss the difference between non-Western gender categories and historical ones. Very often in academic settings (especially in the field of anthropology, with which I have some familiarity) so-called 'non-Western' social phenomena are strongly associated, or even conflated, with historical or archaic ones. The contemporary, modern gender categories I discuss below are not the same as the historical ones I discuss above, but neither is there a complete dichotomy between them. Most of these gender categories have a long history, though this may not be a written one, and many of them have been influenced, especially in modern times, by Western, colonial ideas of gender, sex and sexuality.

Trying to draw a complete distinction between 'Western' and 'non-Western' cultures creates space for value judgments or categorical assumptions to be made about the people of these cultures: the idea that non-Western or indigenous cultures and their ideas about gender are somehow more organic, essential or 'connected to nature' is only one step away from the idea that these cultures are somehow 'primitive' or otherwise less developed or advanced than their Western counterparts.

Indeed, many analyses, especially in the early days of anthropology and linguistics, in fields of study that were heavily influenced by social Darwinism, did just this: differences and boundaries between loosely defined groups of white, European cultures and implicitly or explicitly *nonwhite* cultures were used to justify colonialism and imperialism.

My intention by including both 'non-Western' alternate categories in the same chapter as historical categories is not to imply that modern non-Western cultures are somehow archaic, or to imply any fundamental difference between people of any culture extant today, but to explore concepts of gender which are *not* based in the biological essentialist, two-sex model so pervasive in anglo-phone and European countries. I include these examples simply to suggest more flexible, more blurred, more ambiguous, more granular or otherwise different ways of thinking about gender.

Documented in over 100 North American indigenous societies at various points in history, including today, two-spirit identity is one of the most established, widespread and visible alternative gender categories in existence. Originally called by the exonym 'berdache', which is now largely considered offensive, two-spirit encompasses a wide range of social roles from a number of different cultures,[53] many of them historically ceremonial, that lie outside of the traditional male/female dichotomy.

Two-spirits can have been assigned either sex at birth, though *traditionally* most two-spirits seem to have been AMAB.[54] Aside from a crossing of gender boundaries in terms of dress and behaviour, which exemplifies the category, two-spirit identities are generally associated with religious, ceremonial and supernatural power, and are generally accorded a measure of respect (though this varies from culture to culture) from within the community. This prestige makes two-spirit relatively unique amongst a world of alternative gender categories, for which liminality so often leads to marginalisation.

There have been a number of well-known two-spirit figures of authority throughout history, such as Hastiin Klah, a Navajo *nádleehi*, or two-spirit, who (among other roles) was both a weaver (traditionally considered a women's activity) and ceremonial chanter and sand-painter (roles conventionally reserved for men). Klah was also an important figure in documenting and preserving Navajo religious art and practices. Bíawacheeitchish, or Woman Chief, who lived in the 1840s, was assigned female at birth but, after being captured and raised by the Crow people, showed a strong interest in the male pursuits of riding, hunting and marksmanship and became a renowned warrior and leader in her father's lodge after his death. While Bíawacheeitchish performed various male roles, she apparently did so while maintaining a female style of dress. This expression of third gender by way of mixed dress also seems to have been widespread: Charlie, a Navajo *nádleehi* pictured in Will Roscoe's essay, 'How to Become a Berdache: Toward a Unified Analysis of Gender Diversity',[55] wears a style of dress 'distinct from that of both men and women', along with silver jewellery suggestive of wealth and prestige.

There has been extensive anthropological study of two-spirit people, which has necessarily been coloured by the perspective of the anthropologists. In addition, the history and contemporary context of two-spirit people can't be separated from the violence all indigenous Americans faced and are still facing at the hands of the Euro-American majority. For the last three hundred-odd years it's been nearly impossible for any indigenous American community to avoid being influenced by Euro-American culture, and the definition and specific roles of two-spirit people have necessarily been influenced by mainstream American LGBT culture. Often conflated with both homosexuality and transgender identity, two-spirit is distinct from both and tied inextricably to the Native American cultures in which it originates.

Two-spirit-identified people today, like any genderqueer, agender or genderflux person, will define their own identity in a nuanced way unique to them. Though two-spirit people often consider themselves part of the larger trans community, their identities are tied to both their experience of gender and culture.

There are a number of loosely connected gender categories outside of man and woman that exist in various Polynesian cultures today. The many cultures of Polynesia are, to an extent, culturally and linguistically connected. It's not therefore surprising that many of these island cultures have a shared,[56] long-standing culture of what Niko Besnier[57] calls 'gender liminality',[58] a term which I will use to describe the phenomenon for the duration of this section, so as not to apply the name from one culture to the identity from another.

Polynesian gender liminal people are known by different names in different cultures, *Fa'afafine* in Samoa and Samoan diasporic communities, *Mahu* in Hawai'i, and *Fakaleiti* in Tonga, to name a few.

All members of these gender liminal categories were assigned male at birth, and all seem to be distinguished by a gender expression that blurs the boundaries between man and woman, though not by any specific mode of dress or behaviour. These people do not consider themselves women,[59] and their presentation doesn't precisely match that of conventional women of these cultures.

Gender liminal people in Polynesia tend to have occupations which are traditionally considered 'women's work', and are generally held to be adept at them, sometimes to the extent that they're considered better at them than the average 'biological' woman. According to Besnier, Polynesian gender liminal people are sought after as secretaries and domestic helpers.

An important distinction between Polynesian gender liminal people and Western trans women is that they do not live full-time as women, or even full-time as the same or a consistent mix of gendered signifiers: Besnier takes care to note that Polynesian gender liminal individuals can and very often do alter their presentation, choosing to display or hide their gender liminality depending on the social context. There are also distinctions between liminal and normative Polynesian women as well: though young gender liminal people socialise more often with young cisgender women in some Polynesian societies, their 'womanhood' is more commonly associated in the popular imagination with older, nonvirginal women, regardless of the age of the gender liminal person in question.

In his article, Besnier laments a 'paucity of detailed treatments... in specific Polynesian contexts', which makes it difficult to determine the true origins of the phenomenon, and the extent of the similarities and differences between different Polynesian gender liminal traditions. According to Besnier, these liminal gender categories – or some contemporary form of them – are especially prominent in regions that have experienced more limited colonisation, such as Tonga, as compared to Hawai'i and New Zealand. Until more historic sources are found (the likelihood of this wanes yearly) and more research conducted, it's imperative that any study of collective Polynesian gender liminality avoid generalisations, and mistaking the idiosyncracies of a single gender liminal individual for an archetype.

In short, this is a sparsely documented phenomenon, occurring in a collection of cultures that have been historically (and contemporarily) subject to all the destructive influence of European colonialism, an influence which was strongly in favour of erasing anything the colonisers deemed aberrant, sinful or otherwise morally questionable – as so many non-normative expressions of gender and sexuality have been.

The Bugis people are an indigenous cultural group in south Sulawesi, Indonesia. The Bugis consider there to be five genders. Two of these, *makkunrai* and *oroané*, are equivalent to the Western categories of cisgender men and women. Two others, *calalai* and *calabai*, are similar to the categories of trans men and trans women, which are also becoming more visible in the West.[60] The fifth category, which I'll focus on here, is called *bissu*, or 'gender transcendent'.

Bissu are considered to embody qualities of both male and female, as well as of the mortal and divine. They act commonly as priests and religious authorities, bestowing blessings for special occasions, for example before a Bugis person makes the pilgrimage to Mecca – the Bugis practice a syncretic form of Islam and an older, pre-Islamic religion.

The criteria by which a person is considered or 'becomes' a *bissu* are variable and often depend on individual choice and personality. If a child is seen to have a propensity for gender ambiguity, rather than being punished and coerced towards a normative male or female presentation, they are groomed for the social role of a *bissu* shaman. Many *bissu* are people who were born with ambiguous genitalia (i.e. intersex people), but many people with unambiguous male or female genitalia also become *bissu*. For example, if a person with a penis becomes a *bissu* it is commonly held that they are 'female inside', and vice versa.

The inextricable link between *bissu* and spirituality raises a few questions about the relationship between gender, religion and society in Bugis culture: is the acceptability or legitimacy of the fifth, *bissu* category enabled or facilitated by the two 'trans' categories, *calalai* and *calabai*? This is a difficult question to answer: other cultures do have a simpler three-gender system, and it would take a great deal of comparative study to see if there are any differences in the relative acceptance of these categories in their respective societies. Further, nowadays it is possible for *bissu* to have jobs other than shaman or priest. According to Sharyn Graham Davies in her article 'Sex, gender, and priests in South Sulawesi, Indonesia',[61] in the past *bissu* would usually be expected to play a role in the royal court.

Nowadays, however, many Bugis youth who don't identify as strictly male or female consider the training and initiation rituals to be too strenuous. Because many of them find themselves and their gender identities accepted socially as *calalai*, *calabai* or simply as a Western-style trans or nonbinary person, the tradition of *bissu*-as-priest is in danger of dying out.[62]

The Buginese, or Bugis people, are the most numerous linguistic and cultural group in South Sulawesi, Indonesia. Though the majority of Bugis people are farmers, many live in major cities and as a cultural group the Bugis have political clout; the current prime minister of Malaysia and the vice president of Indonesia are both Buginese. I include this information not only to discuss an alternative way of thinking about gender but to suggest that alternative gender categories need not be 'obscure' or 'sub-cultural'.

Conclusion

Creating binaries – discrete, inflexible categories – is a human instinct. But as easy and clean as they are, binaries are not supported by the evidence, be it historical, biological or psychological. There is a vast weight of evidence that supports the idea that the boundaries between 'male' and 'female' are not as immutable as we are generally led to believe. There have always been people who pushed those boundaries, whether their respective societies chose to acknowledge them or not.

The higher significance which is placed on the state of being trans or gender-nonconforming in some way is an interesting and persistent one. A great many of the categories of people that I discuss in this chapter are associated not only with 'liminal', ambiguous or in-between sexes and gender presentations but also with states of being which themselves can be considered liminal or transitional. Throughout history people of marginalised genders, such as eunuchs and India's hijras, have been given roles which deal with transitions in states of being such as death rituals, medicine and birth. So, not only can trans and genderqueer people be considered to fit within the worldview of a great many human cultures, in many cases they are considered essential to it, just as much a part of the creation and perpetuation of human culture as men and women.

Even in the past few centuries, it is possible to trace changes in the zeitgeist of gender: how are economic and social changes affecting the way that 'man' and 'woman' are defined, differentiated and associated with different roles? These very changes have been documented throughout history – for example in the West there has been a shift from a socially to a biologically determined concept of gender. The accepted theory has moved from considering physical sex to be fluid to seeing personal identity as fluid – evidence that the barriers we place between the categories are porous and flexible. Ours is not the only way to think about gender. As rigid, logical, natural and eternal as our current model of sex and gender may seem to us now, it has not always been this way, and nor will it continue to be so in the future.

Exercises and discussion questions

1. Apart from contemporary categories like nonbinary, genderqueer and transgender, do you or your family come from a culture that has, or historically had, alternative gender categories? What are or were they?
2. Do some further research into this category to try and find some

more information. As much as possible try to find primary sources: videos, articles, blog posts, etc. in which members of these categories and communities discuss *their own experiences*.

3. What model of gender is implicit in a system that includes this category? Is it a three-gender system? Four genders? Is the alternate category fully neither/nor, or is it a variation on 'man' or 'woman'? Are the boundaries between the genders hard and definite, or porous and blurry?

4. What are the entry criteria for the category? Is it externally applied based on coercion (like eunuchs), sexual, social or other types of behaviour (like sodomites or inverts), or is it based on self-avowed identity, like today's trans and nonbinary people?

5. Can a person choose to join the category, are they considered to be born to it or is there another set of membership criteria altogether? Can a person enter or leave the category in their lifetime? When and how does this occur?

CHAPTER 4

Community

Introduction

The genderqueer community is a nascent one: in the same way that our terminology, our identity labels and our meeting spaces are still in development, so too are we in the process of establishing the boundaries of our community, carving ourselves out a space within the greater LGBT and transgender communities and exploring the ways in which other identities intersect with nonbinary and genderqueer.

In this context, *community* can be thought of as an externalised version of identity. A person who identifies as genderqueer or trans or gay and who also interacts or spends time with other people who identify as such, or does work to help other people who identify in the same way or to raise awareness of issues that specifically affect people who identify in the same way, can be considered to be an active member of that community. At the same time, though, there are active and passive senses in which a person can be a part of a community: since we're still a rather nebulous group and a lot of us aren't out, what 'genderqueer community' or 'nonbinary community' means, and who is considered to be a part of it, will necessarily be different for each of us. In addition, because I've personally benefited a great deal from the support I found in the nonbinary community even when I wasn't active in it, I still think it's necessary to consider a genderqueer or nonbinary person who isn't active in genderqueer spaces as a member of that community, perhaps even if that person doesn't consider themself an active member of their community.

As with the great majority of marginalised social groups, community is an important source of support and growth for genderqueer and nonbinary people. Many of us lack emotional, moral and financial support from within our own families, culture and peer groups, and find it difficult to articulate our experiences to people who don't share them. At the same time, we're still in the process of finding each other. The rarity of examples from history, and the lack of studies and research that frames us as a distinct category, makes this very clear. Nonbinary people are fighting every day to have our voices heard as a group in our own right, fighting for mention on census forms and for our pronouns and titles to be brought into common use, at the same time as this lack of visibility makes it difficult to convince people we're deserving of these things.

Nonbinary people within the wider LGB and T communities

Nonbinary, genderqueer and genderfluid people are in a somewhat tenuous position within the larger LGB community because, though we often claim membership within the LGBT umbrella and benefit from the legitimacy implied by a long, well-established history, and though we have least a certain base level of shared experience, the labels *lesbian* and *gay* imply, to some extent, a binary personal experience of sexuality and gender, an experience which, in some senses, excludes us.

So even if a genderqueer person feels a connection to the gay community, for example if they identified with L or G before they came out or understood themself as genderqueer, they may have cause to step back from L and G of their own volition because of the binary implication inherent in the label. They may feel uncomfortable claiming space in the gay community because they've experienced hostility from gay and lesbian people, or they may feel they don't qualify for or deserve to use the label gay or lesbian.

The problem with this is that, like the word 'feminist', L and G mean much more than their denotative definitions; they are often used as statements of political or cultural values. There's a whole lot of history and culture and community inherent in these terms, and it can be difficult or alienating to be denied entry to this shared experience and network of support simply by virtue of existing outside the binary, and I often see nonbinary and genderqueer people make use of more ambiguous or mixed identifiers like queer, bi- and pansexual. I'll discuss the use of these labels and what they mean later on when I discuss dating and relationships.

More specific identity labels

The Scottish Trans Alliance 2015 report, 'Non-binary people's experiences in the UK', records an extended list[63] of terms that participants use to identify themselves. Because this survey, of almost 900 participants, was focussed only on people not identifying as binary woman or man, there was much more space to investigate precisely what labels nonbinary people currently use to describe themselves – discovering which terms are current is important because our community and its lexicon are constantly changing.

The terms we use are also heavily influenced by the culture and politics of our backgrounds, by feminist and queer theory, and even by our geographic region. Even as I enumerate the terms used in the 2015 survey they may be sliding out of common usage with new ones that I've not heard yet taking their place – though I do suspect that we're approaching a time of relative stability in nonbinary terminology. So the estimates of usage within the nonbinary population should necessarily be taken with a grain of salt, and the individuals who identify with these terms are, obviously, the authorities on what they mean.

I'll include a few terms for identities that are slightly more specific and granular than those discussed in Chapter 1. There's no quiz at the end of the book but being at least familiar with these terms will cut down on the amount of explaining a nonbinary person needs to do when their preferred identity marker is being discussed. The most popular designations in the STA survey (these are not mutually exclusive, and participants were encouraged to select as many options from the list as apply) were *nonbinary, genderqueer* and *transgender*, followed closely by *genderfluid* (n=277) and *agender* (n=253). Other popular labels were *transmasculine*, meaning a person assigned female at birth who identifies as more masculine than feminine (n=133), *androgyne* (n=127) and 'other', as in a label not included in the list provided on the survey (n=116). Out of my 14 interviewees, many of whom listed more than one identity label on their survey, two listed 'genderqueer' and nine listed 'nonbinary'. Multiple people also listed their genders as 'trans' and 'genderfluid', and a couple people identified with 'boi', which is an identity loosely defined (by the Gender Wiki) as 'a youthful, androgynous, queer identity that originated in African American culture in the 1990s'.[64] Boi is an identity I've seen used most commonly in the United States, and usually by BAME people.

Genderfluid

The first identity marker I'd like to discuss here is *genderfluid*. Genderfluid identities are ones that develop, change or fluctuate over time. Of the 895 participants in the STA nonbinary experiences survey more than half described their gender identity as fluid or changing,[65] though these participants may not all use genderfluid as their primary identity label, as the 'fixed or fluid' question was separate from the 'identity' question. Genderfluid, and subcategories like *genderflux*, which will be discussed below, seems to be a growing demographic within the nonbinary umbrella. I don't think this is necessarily because more people are starting to identify with a fluctuating gender, or more genderfluid people are being born, but because more and more people, even outside the trans community, are beginning to see gender as more flexible, blurry and context-dependent than ever before.

Three per cent of those who described their gender as fluid said it depended on circumstances or environment, such as their partner or prospective partner's sexuality, a particular activity taking place or individual mood or attitude. Among the genderfluid participants it was also noted that there was a difference in *what* changed: many people reported that their gender *expression* might change while their identity itself remained the same, or vice-versa, or both. As one participant put it, 'because traditional gender roles feel performative and irrelevant to me'.[66] All of this evidence underscores the idea that gender identity and expression, though intimately linked, are not the same thing: just as a person's outward appearance does not always reflect their personality, so too might a person's gender expression depend on factors other than their identity.

Interviewee VK (who uses female and occasionally *xe/xyr* pronouns) identifies as *genderflux*, a subcategory of genderfluid which refers to an identity that fluctuates between two points on a scale – in VK's case that is usually agender and female. Xe described the difficulty xe had in finding a way to articulate xyr identity: 'I've always known I'm not cis, but I couldn't find myself in a current LGBTQ terminology.' It was difficult for xem to explain xyr gender to xyr cisgender brother, for example, without having a full vocabulary: 'If you don't know that it can change, you might think you don't know what it is, if you don't know that a changing or uncertain gender at a single point in time is a gender.'

VK doesn't know if something causes xyr gender to change, because it's too early to tell. A fluctuation may be triggered by stress, associated with a 'withdrawal' from or discomfort engaging with gender, or it may be influenced by xyr experience of attraction and sexuality: 'I realised last year that I'm attracted to girls for the first time.' VK says, 'At 16 I had to break up with someone I loved because being with him confused me, I felt like I was playing a role.' Again we see the idea of gender roles in relationships feeling forced, artificial or performative, and the intimate perceived link between gender and gender roles causing a genderfluid person to feel uncertainty.

After moving away from xyr home country and the gendered titles and expectations associated with it, and after experiencing an intense period of dissociation and dysphoria, the space to explore an alternatively gendered role in terms of relationships and attraction opened other areas of VK's life up for questioning. VK expressed a hesitancy to present in a feminine way that was always present, even before xe was aware of xyr fluid gender: 'Even when I was feeling feminine, I wouldn't wear female clothes because I wouldn't want to give people a false impression of me (as exclusively and consistently female).' Even now, VK doesn't often wear dresses, 'even though I like the way I look in them'.

VK told me something which I've seen echoed a lot across the queer community, which is the idea that community, family and peer group support, far from simply being a safety net, can be a way for a genderqueer person to explore, develop and articulate their own identity and experiences. VK has experienced a double-bind of exploring xyr identity by talking about it with other people, while being unable to articulate an identity xe didn't have a vocabulary for. Xe described, 'feeling like there's nothing clear in my mind, so I don't want to talk to anyone about it, but it helps to talk about it'.

Another concept which I've seen echoed in the community and which I've experienced myself is the idea that control over one's presentation can have an ameliorating effect on dysphoria, and allow a person to more readily adapt their own presentation in response to a changing identity. VK said that, even before xe figured out xe were genderflux, 'While I didn't know how to identify I started planning a vegan month, I started running, [and] I felt a sense of control over the way my body looks.' I suspect that this sense of control is important for VK (as it is for me since I began my medical transition) not just in the sense of having more control over gender presentation in response to a dynamic and fluctuating gender but in the sense of having more bodily autonomy in general. A great deal of the dysphoria and self-destructive behaviours that can come from it stem from a feeling that one doesn't have control over the way one looks, and over one's life in general.

An added complication is that, even within the larger LGBT community, it's not always accepted that a person's gender identity *can* change. VK describes not having the vocabulary until recently to describe xyr identity, and defaulting to a term even if it didn't feel right: 'up until recently I went by genderqueer – which is something everyone (at least within the queer community) can understand'.

I think a certain amount of resistance to the idea of a fluid identity, even as society as a whole begins to think of gender in a more flexible and dynamic way, might come from the history of invalidation that LGBT people have experienced when they express any doubt or uncertainty about their own identities. A lesbian who sometimes had relationships with men, for example, often had her identity dismissed as 'experimentation', and even now bisexual people are still fighting for their sexual identity to be recognised as more than just 'promiscuity' or 'indecisiveness'.[67] In response to this it's become something of a party line in LGBT discourse that a person is gay even before they have their first gay relationship, that a trans woman is a woman long before she begins hormones and so on.

But just as gay marriage was for many years framed as the ultimate goal of the LGBT rights movement (at the expense of questioning any of the harmful aspects of the institution of marriage and monogamy), the idea of gender as consistent and unchanging is often politically expedient. If a trans celebrity came out as genderfluid, it would be very easy, for example, for an unsympathetic journalist to latch on to this and claim the celebrity 'wasn't really (X gender)', was 'flip-flopping', was 'experimenting' or 'regretted transitioning', and use this to frame the entire trans and queer community as 'changing genders' at random, or as fickle or otherwise illegitimate. So the reality is often much more complex than any manifesto can convey, and the backlash against gender fluidity is at least understandable if it is not excusable.

But none of this changes the fact that fluid gender identities do exist, and likely always have.

In the same way that nonbinary identities *appear* to be an artifact of the twenty-first century, simply because we are only now beginning to assert ourselves as a community and, importantly, develop a vocabulary to define our identities, the development of the gender-fluid community has been limited in the past by the fact that the *word* genderfluid is a relatively new term. It's my hope that we're at the beginning of an upward trend, and that in the next few years gender-fluidity will enter more into common parlance and increasingly be accepted both inside and outside the queer community.

Agender

Agender is an identity I encounter quite often, and one which I feel best describes my own experience of gender. Put simply, an agender person doesn't identify with a gender at all. This can manifest in a number of different ways, from not having a gender or rejecting the idea of labelling oneself, to a wholesale rejection of the entire institution of gender. I have found agender a useful category, though I'm still not sure whether I consider it my primary identifier. For me, and for many agender people, gender is simply not a useful category or characteristic to identify myself by. I don't resonate strongly with any gendered label and, though I present myself as alternately male, female, ambiguously or a combination of the two (most, though not all, styles of clothing giving the impression of one or the other), I don't consider myself particularly male, female or anything in between.

Bigender, polygender and pangender

An identity that seems to be fairly common, and which is in some senses a logical reverse of an agender identity, is a state of embodying and identifying with more than one gender, for example male and female, or a mix of both, or as 'all genders at once', which may include a gender that is neither male nor female.

The most common terms I've encountered which convey this sense of multiplicity are *bigender*, *polygender* and *pangender*. In a similar way to how many bisexuals nowadays are asserting that they don't limit themselves to attraction to two (as implied by *bi-*) genders, and stating unequivocally that they may be attracted to nonbinary people, I consider *bigender*, along with *pan-* and *poly*gender to mean a person who identifies with multiple genders, with a flexible, nuanced definition that will vary from person to person. Certainly a person who identifies as bigender won't necessarily also use the term poly- or pangender to describe themself.

Many people who identify as the terms I've discussed above will give you different and more detailed definitions for them than I do. I advise listening closely when someone you encounter gives you a different definition for one of these labels than the one listed here. Identities – be they gender, cultural, racial, religious – can be intensely personal and the same word will mean something slightly different to each person who uses it. Many of these terms have evolving – or no – standard definitions, and many may indeed fall out of use as they gain or lose connotations, or as gender-queerness gains more mainstream acceptance and recognition. As with any identity marker, it is always best to defer to the person who uses the identity marker, and to listen to them when they explain what that label means to them. Finding out what any one of these words means to someone who uses it can be very enlightening, and can only deepen your understanding of nonbinary identities as a whole.

Do all nonbinary people identify as trans?

Throughout this book I've been talking about both the experiences of nonbinary people and, where information is lacking on nonbinary people as a distinct group, trans people more generally. This raises a logical question, then, of how many nonbinary people also identify as transgender. Up until now I've been using 'trans' as an umbrella term to describe the experiences of a large and varied group of people, for example where nonbinary-specific data is unavailable. This is a good rule of thumb but these categories don't overlap 100 per cent of the time, and though I personally identify as both nonbinary and transgender, the contexts in which I use the terms to describe my experiences are different. I feel it's necessary to discuss these contexts, and the reasons why a person might identify as nonbinary but not as trans.

The Scottish Trans Alliance's 2015 report, 'Nonbinary people's experience in the UK', specifically in the context of services and employment, found that 65 per cent of 895 nonbinary people *did* consider themselves transgender (though this may not be the primary identity label they use to describe themselves). Similarly, the 2015 US Trans Survey[68] found that only 18 per cent of participants who identified as nonbinary *were not* comfortable with being also described as transgender.

But 311 of the STA nonbinary survey participants said that they did not feel 'trans enough' to use the label. This is something I hear echoed frequently in the nonbinary community, and as far as I can tell it comes down to a few key factors, namely discrimination, gender presentation, a desire to (medically and socially) transition and an individual's interpretation of what 'trans' means.

A nonbinary person may feel that being transgender implies a desire to transition in some visible way, either socially or medically. A nonbinary person who doesn't visibly alter their presentation from the norm may feel that the label 'transgender' doesn't correctly describe their experience. This lack of a change in presentation may be because the nonbinary person in question doesn't feel the need to outwardly express their gender identity, or because they are not comfortable doing so in their home or professional environment. A nonbinary person may still identify *partly* with the gender they were assigned at birth and feel that 'transgender' implies a complete break with one's assigned gender.

The majority of participants in the STA survey who don't use the 'trans' label say it is because they don't personally experience discrimination relating to their gender. These people see 'transgender' as a label expressing a shared experience of marginalisation and community solidarity in the face of hardship, and they may feel that for them to take on that label would constitute an appropriation of trans culture – that they would benefit from identifying in the trans community without facing the discrimination that trans people face.

At the same time, nonbinary people may also feel unwelcome in the transgender community for the same reasons. They may have faced hostility (though this seems to be quite rare) from certain trans people who feel a nonbinary presence in their spaces is a threat to the legitimacy of their own identities. A few participants in the STA survey felt that they were actively excluded from the trans community, that the community they had experienced was heavily focussed on the experiences of binary trans people or that the popular perception of transgender was, for example, 'on a journey from male to female'[69]. In addition, only 72 per cent of respondents who used LGBT services felt comfortable being open about their nonbinary identity within those services, which suggests that there is still work to do within the LGBT community towards full nonbinary and genderqueer inclusion.

I personally do identify as trans. I take hormones and am out as nonbinary to my friends and in the workplace. I consider myself a part of the trans and larger LGBT communities, and I feel solidarity with all gender-variant people, binary or not. I find 'trans' a useful label when describing the aspects of my own experience which are specifically connected to a rejection of the gender I was assigned at birth. Further, because of the complex and multilayered connection between gender identity and gender expression, many cis people who encounter nonbinary people undergoing a medical transition may not be able to tell the difference between the binary and nonbinary trans experience. It may also be politically expedient to lump our groups together under one umbrella in some contexts. When I'm speaking about my experience and don't have the time to explain the nuances of a nonbinary identity, or when I'm making a point that's not connected to the *nonbinary* part, I don't always distinguish the two. In many senses, the marginalisation we all face comes from the same sources.

Nonbinary and genderqueer people, feminism and trans exclusion

I first gained the vocabulary to talk about my gender at the same time as I discovered feminism, and largely from the same people. The underlying political ideology of the first queer community I became a part of was based in the intersectional, or third-wave, model of feminism, a community and a model with which I primarily engaged online, and with people my age.

The term intersectionality was first used by civil rights activist and political theorist Kimberlé Crenshaw in 1989, to describe a feminism that addressed the differences in experience, opportunity and marginalisation in women of different racial and sexual backgrounds. Intersectionality proposes that a person who experiences multiple forms of marginalisation, be it due to their gender, race, class or some other identifier, was like someone standing at an 'intersection' through which more than one stream of traffic was flowing. Put simply, the more ways in which a person experienced social marginalisation, the more dangerous it was for them to stand at that intersection; the more traffic they had to dodge.

Intersectionality was entering mainstream political discourse when I first started hearing about it in the early 2010s, and has since become in many ways the standard model. An intersectional feminist doesn't just advocate for women's rights, despite the connotations of the word *fem*inist, because they acknowledge that race, class, sexuality, ability and transgender status all have an effect on a person's life experience as well.

Because of the environment in which I learned it, and because the two theories are ideologically compatible, intersectionality goes hand-in-hand, in my mind, with queer theory. Queer theory challenges the systems which cause the axes or streams of oppression that are acknowledged and studied by intersectionality theory. Queer theory is useful for me and for this book because it's a mindset that causes one to question the rigid binaries and institutions which create labels like 'man', 'woman', 'gay' and 'straight', and allows us to imagine genders and sexualities that exist outside of these categories. So in this way, for many of the politically minded people of my generation, the feminist and transgender communities have considerable overlap.

However, not every person who considers themself a feminist thinks of these communities as adjacent, or even compatible. Intersectional or third-wave feminism not only gives us a new, more inclusive way to talk about the experiences of women and oppressed people, it also represents a political ideology that is in many ways opposed to the previous model of feminism, second-wave feminism.

The dominant narratives and forces in second-wave feminism have focussed mainly on advancing the rights of cisgender, middle-class, white, straight women, rather than on inclusivity and the diversity of all women's experiences. As a result, feminists of this generation can be overtly hostile to the idea of *gender* and *sex* as separate things.

There is a brand of feminism called trans-exclusionary radical feminism (abbreviated TERF), which objects to the inclusion of transgender women – that is, women who were assigned male at birth – in spaces devoted to women's rights and issues, because it considers women to be oppressed due to their biology rather than an innate quality of being a woman. Trans-exclusionary feminist Sheila Jeffreys, for example, has said that trans women who transition medically are 'constructing a conservative fantasy of what women should be',[70] which is to say that by changing their bodies to approach a normative model of femininity trans women themselves are perpetuating patriarchal notions of sex differences (rather than, say, trans women are forced to change themselves to adhere to cultural norms of femininity in order to operate within a society that punishes them if they do not). While the point of contention for TERFs usually centres around trans women, the ideology also often takes aim at nonbinary and genderqueer people. Many trans-exclusionary radical feminists believe there's no such thing as nonbinary genders, and consider nonbinary people to be simply women who hate other women so much that they disavow 'woman' as a self-identifier.

It's important to note before going further that not all radical feminists are *trans-exclusionary* radical feminists. The word 'TERF' itself was coined as a neutral technical term to distinguish between trans-supportive and anti-trans radical feminists. Nowadays application of the term has evolved, such that many of the people who come to be labelled as TERFs are not in fact *radical* feminists: often TERFs are simply bigots who borrow the label of feminist in order to give their beliefs more perceived validity. Radical feminism at its heart advocates for a radical restructuring of society to eliminate male supremacy, and some radical feminists view (cis) women's liberation as the key to liberation for everyone, but many others take a wider view which favours dismantling all the interconnected systems of patriarchy, white supremacy and capitalism. Radical feminist writers Andrea Dworkin and John Stoltenberg, for example, have been recorded as taking it as a given that radical feminism should be trans-inclusive,[71] and there are a large number of trans people who identify strongly with radical feminism.[72]

So, while radical and intersectional feminism are not necessarily incompatible, TERFs see any theory that separates or breaks down sex and gender as incapable of challenging the oppressive system called the patriarchy. TERFs see trans people as a threat to women's equality, and tend to ignore the fact that transgender women are very often subjected to violence because of the intersection of their trans and female status, and the fact that there are plenty of nonbinary people who were assigned male at birth, and plenty who are active campaigners for the rights of all marginalised groups.

It is fact that in many cultures people assigned female at birth are socialised to be submissive, nurturing, and obedient, based entirely on the genitals they were born with, just as there are people who are socialised to be assertive, confident and even violent based on theirs. But I assert that framing gender as entirely based on biological sex denies the lived experiences of actual people. Trans people are often subject to a level of violence that can approach and even surpass the violence that cisgender women face, precisely because they don't or can't conform to conventional gender norms.

The patriarchy is not simply the way in which 'men' oppress 'women'. It's a global system by which the powerful oppress the powerless along multiple axes, and any ideology that ignores the violence all marginalised people, including women *and* trans people, face, cannot possibly hope to combat global inequality. To speak very generally, the patriarchy is the system that uses the gender binary to oppress all people who are not (cisgender, white, straight) men. The very existence of genderqueer and nonbinary folk challenges the gender binary and therefore the patriarchy, and the acceptance and acknowledgement of genderqueer people in mainstream society will be a step towards tackling every kind of oppression.

I shouldn't have to explain why TERF ideology is problematic, in fact I would rather not discuss it at all, but it is an ideology that has a direct impact on nonbinary and genderqueer people, many of whom consider themselves feminists and are active in the feminist community. Further, whether or not a genderqueer or nonbinary person identifies as transgender, they may be perceived as such by other people, who may regard them with hostility. Nonbinary people nowadays are lucky to live in an age, or at least the beginning of an age, that accepts us for who we are. The division between 'man' and 'woman' is becoming malleable enough to admit the existence of something outside either. This is a change that should be celebrated, not decried.

Every single article I write on this subject – and a great deal of my fiction – challenges the normative, heterosexual, white, capitalist system of binary gender. I'm living proof that it is possible to be a feminist, and to challenge the patriarchy, while also holding a 'queer' view of gender. I think the binary should be challenged, bent, transformed, broken and maybe destroyed, but I also don't think that gender itself is *only* a tool for the subjugation of women. I don't have all the answers, but I do know that solidarity across subcultural lines is more important now than ever. There is so much conflict and animosity within the LGBT community, and between generations of activists and feminists, and this can only weaken us all in the long run.

Intersections in the nonbinary community

There's a perception being cultivated in the popular imagination of nonbinary and genderqueer people as a collection of pale, androgynous waifs with floppy hipster hair. This image has been reinforced by celebrities like Ruby Rose, La Roux and Miley Cyrus, all of whom have actually come out publicly as genderqueer, genderfluid or nonbinary. With notable exceptions like Amandla Stenberg, Jaden Smith, Angel Haze and Andreja Pejić the majority of these popular figures are white, and were assigned female at birth. But these wealthy, polished people are only the most visible face of our community: in reality there are infinite ways to be, and present as, genderqueer, and there's no one demographic or type of person who is more or less likely to be nonbinary. Our demographic crosses generational, racial, ability and ethnic lines, and the popular image of nonbinary people as thin, rich, beautiful, white and able-bodied erases the reality of our diverse community, and can contribute to feeling of alienation or inadequacy in nonbinary and genderqueer people who don't fit the model.

A family friend recently asked me whether all nonbinary people were assigned female at birth. After my strong 'of course not!', it occurred to me to wonder where my family friend had got this impression. Certainly the only nonbinary people she had encountered were AFAB, and indeed the statistics seem to indicate that, at the very least, more than half of those who are out and primarily identify as nonbinary or genderqueer are AFAB as well. The 2015 US Trans Survey reported that of all nonbinary participants, 80 per cent answered that they had been assigned female at birth, and only 20 per cent male.

Again we're tripped up by a lack of statistics on genderqueer demographics, so the most I can make is an educated guess. Is it simply that people who are assigned female are more likely to end up identifying as nonbinary? But that still wouldn't answer the question of *why* this was. Is it, as TERFs insist, because the nonbinary category is nothing but a bunch of women who hate themselves and other women so much that they can't stand being called women? Aside from this assertion being both ridiculous and offensive, the fact remains that AMAB nonbinary people *do* exist. I think that, far more likely than there simply being more AFAB nonbinary people than AMAB, there are a number of social dynamics at play which conspire to give that impression.

Part of the issue may be that the same social mechanisms that punish trans women for having left the exalted category of men, and that punish boys more severely than girls for acting like the 'opposite' gender, put pressure on people perceived as male not to transgress that boundary. By this mechanism a person perceived as male who exhibits some feminine tendencies might – if they are not punished severely to try and quash those tendencies – immediately be barred from maleness and categorised as a trans woman, might never be given the option of identifying outside the binary, or the opportunity to experiment with identity and presentation.

This pattern may be connected to the fact that, historically speaking (at least for the last century or so), it's been seen as far more acceptable for women to wear clothing traditionally associated with men (and still be seen as women) than the reverse. Perhaps a contemporary artefact of this is that people perceived as women are given generally more leeway to experiment, and the divide between the cisgender ingroup and the ostracised, trans(gressive) outgroup is not so rigid.

There is a similar double standard when it comes to sexuality, which classes any man who has relations with other men, no matter how many female partners he has, as *gay*, while a woman who has relationships with many female partners and only a few male is still called *straight*, her relationships with women dismissed as 'experimentation'. The boundaries of these gender categories are policed differently but enforced by the same rigid social structure.

A handful of my nonbinary interviewees are indeed AMAB, though the exact number is unknown because I chose not to include a question about sex assigned at birth in my survey. At least one of these interviewees told me that they present as a binary trans woman during their GIC appointments in order to receive treatment: indeed, it's commonly accepted (and will be discussed in the following two chapters) that trans people, especially those assigned male at birth, are often forced to convince their clinicians that they're sufficiently 'committed' to living full-time as their affirmed gender (which is tacitly assumed to be binary) in order to qualify for gender-affirming medical treatment. I can easily see how this could make it difficult for AMAB people who wanted to medically transition to be out as genderqueer in their daily lives.

I suspect there may also be a level of self-policing involved in terms of sex assigned at birth, race and class; I took pains at the beginning of this section to point out that the nonbinary community is more diverse than it appears. In the same way that studies have proven that, for example, girls are more likely to aspire to high-power careers when they see women in those roles, I think it likely that some people who privately identify with a nonbinary gender may not publicly say so because they don't look like the popular image of a nonbinary person. Contrary to the idea of us as fashionable and wealthy, many of the genderqueer people I know have experienced poverty. I also personally know a number of Indigenous, Hispanic, Black and East Asian people who identify as nonbinary, genderqueer or genderfluid, as well as several disabled people. I don't think it very likely that, for example, non-Western cultures are somehow less likely to accept genders outside the binary, rather, different cultures conceptualise gender differently. The concept of nonbinary gender that this book deals with, and that is the basis for our community in most anglophone countries, is one based in – even as it sits in opposition to – a Western model of sex and gender.

Whatever the reason, there are likely far more people who don't identify with a binary gender than there appear to be. Those of us who are most visible are those who are active in the spaces where our vocabulary has been defined, that is, largely English-speaking, middle-class, university-educated spaces. I don't know which factor or factors are responsible for these imbalances, but I'd be very interested to see if there are any visible changes in the makeup of the community over the next few years, as gender-queerness gains more mainstream currency, and I hope to see an increase in the number of diverse, accessible resources for genderqueer and nonbinary people of all backgrounds.

Exercises and discussion questions

This chapter is all about identity and community, concepts with which most people engage daily, by default or by instinct, but are not necessarily consciously aware. Some of these questions concern topics which may be sensitive: if you are answering these questions with other people feel free to treat them as thought exercises rather than a group discussion.

1. Think about the identities and communities that shape who you are as a person: are they cultural? National? Local? Sexual? Religious? Are they related to your interests or your chosen leisure activities? What communities are you most active in, and which labels do you identify most strongly with?
2. How do the communities and labels you identify most strongly with shape how you view the world? If one aspect of your personal identity were different, how would that change who you were as a person?

3. How do your personal identities intersect and interact with each other? How do, for example, your racial and national identities work together to shape you as a person? How does your gender interact with your religion?

4. How did you come to be a part of these communities? Were you born into them? Did you join them voluntarily? Are they considered obligatory for a person in your family or neighbourhood?

5. Sometimes the intersection of two identities can create friction: have you had to leave or been forced out of a community in your lifetime? If you are genderqueer, trans or nonbinary, for example, did your gender identity cause you to be excluded from your culture or religious community? Were you able to reconcile or rejoin that group or did one identity have to win out over another? Why do you think this was?

CHAPTER 5

Wider Society

Introduction

In many senses, nonbinary and genderqueer people represent a snag in the fabric of society: gender is a thread that reaches far and wide, affecting nearly every aspect of our lives. Pulling on the thread anywhere will disrupt the fabric as a whole. Existing as genderqueer or nonbinary affects a person's life in innumerable little ways, and the interstices of gender identity, culture, race, class and sexuality multiply the variations infinitely.

The sheer diversity of the nonbinary community is far larger than a single book chapter is capable of conveying, but this chapter will talk a little bit about what it's like to exist as nonbinary and genderqueer in a wider, largely cisgender, society. I'll discuss what it takes for us to come out and live openly, and some of the obstacles we face in navigating the complex social relationships – familial, romantic, professional – that texture our lives.

Coming out, transitioning and living as genderqueer in a cis world

Coming out, in a transgender context, means letting other people know about one's trans status. It has to do with whether or not other people understand us as nonbinary, and how comfortable we are with other people knowing. This can be done in a targeted way, when a genderqueer person tells someone that they're genderqueer or asks that the other person use certain pronouns for them, or it can be more passive, for example when that person dresses in a mixed or gender-ambiguous way, or undergoes medical treatment to perceptibly change the gender other people perceive them as.

To live as openly genderqueer is a rebellious act, and doesn't happen all at once. There are grades of being 'out', for example, to one's friends but not one's family, or to friends and family but not at work. Nowadays I personally am out to everyone who knows me for more than about half an hour (indeed, anyone who gets to know me has to deal with me talking about all of this stuff pretty incessantly), but I came out to different friend groups at different times, to my friends and even some professors before I came out to my family, and to my father before my mother.

Coming out to one's family can be a difficult experience, especially because coming out to older relatives involves negotiating generational boundaries. Trans people are at high risk of domestic abuse, family rejection and homelessness.[73] We're taught that family members, blood relatives, are supposed to stand by us no matter what, and for many people familial bonds are more important than any other. So when something happens to test those bonds, if an underlying prejudice is revealed and familial support is withdrawn, it can be devastating. Most trans and genderqueer people are not financially independent enough to be able to live on their own. To live everyday with people who don't accept or even know the real you – and to face the threat of violence, abuse or homelessness should you try to be more open about your identity – can be stressful, if not unbearable.

Even if abuse doesn't result from coming out, a curious blindness often manifests itself in our family members and relatives. A number of the nonbinary, genderfluid and genderqueer interviewees I spoke to over the course of writing this book told me that they repeatedly had to come out to family members who would conveniently 'forget' about their gender identities. This is connected to the larger mainstream unwillingness to validate or even acknowledge the existence of genderqueer identities, and a tendency that parents of transgender people often have to think of their children as static, unchanging and defined entirely by the parent's perception.

I have vivid memories of a rather fraught nighttime car ride, driving from Los Angeles to Orange County. It was the first time I explicitly came out as nonbinary to my mother. Perhaps I did it then because we were both trapped in the car with each other; I wanted to get it over with while there was no escaping for either of us. My mother cried. She said 'but you're my little girl'. I'm sure I cried as well. But, to my surprise, after this sentiment had been expressed aloud, it wasn't too difficult to tackle. She'd said what I was afraid she would – that my assigned gender was inextricably tied, in her mind, to who I am. But once it was said aloud we were able to analyse it, and we began to move past it together.

I asked her why I couldn't just be her child. I asked why my gender – something that I considered vestigial to my personhood, that I wished to be rid of – was essential. And to my relief and no doubt my mother's surprise, we found that it wasn't, not really. My mother decided that my wellbeing was more important to her than her own mental concept of me. She realised that I would still be her child no matter how I thought of myself, and she realised that my gender – my belief in and adherence to a set of social norms that she and my dad had imposed on me without conscious thought – was unimportant in the grand scheme of the things that made me who I was.

Ego can be a powerful force with parents, who often find that their idealised version of their child does not match who their child actually is. This can very quickly create conflict between parents and trans children, and though I was lucky enough to have two parents clear-eyed enough to put my own autonomy first, I am painfully aware that most of us are not so fortunate. According to the 2017 Stonewall Trans Report,[14] 24 per cent of nonbinary survey participants were not open about their gender identity to anyone in their family (compared to one in seven binary trans people). I have a few theories as to why this might be, and why it might be easy for the parents of genderqueer people to reject their coming out, to invalidate and ignore their identities.

Nonbinary people whose families reject their identities must walk a fine line: any aspect of their expression which is in accordance with the gender they were assigned at birth is tacit permission to think of them as such, to gender them as man or woman and call them by a rejected birth name. On the other hand, expressing themselves as they really are often comes with a cost of physical or emotional violence.

The variable here, speaking very generally, is the difference between a crossing from one familiar binary option to another and from a binary gender to something that isn't so easily understood for a person who hasn't experienced it, and which may not always be the same. This creates an extra layer of mental adaptation which a genderqueer person's family must do in order to accept them.

Not all of the people I spoke to to research this book are 'out' to everyone in their lives.

The process of coming out, which has historically been heavily associated with social ostracism and the threat of physical violence, is both easier and less clear-cut than it used to be.

Coming out is as much a political statement as it is a declaration about oneself, one's past and, to an extent, one's personal life.

For many trans people, there is a constant give and take between coming out, passing and transitioning. Because our identities have not yet made it into mainstream understanding, there's a certain amount of explanation that a genderqueer person is expected to do if they want to live openly as genderqueer and have their identity respected. Rather than simply declaring that they are genderqueer and being done with it, they will be asked to explain themself to their cisgender friends, family and colleagues, decide when entering demographic forms whether they want to go to the trouble of specifying their gender, and even sometimes justify their presence in trans spaces.

Personal appearance, that is, gender presentation, can do a bit of this explaining. Pin badges with preferred pronouns, and pronouns listed on Facebook, Twitter and email signatures can do a bit more, but there is still a great deal of work involved in coming out and, possibly more importantly, *staying* out as genderqueer. A person who is out as nonbinary cannot just 'come out' once and begin living as their affirmed gender, because there's no such thing as 'passing' for our affirmed genders. A genderqueer person must be continually explaining themself, justifying their existence, 'coming out' again and again each time they meet someone new or enter a new environment or have their identity questioned.

Passing

When a trans person decides to come out and live visibly according to their gender identity they risk everything from public mockery to physical violence. Passing, or attempting to pass, as cisgender is the only option for a great many trans people, for example those who live in cultures or areas which are hostile to gender and sexual minorities. My ability to be both safe and open about my gender identity is a result of privilege which many people do not have, and I try to be mindful of this fact as much as possible. For trans people who don't 'pass', that is, who don't present conventionally as their affirmed gender, the danger is even greater, as they cannot control who knows about their trans status.

The concept of 'passing' is itself the subject of much debate within the trans community. The entire concept is tied up in an ability – or inability – to hide one's membership in a minority group, and for that reason many people consider it problematic. A great many trans people, both binary and not, consider the whole concept of 'passing' to be a flawed goal, dictated and enforced by an oppressive majority. They argue that rather than trying to adhere to a normative and very often unattainable ideal, trans people should try to challenge the system that creates the gender norms we are pressured to approximate. They argue that as long as there is pressure for trans people to 'hide in plain sight', as it were, then we will continue to be oppressed.

On the other hand, passing as cisgender is *not* an option for many people. Aside from people whose bodies react to hormones in unexpected ways, or people whose health makes surgery impossible, for many nonbinary and genderqueer people, to present as their affirmed gender precludes the possibility of passing at all. For many nonbinary, genderqueer and genderfluid people, identity and expression are intimately connected. We express our genderqueer status visibly through our bodies, hair, makeup, clothing and mannerisms. For these people there is no question of 'passing': there is no conventional idealised appearance for us to aspire to, and no commonly accepted ideal of what a nonbinary person should look or act like. For nonbinary or genderqueer people, to be visible is to be visibly nonconforming, alternative or non-normative. In order to present as nonbinary we have to forge our own path, as it were, and constantly battle between facing transphobic harassment and dysphoria and having our identities denied.

On the flip side, many nonbinary people are open about their identities to the people they know, while still presenting as binary-gendered in daily life: these people maintain the core of their identities in their self-image, but are perceived as binary, sometimes because the environment they live in makes it dangerous for them to be perceived as trans, and sometimes because presentation – and the way their gender is perceived by others – is unimportant to them. Other people may maintain a consistent and cis-appearing gender presentation even if their actual gender identity is fluid. Indeed this may be the safest option for many people who aren't out to everyone they know. For these people the question is of passing as fixed-gendered at any given time.

I believe that in the long run there is little to be gained from conformity: striving to imitate a normative ideal can end up a tacit acceptance of that ideal. I believe that the definitions of what is male and what is female can and should be expanded: inclusivity is the only way we can create a society in which binary trans and cis people can be equal. At the same time I also feel that there is room for flexibility in these definitions, and that the institutions of binary gender will still stand up if not everyone in the world fits into them. But for many trans people there is no choice but to pass or attempt to pass, and it's my hope that someday the pressure to do so will no longer be there.

Dating, relationships and sex

> I could tell in talking and meeting in person with cispeople that ultimately they weren't sure if they could be with someone who wasn't also cis, or someone whose gender and appearance might change. I'd gone on several dates with cis gay women, and could tell my genderfluid, masc presenting self didn't fit exactly into who they were interested in. I also felt that the way I present (as NB trans, very transmaculine) limited who was interested in me, as I was often interested in other NB people, men, and transmen who did not share that same attraction.
>
> *Interviewee XX2*

Relationships, sex and dating are a huge part of our culture. The expectations associated with dating are based on a set of cultural norms, conventional behaviours and assumptions based on a largely heterosexual, binary-gendered majority. Being genderqueer while dating can throw a wrench into the works, so to speak, in many respects. There are a number of basic assumptions that we can disrupt or subvert by our very existence:

- the assumption of attraction to the opposite sex, or the idea that there even is an opposite sex
- the assumption of sex being the same as gender, or that a person's genitals look a certain way based on their outward appearance
- the assumption that a person is interested in sex, or will be after a certain amount of time; that sex is the ideal end goal or outcome of a relationship
- the assumption of monogamy
- the assumption that 'matching' with someone based on a handful of surface-level characteristics can be the basis for a meaningful sexual or romantic relationship.

I've often heard the sentiment expressed, even from within the nonbinary community, that genderqueer and nonbinary people are 'undateable': that our gender identities – or more importantly the way these identities are perceived by other people – preclude us from taking part in conventional practices of courtship. Indeed dating and relationships are often framed by popular discourse in black and white terms of male and female, or of only being attracted to men, or only women, with no room for flexibility or the grey areas in between. The entire basis of the culture surrounding dating, sex and marriage is on on a gender binary, in terms of romantic partners being on opposite or the same sides of it. Even the romantic ideal of 'matching' with your 'other half' is distressingly binaristic.

But sexuality and attraction are much more complicated than popular imagination may make them appear, and despite the trope of 'boy meets girl', attraction doesn't always follow clear gender lines. This can complicate things when it comes to finding a romantic partner. For a nonbinary person, it takes a bit more effort to find someone who is open to the idea of dating a person who is neither a man nor a woman, or who might be both, or neither, or different genders on different days. Unfortunately this means that most conventional dating apps, which broadly sort their users based on discrete categories and pair them based on their desire for or compatibility with people fitting other categories – and practices such as blind dating or speed dating – don't work for the average nonbinary person. Even in terms of gender identity options available for users to mark themselves with, most apps aside from a select few, such as OkCupid,[75] are extremely limited. When asked if being nonbinary 'limits their options' when it comes to relationships, interviewee SG said, 'yes, I think when you don't fit into commonplace gender/identity categories people who may be attracted to you don't consider you, because of preconceived ideas of what they like.'

In the community there's also commonly held to be a certain level of danger associated with 'dating while trans'. Because so much of dating relies on outward signals of inward characteristics and preferences, having a gender identity and presentation that doesn't 'match' your genitalia can create a situation in which a potential partner's expectations, their interpretation of the gendered signals a person is giving off, don't match what they expect to see in that person's underwear. This mismatch between expectations and reality is the basis for the harmful and distressingly pervasive stereotype of the 'deceptive' trans woman, who 'lures' an unsuspecting man into bed and then reveals that – shock horror! – she has a penis. The reason this stereotype – and the idea that trans people are in any way *hiding* an aspect of themselves from potential partners – is harmful is that we can't control what gender we were assigned at birth. The suggestion that we should be forced to disclose the nature of our genitalia before dating is invasive and demeaning, but it has been suggested as a 'solution' to the trans dating 'problem'. The idea that we're purposefully misrepresenting ourselves to some nefarious purpose, aside from being not true, contributes to the perception of trans people as bad, aberrant and otherwise 'other'.

There is in some ways an inverse relationship between how much of their identity a nonbinary person reveals to the world and their potential dating pool. For many of the genderqueer and nonbinary people I've spoken to, casual dating and using dating apps simply isn't on the cards, so finding potential partners can in many ways be a more laborious process. As interviewee JRF put it, 'most people are just looking to get their rocks off'. When asked if they use dating apps or websites, interviewee TP said, 'I usually don't. Because being demisexual, first impression "attraction" isn't how I work ever. But I've tried Tinder. I mostly use it to find queer friends in my area, and I make sure to state on my bio that I'm looking for friendship first and foremost.'

When you're nonbinary, especially if your presentation is very ambiguous or variable, it can be difficult to know where you stand with people. I personally present very ambiguously in my everyday life, and I've been asked out on dates by both cisgender men who identified as gay and who identified as straight. These instances have been difficult, not just because I'm not attracted to men at all, but because it's hard to know what aspect of my personality or appearance they were attracted *to*. What in my behaviour gave them the signal that I might be interested in them? What would they expect from me if we dated and what would that mean to my own gender identity?

Dating while identifying as nonbinary is a fraught process that requires both openness and trust on the part of both partners. Each of my interviewees seemed to navigate it in different ways. Interviewee EB2 says that they're open about their gender identity to the person they're in an open relationship with, but when going on casual dates they don't disclose that they are genderfluid. When asked how soon in a date or new relationship they would bring up their identity, they responded 'It hasn't come up yet and I am definitely too scared to acknowledge it yet or even approach the topic.'

On the other hand, interviewee XX2 says that their identity is not something they're willing to hide: 'When I was dating, both online and in person, I was upfront about my gender identity [after I came out], because I didn't want anything to be up in the air or have to deal with the bull of prospective partners reacting negatively towards me because of my identity. If my gender disqualified people from being interested in me, so be it (as hard as a conclusion that was to come to).' TP, too, makes their identity apparent from the start: 'I make sure someone knows my pronouns the moment they learn my name. My gender identity is clearly stated on all of my social media bios, and I try to make it as obvious as possible.' KR says, categorically: 'If someone can't respect your pronouns then they don't respect you and don't deserve to be in your life.'

The experience of dating varies heavily depending on a person's mobility and what environment they live in. Not every area has an active trans community and for someone who isn't able to connect in person with people who are genderqueer or open to dating genderqueer people, it can be incredibly isolating. Interviewee EB2 continues, 'I feel like if I want to pursue any kind of relationships, especially in the town I'm in, I have to be closeted or I won't have any options at all, honestly.'

Sex and attraction

Nonbinary gender identity can make a person very aware of the nuance of the way they experience attraction, and the ways by which their identity subverts expectation. Interviewee TP, on sexual attraction, says 'I'm attracted to mostly femme cis women. I am attracted to men, but have trouble connecting sexually with them. I think some of that has to do with my gender identity and feeling like I need to perform more femininely when I'm engaging sexually with a man, and that makes me feel uncomfortable and not like myself.'

The fact of having an identity outside male or female can disrupt traditional gendered sexual roles. Sexual preference is not always something discussed in detail on a first date, and very often we're not equipped with the vocabulary to talk about these things with subtlety, so a genderqueer person dating a cis person might not know how their partner will react right up until they actually have sex.

Sex can be strange, embarrassing or awkward for almost anyone, but for a person whose relationship with their body is strained the act can be even more difficult. Many nonbinary and genderqueer people experience gender dysphoria, or a discomfort due to the mismatch between their body and the gender they identify with. I'll explain dysphoria in more detail in Chapters 6 and 7, but for now it's useful to know that it can make the person who experiences it very aware of, and very uncomfortable with, their own body, especially their genitals and secondary sex characteristics. Because sex is a physical act, the way that sex is performed and the way that a nonbinary person's partner relates to their body can have an impact on the relationship.

Interviewee TP said that, in the early stages of dating, it's very important to lay ground rules regarding the language their partner uses to describe their body: 'It is important to me that when entering the phase in the relationship where we have to label each other or describe each other, or if we begin sexting, a conversation is required about what descriptive words my partner can use for me at which times, what parts of my body I do and do not want talked about during sex or sexting, and what I words I would be comfortable with my partner using for certain parts of my body.'

A number of the people I spoke to while researching this book said that they felt more comfortable in relationships – sexual, romantic or otherwise – with another trans or nonbinary person. Even for nonbinary people who don't experience dysphoria, the basic fact of sharing lived experience can make them feel safer in a relationship and make intimacy easier to achieve. If a genderqueer person chooses to only have sex with other genderqueer people, they are essentially choosing to only have sex with other people who know something of what they've gone through, and are more likely to understand the relationship they have with their body. XX2, when asked how their identity interacts with their sex life: 'I'd say if anything it's positive. I didn't know for sure until we had sex, but I'd rather be with someone/ have sex as a transperson with another transperson.'

Sexual identities within the nonbinary community

In today's highly sexual culture – a culture that is quick to leap to binary conclusions – being nonbinary can force a conversation in which one challenges the rigidity of categories like 'man' or 'woman', 'gay' or 'straight'. Because of the way that preconceived notions about gender and sex shape dating and relationships, many of the nonbinary people I've spoken to have indicated that they're most comfortable in a dating situation in which these preconceptions have been largely discarded. That is, they're most comfortable in an environment where the culture of dating and relationships has been broken down or *queered*.

Of the nearly 900 people who responded to the STA nonbinary experiences report, 53 per cent identified their sexuality as 'queer', with 'pansexual' and 'bisexual' close behind at 32 per cent and 28 per cent, respectively. There was also a high instance (19%) of asexuality among the participants. Around 20 per cent of participants described themselves as lesbian or gay, and only 5 per cent identified themselves as heterosexual. Only one of my interviewees identified with what could be called a 'binary' sexuality, and described themself as: 'homosexual, attracted to male genitals but people who lean toward a more feminine side.' Interviewee SG's take on their own sexuality was particularly nuanced: 'I generally describe myself as queer, naturally polysexual/polyromantic[76] (my love for emotionally significant people does not affect my feelings for others), on the asexual spectrum – I have a preference/particular attraction for people with traits that I interpret as gender non-conforming.'

Bi- and pansexuality
Seven of my interviewees described themselves as bi- or pansexual, meaning a sexuality that involves an attraction to multiple or all genders. There has been a certain level of debate surrounding the term 'bisexual', namely whether it should be distinguished from

'pansexual', or whether they should be taken to mean functionally the same thing. Some people who identify as pansexual claim that bisexuals are attracted only to *men* and *women*, and thus inherently trans- and nonbinary-phobic; this faction assert that by calling themselves *bisexual* rather than pansexual bisexuals are denying the existence of more than two genders, or at the very least claiming to be *attracted* to only two genders. But I've never met a bisexual person who considers their identity to encompass only male and female. The vast majority of bisexuals I've spoken to have said unequivocally that they don't believe bisexuality precludes relationships with genderqueer people, and that they would consider dating a transgender or nonbinary person, even if they have not in the past. In any case, how do you measure or chart a person's sexual attraction towards someone else? Towards a whole demographic? Sexuality is nebulous and intensely personal, and the precise definition of a sexual identity will be unique to each person who experiences it.

The issue then is one of semantics or nomenclature. Similar to the way that someone may variously identify as nonbinary or genderqueer because of the community in which they first began to explore their identity, many bisexuals simply call themselves bi- rather than pansexual because that is the term used in the community they interact with. The terms were coined at different times and there are different connotations associated with each. There may be a self-described bisexual person out there who is only interested in dating binary, cisgender women and men, but I have never met them. Most of the time in my experience, if a person is attracted to only a smaller subset of gender expressions, they will specify these when stating their sexuality, rather than calling themself bisexual and assuming other people will know precisely *which* genders they mean.

Polyamory

Another pattern that seems prevalent in the transgender community is polyamory, that is, relationships involving more than two people, or a capability of being attracted to and forming a relationship with more than one person at once. Interviewee MG says, 'I identify as pansexual and polyamorous. I tend to develop romantic feelings for people very easily but I also tend to get very worn out very easily.' 'I am currently with 4 partners, two AMAB people and two AFAB people. I also have one prospective partner, an AFAB person.' Again, polyamory isn't the same as promiscuity; lots of polyamorous people spend a long time in committed, consensual, stable relationships with the same group of people.

Again, there haven't been any studies specifically on instance of polyamory or polyamorous attraction within the genderqueer community – I doubt there's been much study of it in *any* community – but nonetheless I know several genderqueer people who are in polyamorous relationships, including three of my interviewees. I imagine that the reasons for this prevalence are similar to the reasons why so many nonbinary and genderqueer people seem so likely to form meaningful relationships based on attractions other than sexual, and to separate romantic, aesthetic and sexual attraction.

Asexuality

Six of my interviewees (and I myself) described themselves as asexual or a related term like demisexual, gray-asexual or aromantic. Asexual (often abbreviated 'ace') means that a person doesn't experience sexual attraction or seek out sexual contact with other people. Someone who identifies as aromantic may still want to have sex but won't form romantic relationships. Being asexual is not the same as being celibate: asexuals simply don't experience sexual attraction. This may be because they've experienced trauma in the past, but for most asexuals this is not the case: asexual and the terms under its umbrella are sexual orientations like gay and straight. Demi- and gray-asexual identities are characterised by rare instances of sexual attraction, or sexual attraction that occurs only in specific contexts, such as only after a deep emotional bond has formed.

Asexuality can be related to dysphoria: interviewee XX1 says, 'I'm not certain whether my gender identity interacts with my sex life, but since my sex-repulsion often happens to directly link to my repulsion of genitalia, it probably does. I do not know who gets to decide if my lack of sex is positive or negative.' But there are plenty of asexual people who don't experience dysphoria, and many who aren't even trans or nonbinary. If someone identifies as asexual all it means is that they are asexual – no other conclusions should be drawn.

Anyone who's spent time in either the asexual or the genderqueer community will notice a considerable overlap between the two. I've wondered for a while whether this was correlation or causation, but as nonbinary gender and asexuality are still both largely invisible communities there have been no studies of this connection, if it even exists. I'm sure part of the prevalence of asexuals in the genderqueer community has to do with dysphoria, but I also think the most likely explanation is that the genderqueer and nonbinary community is simply more tolerant of difference, and more open to the idea that maybe if you don't have to have a gender, you don't have to have sex. Potentially, those of us who are active in the community are more free of the normative expectations placed upon people in binary-identified society: the expectation to pair up, marry and have children. Regardless of whether genderqueer people are more likely to be asexual and aromantic, asexual and aromantic people are an important demographic within the nonbinary community.

It's important to note here that, though they may seem to be diametrically opposed, ace and bi- or pansexual identities are by no means incompatible or mutually exclusive. Plenty of people I spoke to said they identified as, for example, both demi- and bisexual. Bi- and pansexuality have a connotation of being somehow 'promiscuous', but this is a harmful stereotype: bi- and pan- refer to *who* a person may be attracted to, not how *much* sex a person has. A person might be sexually attracted to people of any gender but only after they've become good friends, for example. An asexual person might seek out romantic relationships with people of any gender.

I think that the milieu in which a person learns terms to describe their gender identity with more nuance than 'boy' or 'girl', and to separate sex from gender, is also one in which a person can learn about different types of attraction – such as romantic, aesthetic and platonic – and to be aware that friendships and romantic relationships can be deep emotional bonds, and that sex is not the ultimate goal or validation of any 'serious' relationship. Because it entails fragmenting and analysing different parts of identity, starting with separating sex from gender, being active in the nonbinary or trans community may make it easier for us to separate out individual strands of attraction: physical or sexual attraction, emotional attraction, intellectual attraction and so on. In this way, being nonbinary or transgender can cause a person to question precisely *what* aspect of another person they're attracted to. Our identities already often make it difficult for us to participate in the conventional expectations of courtship, so acknowledging different strands or types of attraction – and acknowledging them as valid and meaningful beyond questions of marriage and sex – is both validating and empowering.

Distinctions can be drawn between relationships based on romantic feelings (a desire for a feeling of closeness or contact with someone), sexual attraction (a desire to engage in sexual intercourse with someone), aesthetic attraction (an attraction to surface characteristics of a person, such as the way they look), even platonic feelings (the love felt between friends).

A person may find themself attracted to different people based on one or more or even all of these metrics, and all these different forms of attraction interact and inform each other.

Many people I've spoken to talk about platonic and aesthetic attraction as the most powerful forces in their relationship lives, rather than romantic and sexual. Interviewee XX3 says, 'I assume I am either pansexual or demisexual. At the end of the day it comes down to how I feel about the person emotionally. If I feel a strong connection with them that's when I'm most attracted to them. It's how I found out I was gay.' Interviewee TP discusses the complex and sometimes fraught connection between sexual and romantic attraction: 'I have much difficulty engaging sexually with people I don't have romantic feeling for. Because of this, hook-ups and casual dating are nearly impossible for me. If I see someone who is aesthetically pleasing, and I become sexually aroused, it doesn't mean that sexually engaging with that person will actually give me any pleasure. I've received zero sexual pleasure several times when engaging with people whom I didn't know for very long or whom I found "hot".'

Interviewee TP discusses how aesthetic, romantic and sexual attraction interacts for them: 'Romantic feelings are a hit or a miss with me. They just sneak up on me, and I can never understand how it happens.' 'All of my relationships have been with women that I wasn't aesthetically attracted to at first. Once the romantic feelings came, my sexual feelings for them followed.' Interviewee EB2 says that attraction can follow displays of affection, rather than those displays being the result of this attraction: 'there's a huge overlap between physical affection (hugging, hand-holding, casual touching) and development of romantic feelings.'

Gender and sexuality interact with each other in complex ways, and the social factors that influence a person's sexuality – or their conceptualisation and articulation of their sexuality – are surely affected in a person who belongs to the LGBT community, even if they don't primarily identify as L, G or B. It may be that only a person who knows sex and gender might not match is more likely to be aware of disconnects in other contexts.

In my experience, by far the most all-encompassing, and most prevalent, way nonbinary and genderqueer people describe them-selves is 'queer'. The connection the term has with the queer theory that I discussed in Chapter 1, and the reclamative sense by which members of the LGBT community have begun to use it as it was once used as a slur for them, makes it uniquely suited to describe the way that we form relationships. In my mind *queer* implies sub-version, complication, the questioning of boundaries and discrete categories. It's an extremely useful label, popular and growing. I've seen it said often by nonbinary and genderqueer people that, 'all my relationships are queer relationships'. Queer is the best way that I've found to describe the idiosyncratic, blurry, inconsistent way that I personally experience attraction.

While entering a relationship can be complicated, and the fragmentation of our identities can make it both easier and more difficult to make ourselves understood to potential partners, what we generally look for in a relationship is the same things anyone would want: commitment, communication, emotional support, to feel desirable and loved.

Some of us feel no interest in dating someone who isn't aware or accepting of our gender identity, but at the same time, some of us aren't comfortable with that level of disclosure a priori. Gender identity is extremely personal, and many nonbinary people reject the idea that it's something we must 'disclose' beforehand, as if it were a communicable disease. This creates a tension between making assumptions about what a prospective partner knows and what we need to tell them.

For the most part, we tend to seek relationships with people who've gone through what we've gone through, that is, other genderqueer people. I personally find that I'm inclined to look for a partner within the trans or nonbinary community. Not only do I find it tiring to have to kill a relationship with a cis person before it begins by disclosing that I'm asexual, but I'm more likely to find someone who generally understands me, and who wants the same things out of the relationship that I want, from within the community. I also find that nonbinary and genderqueer people are generally less obsessed with pairing off and matching up: I value my cisgender friends very highly but, all of them being in their thirties, it can be difficult to always be playing second fiddle to someone else's partner or spouse.

Activism or community engagement of some kind also tends to be important, though not necessarily LGBT activism: interviewee BJS says that in a prospective partner, they look for someone who 'is aware of and actively working against social injustice'. Interviewee XX2 continues, 'openness with one's gender identity can be a political act as well as a personal one, and many nb/gq people are active in their communities. As such, it can be important that a prospective partner is engaged with, or at least aware of, the social issues surrounding our identities.'

Overall when it comes to finding a partner, many of my acquaintances and several of my interviewees stressed the need for self-education and communication in dating. Some of the most common themes were open-mindedness and a willingness to learn and flexibility when it comes to labels and roles. As interviewee XX2 says, when seeking a new partner, 'I looked for someone who, first and foremost, accepted me for who I was, gender, sexuality and all.' Another interviewee said simply, 'a person who won't try to change me'.

Genderqueer in the workplace

The STA nonbinary experiences document found that only 4 per cent of participants were always comfortable being open about their gender identity at work, while 52 per cent were never comfortable.[17] Over 80 per cent of participants worried their identity wouldn't be respected at work, or that it would make their work life more difficult generally. Many cited existing bigotry in their workplace directed at other minority groups, as well as the potential for harassment, as a reason for keeping their gender identity hidden.

The majority of workplaces are not, by their nature, conducive to behaviour that defies convention. The culture that prohibits tattoos from being visible in the workplace, and that pressures women to wear skirts and heels to interviews, also creates an environment in which nonbinary people don't feel comfortable being out. Over half of the nonbinary experiences survey participants felt pressure to pass as male or female, or to adhere to a gendered role in their workplace. Over 60 per cent of participants who were applying for jobs felt pressure to hide their nonbinary status during the application process. Applications are also one of the places nonbinary people are likely to be required to gender themselves when providing personal information. Eighteen per cent of survey participants had difficulty even securing employment because they had official documents that didn't match their birth certificates, or that demonstrated name changes that made it difficult for them to prove their identities during the application process.

Overall, survey participants cite several factors as contributing to their feelings of discomfort and unsafety in the workplace. These mostly stem from ignorance or hostility towards transness at the individual level, and preservation of traditional gender roles at company level, especially in terms of uniforms and dress codes, but also generally speaking in the enforcement of differing standards of behaviour when it comes to male and female employees.

Much of the difficulty that nonbinary people face in institutional settings lies in the fact that work environments can be some of the places where the last vestiges of traditional gender roles are reinforced. For example, one STA survey participant cited a double standard in terms of uniform, where men were expected to tuck their shirts in but women were encouraged not to. In many workplaces people perceived as women are required to wear skirts whether they want to or not. This may seem like a minor point to quibble over but uniforms are just one way in which professional environments reinforce dominant social structures. Further, in the same way that culturally coded clothing and hairstyles such as a turban, hijab or dreadlocks can sometimes unconsciously be perceived as 'unprofessional', unconventional gender presentations can also be interpreted as subversive or disruptive to a professional environment, even when the person presenting unconventionally is doing so because that is simply who they are.

The Scottish Trans Alliance has created a number of excellent resources, and is willing to work with employers and service providers to create more inclusive policies. The STA has created a set of guidelines for employers and service providers who wish to create an environment that is more inclusive of people with nonbinary and genderqueer identities.[78] Overall the guidelines make several basic suggestions for improvement in the following four areas:[79]

- education, training and awareness
- redesigning forms
- names and pronouns
- gender-neutral facilities.

Many of the problems that nonbinary people face in the workplace and in public services come from ignorance rather than conscious hostility. Many nonbinary experiences survey participants ascribed their reluctance to be out at work to the fact that, often, nonbinary people are simply not acknowledged to exist. When a nonbinary employee encounters this attitude in a colleague it's often more trouble than it's worth to try to explain one's entire existence, especially to a relative stranger.

Colleague ignorance, which creates pressure to hide or self-police gender expression, can be a strain on mental health, and creating an environment in which the existence of trans people is acknowledged and understood is a first step towards creating one in which our identities are respected, even celebrated. A good way to start raising awareness is by including trans and genderqueer identities in workplace sensitivity training exercises. Make sure that anti-discrimination rules and posters are inclusive of gender identity. Consider actively seeking out nonbinary and genderqueer applicants when hiring.

A nonbinary employee's colleagues are likely to make mistakes sometimes, especially when they are still getting used to using inclusive language. Ensure that employees who misgender or misname a colleague apologise and correct their behaviour, but keep in mind in these instances that gender identity can be a private thing and that sometimes what a nonbinary employee who has been misgendered will want is for a simple, private apology and for everyone to move on. Try to treat instances of misgendering with discretion, maintain the privacy of the nonbinary person as much as possible, and refer to their preference for how the incident is to be dealt with.

In cases of harassment or bullying, deal with any incidents in the same way you'd deal with a case of harassment based on race or sexuality, for example, and enforce these policies diligently. If you don't have any workplace policies against harassment of any kind, consider creating some. If you do, make sure they explicitly cover harassment or bullying of nonbinary individuals.

Fifty-eight per cent of participants in the Scottish Trans Alliance's 2015 report 'Nonbinary people's experiences in the UK',[80] said that, when engaging with public services like hospitals or the police, the forms they are given to fill out *never* allow them to represent themselves accurately. Examine your company's use of language. In terms of information collection, intake forms and ID cards, changes can start even before a nonbinary employee is hired. On application forms, allow applicants who wish to to select a gender option other than male or female, or allow them not to specify. A number of institutions (like my bank, for instance[81]) are now giving customers the option to use a gender-neutral title, such as Mx, instead of traditional Mr/Mrs/Ms. While I'm a bit sceptical of the need to use honorifics and titles at all, I'm still excited about this development and eagerly select 'Mx' on any form that offers it (in many cases I'm still forced to cheekily select 'Dr' or, my favourite, 'Rev'). Not only will this allow nonbinary applicants to avoid gendering themselves, it will also contribute to the normalisation of nonbinary gender and go towards creating an environment in which all employees recognise our identities as legitimate.

Ensure that names and pronoun choice are respected by allowing for pronouns and preferred title (for example the gender-neutral Mx) to be specified on application forms or upon a first meeting, and make sure that training materials and standard documents are inclusively worded, for example by replacing 'he or she' with 'they', and 'son or daughter' with 'child'.[82] Consider reducing the number of instances in which employees are trained to gender other people. Forcing a situation in which all customers or service users *must* be gendered as male or female (for example, using a standard greeting like 'good morning sir/ma'am') is an excellent way to make a nonbinary person (and the service provider, for that matter) feel embarrassed and alienated.

During the application process and beyond, be mindful of the fact that some trans applicants may go by a name other than the one they were given at birth, or that an applicant's gender may not match that which is on their passport or birth certificate. There are all sorts of reasons why this might be the case, even outside of gender, and approaching these instances with an assumption of good faith, and allowing applicants to explain themselves, can go a long way towards making them feel safe and comfortable in the workplace.

Ensure that there are gender-neutral bathrooms and other facilities available for employees who wish to use them. Consider whether gendered facilities are even necessary: if the existing facilities are single-person and lock, why gender them at all? Consider labelling bathrooms by what they contain, i.e. a toilet, or a toilet and a urinal, and so on. Likewise consider re-evaluating any gender differences in employee uniform or dress code. Reducing gender-based divisions in employee dress will not only make genderqueer employees more comfortable, it will go a long way towards eliminating sexism in the workplace more generally.

Generally speaking, it's very good practice for employers and policymakers to simply be more mindful of their own perceptions about gender, and the way they make gendered assumptions about other people. Managers and supervisors should analyse the way they personally use gendered language, and think deeply about how their own assumptions may affect their trans employees.

Think about ways that you can actively make your company more inclusive, not just by reducing situations that cause people to be gendered, but also by celebrating the fact that you're an inclusive employer. Genderqueer and nonbinary people have a unique perspective that can enrich a workplace. Try not to think of genderqueer employees as defective or strange, and try not to exclude them – consciously or unconsciously – when seeking employee input or selecting someone to represent the company in an outward-facing role. Consider including images and examples including nonbinary people in promotional and training materials. Of course, there's no single way for a nonbinary person to look, but increasing the diversity of these materials will go a long way to creating an environment in which nonbinary and genderqueer employees and customers feel included and valued.

Nonbinary at school

Most of what I discussed in the previous 'work' section, about re-evaluating gender in dress code, facilities and language use, also applies to schools, though there are a few caveats and extra points that should be addressed. The most important of these is that young people are often vulnerable: students, even college and university students, are going through a formative time. Adding a gender-identity crisis to the mix can only complicate things, and thus sensitivity and discretion are important when interacting with trans and nonbinary students. Experiencing harassment or bullying due to being nonbinary or genderqueer at this age can be incredibly damaging, and can have repercussions throughout adulthood. It's very important to make schools a safe and supportive environment for trans and nonbinary students, if we want them to become confident, happy nonbinary adults.

A sentiment I've seen repeated often by politicians, parents and media personalities lately is the idea that gender-inclusive practices in schools are somehow 'coddling' our nation's youth. This claim is usually backed by an argument that goes something like, *how will they function in harsh, gendered society if we hold their hands and let them use neutral toilets, uniforms and locker rooms? Why should we make accommodations for trans youth when the 'real world' will not?*

My first objection to this point of view is a simple argument for tolerance. The children of today are tomorrow's parents, leaders, policymakers and service providers. The sooner we instil in them open-mindedness and acceptance the more likely they are to treat people different from them, such as nonbinary people, with respect, even if they themselves are not nonbinary.

The other, less obvious objection is that, quite frankly, school can be one of the most gendered environments a person will ever en-counter. The 'real world' (as if kids aren't exposed to all the attitudes and trials of 'real life' in high school) is in my experience a lot more flexible and tolerant of variation than cliquey, bully-ridden school. In my daily life I am not expected to shower in front of other people on a regular basis. I'm not at the mercy of roving gangs of 'popular kids'. I'm not forced to line up for exercise class on the same side as people who were assigned the same gender at birth as me. I'm not expected to wear a skirt because my birth certificate or ID says 'F'. School is where gender is taught, and by de-gendering schools, not only are we making life easier for nonbinary students and allowing those questioning their gender identity more room for experimentation, we're also creating a generation, or at least a cohort, of students who are themselves less concerned with gender.

There are a number of resources designed specifically for schools who wish to be more inclusive of transgender, nonbinary and gen-der-questioning students. Here are just a few:

- The Mermaids UK Trans* Inclusion Schools Toolkit:[83] designed for schools in East Sussex to help them more effectively support trans students and prevent transphobic bullying. This guide includes a 101 on trans umbrella identities, information on the Equality Act 2010 for schools to use to check compliance and suggestions for policy changes.
- A guidance document developed by the Gender Identity Re-search and Education Society (GIRES) on preventing transpho-bic bullying in schools:[84] this document includes guidelines for governors, head teachers and teaching staff on how to prevent transphobic bullying from negatively impacting both trans students and staff.
- The National Student Council have created a video[85] featuring some nonbinary-identified students who talk about their ex-periences as students and what they'd like to see in schools in terms of policy and teacher behaviour. This video was created

by the Gay, Lesbian & Straight Education Network (GLSEN), who currently maintain a nonbinary student council.

I feel it's also important to point out a resource that I would strongly recommend *avoiding*. There's an organisation called Transgender Trend which sets itself up as a parents' organisation but which is in fact an anti-trans group with rather insidious tactics. Threatened by or disapproving of the rising number of people who are comfortable being out as trans, Transgender Trend have created a 'schools resource pack' which frames the rise in gender-questioning and trans-identified students as a 'trend' (as implied by the name), and advocates discouraging students from experimenting with their gender identity. This 'resource pack' is not based on evidence, and it has the potential to actually harm trans students. In response, LGBT advocacy group Stonewall have created an excellent page[86] on supporting trans students, which explains a bit more about why Transgender Trend are a dangerous organisation.

The resources listed above will go into more detail than I do but here are a few basic suggestions, geared specifically towards nonbinary students, which can help schools and teaching staff more fully support them:

- Have a zero-tolerance policy when it comes to transphobic bullying, and make sure it explicitly includes nonbinary and genderqueer people. In addition, make sure that counsellors are educated on, accepting and supportive of nonbinary identities. A zero-tolerance bullying policy is useless if nonbinary students aren't comfortable coming forward because they believe school authorities won't be respectful of their identities.
- Consider de-gendering or creating gender-neutral toilets, showers and other facilities. These are some of the spaces where trans students feel most vulnerable (I know I always did), so consider creating designated facilities for nonbinary students who wish to use them.

- Consider de-gendering uniforms and dress codes or allowing students to wear whichever uniform they are most comfortable in. Rather than creating a rule that only applies to trans students, consider allowing boys and girls to wear whichever uniform they are most comfortable in as well. Reducing the instances in which boys and girls are expected to behave differently can only create a more tolerant and equal environment, and serve students well during adulthood. In addition, since clothing is one of the most important ways in which we express gender, allowing for experimentation in clothing can make school a safer environment for students who are gender-questioning.
- Make curricula (especially sex education, history and social studies) more inclusive of trans (and LGBT more generally) identities. Acknowledging and celebrating our identities will enrich every student's education.
- Examine language use throughout the school. Respect individual students' pronoun preferences. Consider using more inclusive wording in educational materials. If titles are used for any students or staff, consider allowing the use of a gender-neutral one like Mx.
- Generally, ask genderqueer or gender-questioning students what they need from you. They'll be more aware of restrictive policies than you will, and may be able to help create more inclusive ones. Do what you can do accommodate them. Remember too that school students will be going through their formative years and many will be questioning their own identities and trying to find the right fit. Don't punish students for experimenting, for example by trying out new names and pronouns.

Recommendations

In general, the best way to learn about the lived experience of genderqueer people is by educating yourself on the issues that are important to the people you're interacting with: many of us are more than happy to chat about our experiences, especially if we're already friends, but it's a good idea to first read up on nonbinary and genderqueer issues as much as possible, *rather* than asking nonbinary people to explain themselves. For one thing, the experiences of a single person won't necessarily be representative of the community as a whole. Aside from this, any member of a minority group can tell you how exhausting it is to have to constantly be educating outsiders.

Keep in mind that every person is an expert in their own experiences. When you encounter someone whose gender identity or presentation is ambiguous or inconsistent or doesn't make sense to you, remember that gender is a fluid, changing, complex entity. That person has had years and years to consider and explore their own gender and they may still be in the process of doing so. In addition, gender presentation is just the tip of the iceberg, as it were, of gender identity. What a person chooses to show you may not be the entirety of their identity, and each person will have different reasons for the way they present. Be respectful, remember that a lot of trans people are constantly interrogated about their genders and keep in mind how tiring this can be before you ask questions.

Generally speaking, be flexible and open to new ways of thinking about gender and sex – this should be the case with any new friend or partner, be they cis, trans or otherwise. Interrogate your own preconceived notions about what gender is and how you relate to it. What's your place in the gender system? If your concept of your own gender were different, how do you think that would change the way you relate to others? Think about the ways that your own gender identity informs the way you present yourself.

There are a wealth of blogs, videos, articles and a growing number of books that are written by nonbinary and genderqueer people who actively want to educate others. Rather than assuming a nonbinary person has the time and energy to educate you, seek out these materials. One of the best resources I've come across is the YouTube film series My Genderation. The videos touch on a wide range of topics and all are created by trans and nonbinary people. At least two of the creators of the series, activist and filmmaker duo Fox and Owl, identify as nonbinary. I'll include a few of these in the resources section at the end of the book, but any internet search can generally find you blog posts and articles that have been written by nonbinary and genderqueer people themselves, which will give you a good idea of our experiences from a diverse range of perspectives.

Exercises and discussion questions

The answers to some of the questions in this section may be sensitive for some people. If you are discussing the answers as a group, feel free to think about and answer privately any that you are uncomfortable sharing aloud.

1. The concept of 'coming out' doesn't have to just be related to gender and sexual identity: it applies to a lot of different identities, especially minority ones, which are often hidden. If applicable, think about a time when you've made a conscious decision to be open about an aspect of yourself you had previously kept hidden – this could mean illness or mental health status, religious or cultural background, or even what sports team you support. Did your openness about this identity change anything about your interactions with other people? How so?
2. How do you think your identities, hidden or otherwise, affect the way you interact with other people who don't share those identities?
3. How do the groups and categories you identify most strongly with, and signal most strongly to the rest of the world, affect the way you navigate a professional environment? An educational environment? When seeking out or interacting with romantic and sexual partners?

CHAPTER 6

Mental Health

Introduction

Gender variance is not a mental illness. There is no brain abnormality or dysfunction that 'causes' a person to be genderqueer, and the state of being genderqueer or trans is not something to be treated or solved. The idea that being transgender is an illness, an idea which has cropped up repeatedly throughout our history, is rooted in Western medical definitions of 'abnormality', and ideas about the psychological causes of variant behaviour, which are based on relatively recent historical developments. The medicalised concepts of 'gender identity disorder' and 'transsexualism'[87] are used as justification for the harmful practice of so-called 'conversion therapy', which seeks to cure a transgender person of being transgender. More generally, these 'diagnoses', which were until recently considered the standard way of thinking about anyone with a variant gender identity, leads to us being treated with an automatic assumption of mental ill-health, and a perception of us as fundamentally 'abnormal'.

This being said, there has been some research done recently into finding the neurological origins of gender variance, which readers may have encountered. These studies have suggested that gender identity and sexuality are formed in the brain at various stages of natal development, while the brain is under the influence of various hormones.[88] While the results of these studies may very well be sound, I'm highly sceptical of any conclusions that might be drawn from them, because any scientific practice that seeks to find a physical cause for natural variance veers, in my mind, dangerously close to the ideas which have been used to justify conversion therapy and other 'cures'. There is a history of mistrust between the trans and larger queer communities and the medical establishment. The idea that we're afflicted with a 'disease', implied by a diagnosis of 'transsexualism', is rather pernicious. Like a chronic illness itself, it's proved difficult to get rid of.

But many trans people *do* suffer from mental illness. These are most often due to two interconnected causes: gender dysphoria and minority stress. These causes are themselves the result of existing as genderqueer within a society that doesn't accept us: these two stressors both stem from the strict conventions associated with gender that are ingrained in our society. The idea of gender as an immutable, strict binary of male and female, gender as connected innately to certain body parts, or to a certain shape or type of body, and gender as inborn, have repercussions for people who don't fit into them. They create both an internal dissonance between a trans person's sense of self, and social expectations, which can adversely affect mental health. Externally, mainstream hostility towards people who are openly outside the norm leads to social marginalisation and a number of associated stresses. This creates an environment in which nonbinary people must police themselves in order to conform, or risk ridicule and violence if they don't.

The purpose of this chapter, then, is to give the reader an idea of the factors likely to adversely affect the mental health of a genderqueer or nonbinary person. I'll put the dry statistics into context with some discussion of my own experiences with mental illness, and plenty of anecdotal evidence from the nonbinary, genderqueer and genderfluid interviewees I spoke to. I'll discuss the myth that claims that gender variance is a mental illness in and of itself, and I'll discuss some of the actual causes, both internal and external, of mental illness in nonbinary people. I'll discuss the most common symptoms of mental illness that manifest in genderqueer people – primarily as anxiety and depression – and include a discussion of some of the patterns I've seen in nonbinary experiences with mental health professionals and institutions, including what mental health professionals have done that was supportive or helpful. I'll end the chapter with suggestions and recommendations from nonbinary and genderqueer people about what mental health professionals and institutions could be doing better, and a few resources for genderqueer and nonbinary people in need of mental health support.

Definitions and acronyms

DSM[89]: the *Diagnostic and Statistical Manual of Mental Disorders*, a book published by the American Psychiatric Association. The DSM is used by clinicians and mental health care professionals in the United States to diagnose mental health disorders, and I refer to it here because its treatment of gender identity and dysphoria is exemplary of changing perspectives on non-normative gender identities, as well as of the medicalisation – for which it has repeatedly come under fire – of behaviour and mood patterns that may not be best treated with medication. As most psychiatric disorders or symptoms aren't independently testable through, for example, biopsies and blood tests, 'false positives' can easily occur, and much is left to the discretion of the clinician, and the extent to which patients self-regulate their own behaviour during diagnosis.

ICD: the World Health Organization's International Classification of Diseases, a comprehensive manual used primarily by medical professionals in the UK and other WHO members to diagnose mental health and other disorders. Whereas the DSM is the inspiration for and beneficiary of much research and associated funding in the US, the ICD receives comparatively little funding, and takes an approach leaning towards fewer diagnoses, a focus on primary rather than secondary care, and a focus on care in low- and middle-income countries.[90]

In many ways the ICD and the DSM are representative of the differing priorities and values of the regions in which they are used and the organisations that have developed them: the ICD is developed by the WHO, an organisation very much concerned with international public health, especially in vulnerable populations, whereas the DSM is funded in large part by the pharmaceutical industry and the American Psychiatric Association, which by dint of the expense of psychiatric care and the differing levels of quality between private and public health insurance, caters primarily to middle-class patients with access to this care.

(gender) dysphoria: derived from the Greek for 'difficult to bear', gender dysphoria is a condition experienced by some trans people who feel a discomfort with the incongruence between their gender identity and their body, the way they are perceived and expected to act by others. Symptoms of gender dysphoria may be alleviated by transitioning socially, with patients expressing themselves according to their gender identity, telling people about their gender identity and asking them to use the correct pronouns, and pursuing legal recognition on identity documents of their correct gender and pronouns. People with gender dysphoria *may* also wish to medically transition, that is, to pursue medical treatment in order to change one or more of their physical sex characteristics. There is some debate as to whether cisgender people can experience *gender* dysphoria – there are other types of dysphoria not related to a trans identity.

gender identity disorder: an outdated diagnostic term (used most recently in the DSM-IV) that has historically been used by medical professionals and academics to pathologise gender variance.

Gender identity disorder, or GID, was used to describe the incongruence between assigned gender and identity, the implication being that there is something inherently wrong with that incongruence.

The interaction between mental health and gender

As I sit down to write this introduction, my eye strays repeatedly to an opened letter, sitting on the table next to my laptop. After several months of waiting I've finally got an appointment with a mental health specialist with the rather obscure title of 'Adult Mental Health SE OPD', in a little over a month's time. I'm wondering not only what I'll say to this person, but what I'll be *allowed* to talk about. There's a lot I'd like to discuss. This particular appointment is ostensibly to talk about ADHD (attention deficit hyperactivity disorder), with which I was diagnosed long before I had any inkling of my transgender status and that, on the surface, has little to do with gender at all. But mental health symptoms and causes are so closely interconnected that nearly everything seems relevant to that diagnosis. In any case it took me about six months to get an appointment, so if the SE OPD lets me, I'll talk about anything and everything.

I've not had treatment for ADHD since high school – other mental health issues always seemed to eclipse it in terms of urgency – so it's not until now that I've even thought it might be something I'd want to see a professional about. The last time I saw a psychiatrist was four years ago, after an intense bout of chronic depression and anxiety that was, I came to realise, intimately connected with my gender identity and transition. It was through this psychiatrist that I first obtained a referral for gender-affirming medical treatment, treatment that had a direct, positive impact on my mental health.

Being genderqueer or nonbinary is not a mental illness, yet the vast majority of people I spoke to in researching for this book said they had experienced or were currently experiencing, mental illness. More nonbinary and genderqueer people than ever are seeking the services of mental health professionals. But it's important to understand the difference between predisposition and frequency of diagnosis, between correlation and causation, in order to fully understand our experiences, to effectively implement treatment, and to understand why transition-related healthcare such as hormones and surgery can be so effective in treating mental illness in trans and nonbinary patients.

Transgender mental health – indeed mental health in general – is an increasingly popular topic for academic papers, petitions and surveys, but very little research has been conducted specifically on the mental health experiences of nonbinary and genderqueer people. At the same time, nearly every nonbinary or genderqueer person I've ever met has had to deal with some kind of mental illness. Nearly every interviewee I spoke to while gathering data for this book had been diagnosed with a mental disorder, diagnoses which run the gamut from depression to anxiety to borderline personality disorder to post traumatic stress disorder (PTSD.)

Despite, or perhaps *because* of our growing visibility, increasing numbers of genderqueer patients are seeking all kinds of mental health treatment, which may be contributing to the false impression of us as a demographic composed entirely of fragile attention-seekers. Whether this is the case, or if we're simply the newest target for the ire of an older generation that was largely unable to be open about mental health, we *are* seeking treatment, often at facilities that are ill-equipped to deal with the influx. I'm pining after the biweekly – and distinctly unproductive – psychiatric sessions that accompanied my childhood ADHD treatment: I'd kill to have anything approaching that level of care today, and regret being cagey with my therapist at the time.

So mental health and mental illness do play a large part in our daily lives. Maybe this won't always be so, but for now it's important to talk about these issues and what we can do to address them, especially in the context of a health service that doesn't always provide adequate or culturally competent mental health support for the most vulnerable people in our society.

A question that has been asked but, in my opinion, not fully answered, is whether the mental health issues most likely to affect members of the genderqueer and nonbinary community are different from those affecting the trans or LGBT communities more generally. If these differences exist, are they in kind or simply a matter of degree? Extensive study has gone into plumbing the depths of the transgender psyche – for better or for worse – and I think that, probably, the mental health issues affecting binary trans people are pretty similar to those that affect nonbinary individuals. Many of our sources of marginalisation are the same, after all, and some of the internal conflict we may feel between our identities and the gender we were assigned at birth will resemble that felt by binary trans people. The issue is made complicated, though, by a general lack of valid, reproducible statistics, and it presents a thorny problem for policymakers and medical practitioners to deal with if they are going to meet the growing demand for inclusive mental health services.

In a 2017 article on the mental health of nonbinary and binary transgender youth[91] researchers found that, of a sample size of 677, there *were* some differences between binary trans and nonbinary participants. But these differences were not consistent across questions or subgroups: when asked whether mental health issues interfered with daily functioning, there was no significant difference between binary and nonbinary participants; sex assigned at birth was the main factor in determining their answer. On the other hand, when asked if they had sought treatment for depression or anxiety in their lifetimes, whether a person identified as binary *was* a determining factor: specifically, nonbinary people who were assigned male at birth (AMAB) were less likely than everyone else to seek mental health help, and less likely to have attempted suicide in the past.

The reasons for this pattern are difficult to determine. It may be because AMAB nonbinary people are less prone to mental illness, but I think it's more likely that the reason is tied up in sociological factors, as well as variables the study didn't test for and in the way the results were gathered. It's also important to point out that AMAB nonbinary people only made up about 14 per cent of the overall sample of participants: the smaller the sample size, the more easily it will be affected by a few extreme values or outliers. The limited age range of the participants (16 to 25 years) may also have affected the results. In any case, and perhaps *because* of their relative rarity within the non-binary community, more research is needed on the specific subgroup of AMAB nonbinary people before any firm conclusions can be drawn.

The only metric on which the responses of nonbinary participants on the whole were different from binary trans participants was that nonbinary participants reported an average of 2 per cent higher life satisfaction than their binary trans counterparts. To complicate matters further, a 2017 study[92] found that nonbinary youth had gen-erally *worse* mental health outcomes than their binary counterparts, and a 2015 study[93] found that nonbinary adults struggled more with substance abuse than their binary trans counterparts.

On the whole, the research on differences between binary and nonbinary trans people has tended to be contradictory, slight, sporad-ic or not statistically significant.[94] Very few studies have attempted to discover whether any other variables might affect the mental health status of the average nonbinary person– do age, race, class, ability or gender assigned at birth make a difference in genderqueer and nonbinary mental health outcomes? Again we see the same problem that emerges in the demographic studies I discussed in Chapter 1: we're a population that's just now becoming visible. Our boundaries are fuzzy and the factors that determine membership in our group are contested. There will no doubt be hidden factors that influence the results of any research on nonbinary people, and only further study will uncover them. There need to be more surveys, more studies, more focus groups and generally more attention on genderqueer people as a group in and of themselves before any clear conclusions can be drawn. At the same time, the only way that this data can be accurately and ethically gathered is if more trust is built between the genderqueer community and research institutions.

In any case – and regardless of whether our mental health

status is on average better, worse or the same as any other community – mental illness *does* affect us. We experience higher levels of social stigma and resulting minority stress than the cisgender, straight population, and that takes a toll. The same goes for any minority population: a 2016 report[95] from the Mental Health Foundation found a close connection between poverty and mental illness, and there have been multiple studies that have found that a person's sexuality[96, 97] and race[98] can be a determining factor in whether they experience minority stress, and that minority stress has a negative impact on mental health. And while there may be little evidence to suggest that genderqueer people are more likely to experience these symptoms than binary trans people, the fact remains that if you encounter a genderqueer person in your everyday life, chances are they've experienced mental illness in one form or another.

My experience with mental health and gender

I've got a long personal history with mental illness, which interacts in various ways with my gender identity. I now believe that many of my early symptoms of mental illness may have been early manifestations of a dissonance I wasn't fully aware of until my twenties. I can divide my life so far broadly into various periods defined by the experience of one or another mental disorder: ADHD, anxiety, insomnia, depression. I include some detail here to give you an idea of the various ways that gender variance and accompanying social stigma can lead to, interact with or worsen mental illness.

My 'story', as it were, is typical for a trans person. I first started to question my gender identity in my early teens. This was the time during which, having left the relative shelter of my liberal suburban home for the more normative environment of school, I began to be more aware of the social roles I and my classmates and friends would be placed in, based on our perceived genders. This was a time during which I realised I had to conform to social expectation. I had never really been comfortable with the binary pronoun people used to describe me, but it was peripheral, easily ignored, and my parents were pretty laissez-faire: it didn't seem to matter much to them if I did 'boy things' like karate or 'girl things' like playing with dolls, or both.

Now, it did. In middle school (the American analogue for the first few years after primary school) I had to change for and shower after gym class with the other 'girls': I have distinct memories of anxiety and stress associated with using the showers, but I didn't yet understand what was upsetting me. I was too young to be fully cognisant of the differing expectations placed on girls and boys– or more precisely, cognisant of the idea these were something someone could be *uncomfortable* with. This was a time during which a more flexible or mixed school environment would have made me a great deal more comfortable.

At the end of middle and the beginning of high school my friends also began to pair off, almost exclusively into heterosexual units (neither half of which I felt comfortable in), which brought the gender divide into even sharper focus.

Around this time, though starting in elementary school (the American analogue to primary school) and extending through all of middle and high school, I was also taking medication for ADHD, following a diagnosis in second or third grade. I don't think there's necessarily any correlation between instances of ADHD and instances of nonbinary gender, but I've recently come to fully comprehend the influences that ADHD and the medication I took for it had on my physical development, which in turn affected various other aspects of my mental health, and my self- and body-image.

After a series of detentions and notes home to my parents (and in a decade when doctors and parents were, perhaps, a bit heavy-handed with their ADHD diagnoses), I was put on Ritalin and later Dexedrine – described by *ADDitude* magazine as 'stronger than Ritalin,'[99] with a litany of side effects including:

False sense of well-being; irritability; nervousness; restlessness; trouble sleeping. Note – after these side effects have worn off, the patient may experience drowsiness, trembling, unusual tiredness or weakness, or mental depression...

Thinking back on it now, I worry that my young self was at the mercy of drugs that were probably far too strong for my developing mind. The overall impression I have of this time is of several years of neurotic behaviour, which approached obsessive-compulsive disorder. I washed my hands obsessively, I couldn't step on sidewalk cracks (I even still retain a peripheral awareness of them when out walking) and I had facial tics. It was very difficult for me to sleep, and this time marks my earliest experiences with insomnia, the most long-standing of my mental health issues.

The medication also had a distinct dampening effect on my appetite. I went through my childhood and early adolescence, a peak period for bone growth, eating far less than I should have been. For this reason, I'm convinced that ADHD has had a direct effect on my body image: it led to my small hands and feet, my short stature and thin body type, which were sources of personal anxiety for many years.

I don't include this information here just to tell you a sad story about my wretched childhood – for the most part I was safe and happy. I include it instead to illustrate that, when it comes to mental illness, especially for the patient themself, it can be very difficult to differentiate between root cause, illness and symptom. This is the case, I imagine, with the majority of comorbid people: mental illnesses are not isolated, and having one can exacerbate the symptoms of another. The line between cause and effect, between illness and symptom, can easily become blurry. So it has been for me with ADHD, anxiety, insomnia and various other sorts of symptoms for about as long as I can remember. So tangled were the conditions that characterised my young adulthood that I'm hard-pressed to partition them out into individual causes and consequences. The reality of mental illness can be much more complex for patients than they themselves may be able to articulate.

Gender identity comes fully into play for my own mental health about five years ago, during my final year at university. My degree is beginning to wind down, I'm busier than ever and I'm beginning to think of the future. I've realised I'm transgender, though from around first year to around third year I didn't think very much about what my precise gender identity might be. For a while I thought I was simply a binary trans man, though when I tried to get people to call me 'he', I found that didn't fit either.

I remember the second half of fourth year as a nasty black hole of depression, set off by relationship troubles and an unpleasant experience in the trans community – a community I wanted desperately to be a part of. I had begun at this time to realise that I couldn't go on without transitioning, but I had no idea what treatments were available or how I would get them.

At the time, transitioning seemed an insurmountable task, one that my friends and family (with the exception of a couple of trans friends) didn't understand or know how to tackle. All the while, my depression was telling me that what I was feeling didn't merit any action, that I didn't have the right to ask someone more knowledgeable for help, that there was no hope for me.

But I did it anyway. I went to my campus LGBT centre, to which I now realise I was incredibly lucky to have access, and signed up to see a psychiatrist specialising in gender identity disorder, anxiety and depression. I began cognitive behavioural therapy (CBT) sessions once a week. I don't have much memory of our actual sessions but three things came out of them that I do remember: I ended a relationship that was no longer healthy for me or my partner, I started to break into manageable parts the monumental task of sorting out insurance coverage and finding a doctor to start my medical transition, and my mental health began to improve, dramatically and quickly.

Without the LGBT centre therapist I don't know what I would have done. She didn't specifically tell me how to start transitioning, but she did give me the tools to start figuring it out myself. She didn't cure my anxiety and depression but she did help me figure out which parts of it were coming from me and which from my environment.

I can't overstate how helpful and necessary therapy, specifically CBT, was at that time in my life, and I'm painfully aware that a great many people go through what I went through without that level of support.

The moral of this story, then, is that mental illness, especially in a context where other factors such as gender identity and minority status interact, can be incredibly complex, and a sensitive, flexible approach is needed. The benefits of specialised, culturally competent mental health treatment, and support in figuring out medical and social transition, cannot be overstated.

Common nonbinary experiences with mental illness

The 2015 US Transgender Survey found that 39 per cent of participants were experiencing 'serious psychological distress', which is almost eight times the US average of 5 per cent.[100] The same survey found that instances of suicide ideation were ten times more likely among participants than the national average. Transgender youth have been shown to have high rates of depression, anxiety, suicidality, self-harm and substance abuse.[101] Transgender university students exhibit a higher rate of suicidality than their cisgender peers,[102] especially when they are attending universities that do not grant them access to spaces that correspond to their gender identities.[103] On a more anecdotal level, almost all of my interviewees had been diagnosed with anxiety, or depression, or both, and many have told me they struggle with self-harm and suicide ideation. Here's how a few of my interviewees described their experiences of mental illness:

BJS: I have a Generalised Anxiety Disorder diagnosis, which mostly manifests itself in debilitating perfectionism and/or not doing things because of a fear of failing.

CM: I was diagnosed with depression in 2014, although with hindsight I've had it on and off since my teens.

EB1: I do alright most of the time, but I have had mild depression before, at least twice.

EB2: Diagnosed major depressive, generalized anxiety.

HW: I was diagnosed with depression nearly two years ago and have had ups and downs with it since.

KR: I experience symptoms of PTSD including bouts of depression and anxiety. Previously diagnosed with emotional instability disorder/borderline personality disorder.

MG: I've been in and out of therapy from a very early age due to trauma. I've been diagnosed with severe depression several times and have a diagnosis for dysthymia/chronic depression since 2013 having been previously diagnosed with cyclothymia.[104]

SG: I have a diagnosis of depression and anxiety, and am waiting for an assessment for ADHD which I believe I have.

TP: My mental health is quite poor. I have CPTSD, depression, and anxiety.

XX3: I deal with anxiety and depression. I was diagnosed with anxiety when I was in elementary [school], I remember taking Zoloft. When my family discovered how sad I was in middle school, the school psychologist believe [sic] I was dealing with depression.

Overall our experiences in mental health treatment tend to be very patchy. The Royal College of Psychiatrists Good Practice Guidelines suggest:

There is growing recognition that many people do not regard themselves as conforming to the binary man/woman divide. This will affect their treatment choices. A few people who reject the gender concept altogether and see themselves as non-gendered may require gender neutralising treatments from appropriate clinical services.

Therefore, not all of these elements of treatment will be necessary or desirable in every case, nor will their sequencing conform rigidly to a standard pattern. For some people extensive surgery may not be appropriate or possible.[105]

In practice, however, the experiences of genderqueer and nonbinary people in accessing mental health services such as counselling and therapy (be it related to gender identity or not) can be fraught. Despite the fact that mental health counselling and support has been empirically shown to improve outcomes of both child and adult gender-identity care,[106] and is strongly recommended as a service specification in many gender identity standards of care, it is often very hard to access these services, which are almost always underfunded and understaffed, as there is generally a lack of standardised protocol for trans patients and a dearth of specialised and culturally competent staff. In addition, due to a lack of transparency regarding the criteria for granting referrals to gender identity clinics, and general access to treatment, many patients fear that if they express any doubt or ambiguity with regards to their gender identity, for example during a session with a counsellor, they'll be denied access to treatment.

Many of my interviewees have had to navigate mental health institutions, and often for reasons unrelated to their gender identity. However one of the biggest commonalities I see between interviewees is the fact that it's almost impossible to avoid bringing up gender identity when interacting with a mental health professional. Many of my interviewees have experienced firsthand the way that a nonbinary gender identity can complicate a person's relationship with their counsellor or therapist.

Interviewee MG, who lives in Portugal, described their experience with mental health professionals as 'confusing and unsatisfactory. There is very little information and training for mental health professionals about gender identity, ethical non-monogamy or kink.' Interviewee XX3, who is American, says:

I was young when I started speaking with a psychiatrist, she was the one who told my parents I had anxiety. I took the medication I was instructed to take, granted I was a kid and didn't always take it consistently, but I never felt like my anxiety 'changed', or 'contained'. Ironically I felt more anxious because the medication 'wasn't working'.

Interviewee EB1, who has lived in both Scotland and the United States, describes frustrating experiences with counsellors:

I have used counselling services multiple times in many different situations. Due to my self-awareness and acceptance of gender as not being linked to physical traits I have often found councillors [sic] unable to meet me with the issue I think I have, and instead they tend to think my issues are more fundamental/related to queerness or that I am not able to articulate what I need/am really looking for. It is hard to explain, but I don't ever get what I explicitly ask for, and often much later realize how strange the interaction was. The responses have been things like I ask for couples counselling and get told I need long term therapy, or I ask for them to articulate my options and they ask me what I want to hear, or I ask for help in motivating myself in a tough situation and I get told something articulating an emotional anchor that is very distant to my present situation.

Interviewee EB1's experiences demonstrate the way gender identity can complicate mental health diagnosis, not because it worsens a person's mental health status but because it adds a new variable to the equation which can distract from the underlying causes of mental illness. Interviewee KR, who lives in Scotland, describes their experience as 'very mixed', and says:

I have been involved with mental health services since I was a child and experienced abusive psychiatrists, disrespectful hospital staff, sexual harassment on a psych ward, religion forced on me in a psych ward. In recent years, I have had more positive experiences. I had a support worker who believes in me and treated me with the respect I deserve. I have also had a number of counsellors who I've built very healthy and therapeutic relationships with.

Interviewee KR's experiences are a good example of the way that individuals working within any institution can make a huge difference. Personally speaking if I hadn't had the support of my psychiatrist at university I have no doubt that my mental health outcome would have been far worse.

Interviewee XX1, who lives in the United States, said:

In my experience, most mental health professionals are either too medication happy or completely anti-medication. Getting to a better mental place sometimes requires medication no matter how opposed we may be, and folks in toxic environments/relationships will never be in a better mental place if their circumstances do not change. I was surprised to find that many professionals do not understand trauma, either. I had to explain to multiple professionals what I meant by 'triggers' and why they are important. These professionals claimed to specialize in trauma.

One interviewee, JRF, said that within medical institutions, 'I feel I'm reduced to a child in these environments, and I don't feel I'm being taken seriously.' Many of my interviewees and the people I've spoken to have described similar experiences: a therapist or counsellor has denied or even mocked their gender identity. Mental health services are places where people come when they are vulnerable, so a single negative experience can have a disastrous effect on their mental health.

Interviewee CM, who lives in Scotland, had a particularly nuanced view of the mental health system in the UK, and has experience using both public and privately-funded mental healthcare. Interviewee CM's account of public mental health services are grim indeed:

They're [the NHS] overworked and understaffed, and unfortunately sometimes you get a counsellor who's out of their depth with anything remotely unusual. The NHS mental health counselling was disastrous: I was genuinely told to remember that while things may have been sad for me, there were little brown babies in Africa who were starving. Other excellent advice included 'get a wee part-time job' – I'm a full-time freelance writer who works every hour God sends – and 'try to meet new people'. The counsellor also told me that 'Yes, on Wednesday' wasn't the correct answer to 'Have you felt any suicidal feelings since your last appointment': apparently the question really meant 'are you planning to kill yourself right now, at this second, here, now?'

When asked whether her gender identity was acknowledged within the institution, Interviewee CM said:

In the NHS, no. Partly because I was still in denial but largely because I felt the counsellor wasn't competent. The difference between that and the private sessions was dramatic. It wasn't that the private system is better; it's that the counsellor was. And I knew that if I didn't get on with the counsellor I could ask to see somebody else, because I was a paying customer. I think there's an undercurrent of fear when you deal with the NHS too: if I upset this counsellor, what's going to end up in my file and reported back to my GP?

Interviewee CM's experiences demonstrate the difficulty that genderqueer and nonbinary people can have when trying to be open about their identity while accessing mental health treatment. Often patients who seek out this treatment must walk a knife edge between exploring the link between their mental health status and their gender identity, and getting into a situation in which their mental illness is attributed entirely to that identity without any attention paid to environmental stressors or other causes.

Overdiagnosis and queer as mentally ill

For much of its history, non-normative gender identity, or 'transsexualism', has been considered a mental disorder. In much the same way as homosexuality[107] and any kind of subversive or disobedient female behaviour, for example 'hysteria',[108] were categorised as illnesses, with an accompanying implication that there might be a 'cure' for what was essentially rebellious behaviour, so too has transgender identity been treated as an illness. This mentality, rooted in a Victorian obsession with 'scientific' explanations for all types of behaviour, as well as the use of anatomy and physiology to reinforce the oppression of women, disabled people and even people of different races, suggests the logical conclusion, however unconscious or unintentional, that people who are ill or 'abnormal' in any way are inherently inferior to their fellow humans. Indeed, as Gert Hekma discusses in his article 'A Female Soul in a Male Body',[109] it wasn't until the 1860s and '70s, when theories like forensic psychiatry and sexual psychopathy became fashionable in medical circles, that non-normative behaviour such as homosexuality first started being thought of as an illness. And though this idea contributed to the decriminalisation of homosexuality, it also had unforeseen knock-on effects in the form of gay conversion therapy, a harmful practice that persists today.

Unfortunately, non-normative gender identities are still considered to be mental illnesses or disorders in some circles. The biological essentialist attitude has repercussions across many aspects of our lives, and the language surrounding trans issues is rife with connotations of deformity and aberrance. My interviewee BJS described their experience thus: 'I find it incredibly hard to find healthcare services that can adequately respect my gender identity without inappropriately using it as a "symptom".'

As recently as the DSM-IV,[110] 'gender identity *disorder*' was described as 'a strong and persistent cross-gender identification and a persistent discomfort with his or her sex or a sense of inappropriateness in the gender role of that sex'. Individuals, especially 'males' (meaning people assigned male at birth) are said to commonly experience 'transvestic fetishism' (Section 302.3), which was listed in the DSM-IV as a paraphilia, or 'a condition in which a person's sexual arousal and gratification depend on fantasizing about and engaging in sexual behavior that is *atypical and extreme*'.[111] It was thought that most children who exhibited GID would outgrow it, and those that didn't would continue to experience a '*chronic* course of gender confusion or dysphoria'.

It is clear from a perusal of the diagnoses for GID[112] in the DSM-IV, the language of the diagnosis itself steeped in connotations of illness and deformity, that it is the non-normatively gendered behaviour that was considered the problem, not any psychological distress that the patient may have experienced as a result of social ostracism or discomfort with their own body. The fourth edition of the manual made no recommendation as to how to alleviate the stress caused by social stigma. It states that some patients may *request* genital reassignment surgery but does not recommend such a course, with the rather feeble excuse that the DSM is classed as a diagnostic tool rather than a treatment guideline. Ironically, this meant that the very treatment that would alleviate gender dysphoric patients' *actual* psychological symptoms – respecting their identities, social and medical transition, support from their own community – would have been denied them, and thought of as aggravating a 'condition' rather than treating it; after all, the 'condition' in question was the identities themselves.

Nowadays, things are looking a bit brighter. The DSM-5 separates gender identity from sexuality and sexual 'dysfunctions', and includes a definition of gender *dysphoria*, rather than identity disorder: it acknowledges that it is the feelings of depression and discontent that come from an incongruence between oneself and one's assigned identity, rather than the fact of wanting to transition, that is the problem.

The new version of the DSM stresses that medical practitioners should respect patients' gender identities, and acknowledges that trans people are perfectly capable of being happy, and of being at peace with themselves, if they are treated with a modicum of respect and given the opportunity to present themselves as they feel appropriate. It's only now that we've managed to distinguish illness from symptom that we can begin to effectively treat the mental distress so often experienced by trans individuals.

Unfortunately, however, many of my interviewees still report struggling within mental health services with the very attitude exemplified in the older versions of the DSM. Interviewee BJS says:

> My mental health is definitely affected by my gender identity in so much that I find it incredibly hard to find healthcare services that can adequately respect my gender identity without inappropriately using it as a 'symptom'. At this stage, my options are between being addressed and treated as a woman, or spending an hour every week talking about my gender identity rather than my actual mental health issues, neither of which I'm particularly keen on.

Interviewee SG described their worry around seeking a more complex diagnosis, saying 'I also believe I have a cluster B personality disorder (probably BPD) but don't dare seek a diagnosis of that due to the negative effects that would likely have on receiving transition related healthcare.'

In general, we have to choose between hiding our identities and getting treatment that doesn't actually reflect our experiences, and dealing with the consequences of being open. Interviewee JRF told me:

> The reason I don't insist on, 'actually can you refer to me as this or that', is because when medical professionals say things like, 'I've never heard [of] that before', it doesn't inspire much confidence. It makes you hesitant to mention because you don't feel you'll be taken seriously.

And interviewee CM reported:

I first went to see a counsellor in my early twenties, and didn't mention the trans thing; I didn't get good advice because I didn't tell the
counsellor the truth. Twenty something years later I made the same
mistake. Shame and denial about being trans meant I didn't seek the
help I now realise I needed.

Many of my interviewees have been forced to withhold their
nonbinary status in order to more effectively receive both mental
health and transition-related medical treatment, or have been open
about it and had a medical or mental health professional's personal
biases or ignorance interfere with the administration of treatment.
Interviewee SG described how they must police themself in order to
navigate the mental health system:

I am well spoken, avoid disclosing my status as being non-binary (i.e.
I present as a binary trans woman), have had training/experience
in health advocacy, and have the ability to do sufficient research
prior to accessing services to ensure that I say the right thing and act
appropriately to get the healthcare I need.

The need for self-regulation, be it researching answers to evaluations
or presenting as binary in meetings with clinicians, is exemplary of
a disconnect that I'll discuss further in Chapter 7, where I discuss
genderqueer experiences in medicine and medical institutions. In
short, it demonstrates that very often there is an assumption within
these institutions of bad faith on the part of trans patients, which
leads to patients and medical staff being unable to take each other
at face value. This disconnect complicates the diagnostic process and
contributes to the culture of mistrust between the trans and medical
communities.

The more complicated the relationship between a nonbinary
gender identity and mental health, the more likely a diagnosis is
to be wrong. When nonbinary patients are forced to simplify their
situations, to foreground one aspect of themselves and hide others,

they are essentially being forced to choose what they want to have treated. Interviewee SG says with distressing clarity, 'I have to deliberately misrepresent myself to all NHS services as a "model case binary transgender woman", both to avoid displaying any symptoms of a disordered personality or gender nonconformity, and so avoid anything which might hamper my gender treatment.'

A lack of communication between patients and physicians leads to stunted, incomplete or ineffective treatment. In turn, this causes a stronger association between nonbinary status and mental ill-health, and a perception of nonbinary status as a symptom rather than an unrelated aspect of a patient's personality. I think it likely that in some of these situations an extreme diagnosis is settled upon when a more nuanced understanding of the interaction between gender dysphoria and marginalisation stress would have yielded a more appropriate one.

Overdiagnosis is a commonly accepted problem for genderqueer people; my interviewee XX1 worries, 'Will my identity make my therapist/psychiatrist misdiagnose me with something else?' According to interviewee XX1, 'Some folks have mentioned their therapists claiming they have schizophrenia or they have multiple personality disorder when they are just dysphoric and depressed.' Interviewee EB1 says that counsellors 'tend to think my issues are more fundamental/related to queerness or that I am not able to articulate what I need/am really looking for'.

Perhaps in these instances cisgender doctors, lacking access to the complexities of our gender identities, or even patients, lacking the tools to fully articulate them, might be affected (consciously or unconsciously) by a popular perception of trans people as 'inherently ill', and reach for psychological diagnoses, which can ultimately do more harm to the patient than good.

All of this underlines to me the importance of culturally competent courses of treatment, which take into account all aspects of a genderqueer or nonbinary patient's circumstances. The organisation LGBT Health and Wellbeing deliver excellent counselling services for LGBT people in Scotland, on a pay-what-you-can basis. X, an interviewee I spoke to who works with the NHS, guessed that their presence might be used as an excuse by some clinics in Scotland *not* to provide mental health support and counselling services. But some people feel that these mental health services *should* be made available by third sector organisations rather than within clinics themselves, because patients may feel more comfortable being open about any doubts and fears they have regarding their identities. Being able to seek gender-related mental health support *outside* clinics may give patients more space to explore the complexities of these identities without the fear of being denied treatment, and while we may not immediately be able to create an environment that is completely respectful of genderqueer identities, the availability of mental health treatments in environments where patients need not fear the medicalisation of their identities could go a long way to ensuring the availability of effective treatment and mending the rift between service providers, institutions and the genderqueer community.

Dysphoria

In light of the negative experiences many of us have had when trying to access mental health services, and the ease with which cisgender mental health personnel seem to connect our mental illness to our gender identities, the obvious next question is what *are* the underlying factors that cause such a high prevalence of mental illness in the trans and nonbinary community, if not our identities themselves? Two intimately connected causes stand out that research has shown can predispose a patient to symptoms of mental illness. These are gender dysphoria and minority stress.

Gender dysphoria can manifest as an intense anxiety associated with gendered activities and expectations, specifically where the person is expected by those around them to act or present themself as the gender they were assigned at birth, rather than the one they identify as. Interviewee XX1 described their experiences with dysphoria in this way:

> I feel my gender identity magnifies the uneasiness I feel in my own skin. When a spike of dysphoria occurs, it can ruin my entire day or affect my mental health for days afterwards. That said, I don't feel that my gender identity hurts my mental health, but living in a transphobic heteronormative world as a non-cis person does.

XX2 said:

> Gender dysphoria directly links my gender with my mental health. I feel most dysphoric before and around my period (which I get every month; I'm not on birth control), and even the period symptoms themselves now directly result in my dysphoria. I've no problem not being on T or any other hormones for HRT [hormone replacement therapy], however my period reminds me of my AFAB body, which directly conflicts with my desire to not experience period symptoms/ have a period/to not be a woman or identified as a woman.

In the past, dysphoria has been conflated with the state of being transgender itself (for example in older versions of the DSM, and even still on the NHS website[113]). It's been called misleading names like 'gender identity disorder' and 'gender incongruence', which imply that the patient's distress is caused by their own state of being, and not a reaction to an unreasonably strict set of social expectations that have been impressed on them from birth. Dysphoria can manifest as feelings of hopelessness and frustration, and a deep discomfort with your own body. My interviewee HW says, 'I believe my gender dysphoria causes my depression. I feel it comes from a sense of hopelessness over getting people to perceive me the way I want to be seen.'

It's been proven by countless studies[14] that medical transition can alleviate dysphoria and the mental illness symptoms that accompany it. Many of the genderqueer and nonbinary interviewees I spoke to confirmed this. Interviewee CM says, 'I was diagnosed with depression in 2014, although with hindsight I've had it on and off since my teens. I was on anti-depressants for several years but managed to come off them in late 2017 as HRT started to make some pretty major psychological changes.'

But dysphoria can be tricky to manage for nonbinary people, both because our access to transition-related healthcare is limited by gatekeepers' perceptions of our identities, and because it can be difficult to determine a 'goal' or 'desired outcome' for a person whose identity doesn't necessarily correspond to an established category. As interviewee EB2 explains, 'Dysphoria triggers my anxiety, sometimes also depression... I usually isolate myself when dysphoria kicks in, because being misgendered is the worst but *not having an actual solid identity to affirm means that seeking affirmation is useless*' (my emphasis).

For a genderqueer person, it can be very difficult to prove to a doctor or an institution that you're 'trans enough' to qualify for gender-affirming medical treatment, even if you do experience dysphoria: interviewee MG says, 'In Portugal, as with many other countries in the world, dysphoria is still addressed as a mental health issue and patients need to go through a series of appointments with therapists to see if they are "legitimately trans" and are then authorized or denied HRT.' For a patient who experiences dysphoria but who doesn't have an unambiguous and fixed gender identity or presentation, and whose doctor doesn't think they qualify for gender-affirming medical treatment, one of the most important avenues for improving mental health is essentially denied them.

As trans healthcare, and mental healthcare, have developed over the last few years, it's become generally accepted that dysphoria is best treated by affirming and respecting the patient's gender, by facilitating social and medical transition. But for me, and for other nonbinary and genderqueer people, things may be a bit trickier. Dysphoria experienced by nonbinary people is still treatable with transition but the definition of transition, especially medical transition, is a bit more obscure. What transition means for us will be discussed in more detail in Chapter 7.

At the same time, however, not all trans or nonbinary people *do* experience dysphoria. This is a hotly contested issue in transgender circles, in fact. There are some members of the binary trans community (commonly called transmedicalists, transfundamentalists or 'truscum'), who think that having gender dysphoria is a prerequisite for being trans, and that people who *don't* experience it are merely 'transtrenders': faking their identity for attention, or even appropriating transgender culture.

But for the very same reason that having to prove yourself to a doctor limits genderqueer people's access to trans healthcare, the idea that all people who are trans must experience dysphoria, and that people who don't experience it *can't* be trans, is inherently dismissive of the experiences of many nonbinary people. This mentality tends to frame medical transition, with a view to approximating as closely as possible the *normative ideal of male or female* (rather than self-acceptance, or greater social acceptance for non-normatively gendered bodies) as the only possible treatment for any distress a trans person might feel. This view is harmful to the significant number of genderqueer people (and binary trans people, for that matter) who *don't* experience body dysphoria, and who don't feel the need to undergo surgery or receive hormone treatment, but who still want their gender identities to be acknowledged, celebrated and given legal recognition, and who may still experience mental illness related to their gender identity.

Minority stress

Studies have shown that LGBT people often experience minority stress,[15] which is defined as a chronic elevation of blood pressure and anxiety that adversely affects the mental and physical health of a minority population experiencing high levels of abuse, discrimination and prejudice, internalised stigma, poor social support and low socioeconomic status.

When asked how their gender relates to their mental health, interviewee SG said:

> Largely: most of my mental health problems as they are in their current state have root in social and environmental stressors that stem from or are related to me being transgender... Certainly if I were cisgender my neuro-diversity would be much easier to live with due to the lack of stressors and increase in support in my life.

CM says that her gender identity has had a big influence on her mental health:

> I spent from my early teens effectively pretending to be somebody I wasn't, and that put huge strain on my mental health. Self-policing to try and make sure nobody spotted I wasn't 'normal', the constant fear of being outed, constantly seeing people like me mocked on TV or in the newspapers, the nagging feeling that I was the butt of some huge cosmic joke. That's a lot to carry around inside your head.

Interviewee XX1 had a particularly nuanced view of the impact of dysphoria and marginalisation on XX1's mental health (italics mine):

> As non cis, I am constantly wondering: *will I be attacked for who I am? Am I presenting in a way that I won't feel misgendered (even though I know it will always be no)?* How many people will I have to come out to today? Will I have particularly bad dysphoria today? Will my dysphoria ruin a fun engagement? Will my dysphoria ruin my mood for the next few days? Will my dysphoria make me cry in a public bathroom again while my friends and family wait for me outside? ... Why do all of these pronouns feel wrong? *Will people scoff at me for mentioning another pronoun system other than he/she/they/zher?*, etc.

Conclusions, recommendations and resources

In light of the striking concurrences between the mental health experiences of my interviewees and the anecdotes and statistics I've seen so far, it's fairly obvious that something is going on beneath the surface besides trans people simply being more mentally ill than cis people. I feel it may even be inaccurate, in this context, to say that a genderqueer patient was 'diagnosed' with anxiety and depression because, to me at least, it suggests that anxiety and depression are illnesses and not symptoms. To *diagnose* someone with anxiety or depression, especially if they belong to a marginalised group, suggests that the diagnosis is the end of it, rather than the beginning. It seems to me that in most of the cases I've discussed, treatments like antidepressants or mood stabilisers may be bandaid solutions when a more nuanced approach would be better.

Apart from the harmful association of gender diversity with misery and unhappiness, this kind of thinking is also counterproductive, because as more and more research has shown, the *why* of our mental health issues represents where real change can be made. Often gender dysphoria is framed as a cause of mental illness *separate* from minority stress – even in this chapter I had to think hard about discussing dysphoria and minority stress separately.

The evidence makes it fairly clear that dysphoria is more complex than just a sense of dissonance between personality and body. In my research, I've come to think that dysphoria and minority stress may be two sides of the same coin: gender dysphoria seems to me to be what happens when a person has internalised the way society legitimises and stigmatises different types of gendered expression. To put it another way: I think that if children were to be raised with a wider and more open understanding of what 'woman' and 'man' meant, if those categories were not so closely tied to, for example, breasts and penises, and if children were taught to respect people whose identities, self-expression and bodies were *neither* man nor woman, then those children might grow up feeling they had a right to inhabit the category or identity they felt most comfortable with. When a nonbinary person hates their penis or their breasts it's not because those things are inherently in opposition to the state of being nonbinary, or even inherent to a state of manhood or womanhood: it's because they've been taught their entire life that breasts are *only* compatible with womanhood and *no other identity*, and a penis *only* with manhood and *no other identity*.

I don't necessarily think this is something any of us can fix in our lifetimes. A lot of human culture has been built on these assumptions and associations. But I also don't think we need to destroy that culture in order to make society more accepting of genderqueer and nonbinary people. Rather I think that if we start acknowledging the way culture and history, even recent history, has influenced our ideas of what the genders are and how they should act, then we can start seeing the forest for the trees. If we can widen our definitions and create an environment in which people feel comfortable expressing their gender as it is, rather than how others dictate it should be, then we can improve the mental health, quality of life and life chances of trans people.

But until we create this environment, there are a number of ways we can improve the experiences of genderqueer people accessing mental health services in the meantime. The immediate solution that might spring to mind for any reader who is trans or genderqueer is facilitating transition, both medical and social. In the early 2010s a task force was formed by the board of trustees of the American Psychiatric Association for the purpose of investigating evidence for the efficacy of medical treatment of gender identity disorder and gender dysphoria.[16] This task force found that, though the quality of evidence was generally low – due to a lack of rigorous methodology and small sample sizes, among other factors – the broad clinical consensus was that gender-affirming medical treatments were effective in treating gender dysphoria.

I asked my interviewees specifically what their mental health professionals have done that was helpful or supportive, and what they could have done better:

CM: I think it might be helpful if they could ask about gender identity in the initial assessment, and make it clear that they're non-judgemental about NB/GQ people. I was asked about my sexuality and my sexual activity but not my gender identity... I found the private counselling was both (helpful and supportive): it didn't feel like a chore or an exercise in form-filling like the NHS counselling did. The counsellor was empathetic, engaged and unafraid to ask really awkward questions. The organisation around the private GP is very welcoming too – it's a service specifically created for trans people.

SG, on what mental health services could do better: lots – not assuming gender, having accessible facilities and forms for trans people (e.g. toilets and gender options and pronoun preferences in their forms) and openly adopting gender accepting policies for dealing with clients would be a great start.

SG, on what they did well: LGBT switchboard, who provided me counselling, checked my gender preference and queer life/issues experience when finding the most appropriate counsellor.

KR: I had a support worker who believes in me and treated me with the respect I deserve. I have also had a number of counsellors who I've built very healthy and therapeutic relationships with.

CM also makes clear the importance of training and hiring more mental health service workers, counsellors and therapists who are themselves trans: In late 2017 I had six sessions of private online counselling, which were much better, and where the topic was being trans. The counsellor was a trans woman who was very good at calling me out on my bullshit and the sessions genuinely helped: I developed a much better understanding of the world and where I fit in it.

XX1: Really, the main reason my gender identity causes me distress is the society we live in. Change society and then we'll talk. My health professionals who were my exceptions admitted they do not know everything. They are not me, so they cannot know my truth. Even if they don't understand or relate to what I am going through, it is their job to help me get through it.

Interviewee CM says that coming out had a noticeable positive effect on her mental health:

I think it's [coming out and transition] a huge part of it. I had frequent bouts of suicidal ideation before I came out as trans/NB in early 2017. A year on and that's a very rare and easily dismissed cloud based on circumstances, not a deep-seated unhappiness.

But there is an ironic conundrum that many transgender and nonbinary people find themselves in. Often, trans people are not considered competent to make decisions regarding their own care. This assumption is in direct opposition to the fact that, generally speaking, we *are* expert patients; we know what we need from doctors and mental health professionals, because we often have to do our own research. So the best way for a counsellor or therapist to start, if they want a genderqueer patient to feel validated, supported and comfortable being open about their gender identity, is to listen to what that patient has to say about their gender and mental health.

There is a dearth of training materials that discuss transgender and nonbinary life experience. But at the same time that I advocate fixing this by creating more materials, I also want to assert that the absolute best way for a cisgender counsellor or therapist to learn more about trans people is to meet them, talk to them, to listen to them speak about their experiences. Seek out resources created by genderqueer and nonbinary people themselves, and listen closely when they say something is wrong. Listen to what they think they need from you in order to fix it.

Resources and further reading

LGBT Health and Wellbeing Scotland offer a range of online resources for LGBT people dealing with mental illness, as well as a range of films, helplines and resources for service providers and organisations who work with LGBT people. These can be accessed at: www.lgbthealth. org.uk/online-resources

This 2018 article by Vic Parsons for The Pool describes the trauma that can come with trying to access mainstream and public mental health services, which often lack cultural competence and awareness of the trans community, and how that trauma can lead people to avoid using those services even when they need them: www.the-pool. com/health/mind/2018/20/vic-parsons-how-mental-health-cuts-are-affecting-the-LGBTQ-community

The article specifically mentions CliniQ, an alternative sexual health and wellbeing clinic specifically for transgender people. More information about CliniQ can be found here: https://cliniq.org. uk/about

Trav Mamone's article for Ravishly specifically discusses how nonbinary invisibility negatively impacts mental health, creating feelings of isolation and a lack of support: https://ravishly.com/ non-binary-invisibility-affects-mental-health

Mind Out is a third sector organisation that provides LGBT-specific mental health services. More information can be found here: www. mindout.org.uk

Lev, A. I. (2004). *Transgender Emergence: Therapeutic Guidelines for Working with Gender-Variant People and Their Families*. Binghamton, NY: Haworth Press. ISBN 9780789007087. This book is well-loved by clinicians, however it is quite an old edition and at least one trans reader (being in the best position to evaluate the accuracy of such a text) has pointed out that some of the terminology is outdated.

Chang, S. C., Singh, A. A. and dickey, l. m. (2019). *A Clinician's Guide to Gender-Affirming Care: Working with Transgender and Gender-Non-conforming Clients*. Oakland, CA: New Harbinger Publications. ISBN: 9781684030521. This is a new book that 'provides up-to-date information on language, etiquette, and appropriate communication and conduct in treating TGNC clients, and discusses the history, cultural context, and ethical and legal issues that can arise in working with gender-diverse individuals in a clinical setting.' The lead author, Sand C. Chang, identifies as nonbinary.

Exercises and discussion questions

A lot of the stress, anxiety and depression experienced by nonbinary and genderqueer people is caused by the way our society explicitly or implicitly invalidates and delegitimises their identities and experiences.

1. What do you think are some of the very small, everyday ways this might happen? Think about all the situations you encounter every day that might be experienced differently by a genderqueer or nonbinary person, and how might this difference affect them?
2. How might small things, like gendered changing rooms, medical forms that only allow patients to fill in 'male' and 'female', or someone refusing to use a preferred pronoun, contribute to feelings of invisibility, powerlessness or hopelessness?
3. If you don't experience gender dysphoria, how do you think these factors might exacerbate dysphoria? If you do, how are your feelings of dysphoria affected by small, everyday invalidations and microaggressions like the ones discussed in question 2?

4. What are some tangible, everyday changes we might all make on an individual level to change this?
5. What are some of the things (scenarios, fears, situations, environments, etc.) in your life that cause you anxiety or stress?
6. Even if you aren't trans, genderqueer or nonbinary, how does your gender identity interact with the way these situations or causes make you feel? Do you feel these factors would affect you differently were your gender identity different?

CHAPTER 7

Medicine

Introduction

When I was blocking out the structure of this book, this was one of the first chapters I *knew* had to be in it. The pervasive binarism that exists in medical institutions, and the pathologisation of our identities, represent some of the biggest barriers genderqueer people – and most people under the trans umbrella – face when trying to access the services of gender identity clinics, and healthcare more generally. Further, the challenges nonbinary people face in the medical system is a manifestation of a number of larger issues, such as the way that binary thinking is ingrained in our society, and the ways that acknowledgement and understanding of nonbinary and trans lived experience is necessary in order for policies and resources to properly address our needs.

But the issues that make this chapter important are also its caveats; there is a long and sinister history in the West (especially in the anglophone countries with which this book is concerned) of medicalisation of transgender and nonbinary identities. What I mean by this is that the medical establishment in the US and the UK tends to view our non-normative genders – whether we're seeking gender-related healthcare or not – as an illness or disorder. For a long time and still in some contexts today, doctors have sought to cure us of our identities.

This practice originates from a nineteenth-century obsession with finding a scientific explanation for all phenomena, and with attributing any kind of variant or subversive behaviour to medical and psychological causes – a mentality which itself is rooted in Western Enlightenment and the Scientific Revolution. Before the Scientific Revolution, as discussed in Chapter 3, the way gender was conceptualised was likely very different from today. It was thought that the salient feature of a person's maleness or femaleness was based in their behaviour, and that, crucially, a person who behaved more like the 'opposite' sex would begin to take on physical attributes of that sex. Under this model, while it would be naive to say trans people would have been more socially accepted, it's conceivable at the very least that we wouldn't have been interrogated daily on the nature of our genitals: it would have been assumed, based on the way we spoke and acted, that we were what we said we were.

An unfortunate result of this academic and medical preoccupation with pathology and psychological abnormality is that there is pressure placed on the trans community to pursue medical treatment to 'correct' our gender abnormality, and medical procedure is thought to be a necessary prerequisite for our state of being: 'transgender' is assumed in the common mind to mean a person who has had 'the surgery' or who undergoes hormone replacement therapy. And there is great pressure for trans people to try as much as possible to undergo these procedures in order for them to be acceptable in the eyes of the cis majority.

I don't think a desire for surgery and hormones is *always, entirely* due to external social pressure, nor do I think that people who seek gender-related medical treatment always feel dysphoric. But I will assert that in order for a transgender person to move through our world safely and with the tacit approval of the general public, we generally must, as much as possible, fall within the acceptable range of what someone of our gender is supposed to look, sound and act like. If we are 'clocked' as trans, or as anything outside the norm, we face mockery, harassment and even violence.

A great deal of energy, then, is spent by trans organisations to establish in the mainstream view that gender-affirming treatments are medically necessary, and to secure them as a legal right for all trans people. These efforts have had a measure of success: the NHS makes many of them available for free, to an extent that will be explored later in this chapter, as do some American insurance companies. But it's also becoming increasingly clear, at least in the UK, that the services and resources we have are unable to keep up with a demand that has been growing steadily in the last few years, proportional to the level of trans visibility and acceptance.

This institutional focus on the body and on medical procedure, rather than on the nuances of our internal identities, has fomented a debate within transgender circles as to whether dysphoria, and an associated desire for medical intervention in order to change one's physical sex characteristics, is necessary for a person to be considered transgender at all. My personal view, which I think will win out eventually, is that while gender reassignment services are indeed medically necessary to a great number of trans people, they're not, nor should they be, a prerequisite for membership in the trans and nonbinary communities. A person is trans if they don't consistently identify with the gender they were assigned at birth,[1] and what they do about it from there is up to them. It's reductive and exclusionary to set up gender-affirming medical treatment, and the desire for it, as the defining feature of all people existing under the trans umbrella.

This debate, and the use of medical procedure as a synonym for authenticity or 'true transness', raises a further question: it's undeniable that a large number of trans people *do* feel the need for some kind of gender-affirming medical treatment. It's also undeniable that the trans community contains people whose identities are not binary male or female. What, then, should become of these people if they want to transition medically?

The Gender Reassignment Protocol (GRP)[118] and other treatment guidelines used by professionals providing gender-affirming medical services have mostly been written by cisgender physicians, in a context where the only accepted models of transition involved a 'sex-swap' from one side of a binary system to the other. Most of these materials are phrased in such a way that precludes the very existence of nonbinary identities. This linguistic binarism begets institutional binarism: environments in which nonbinary and genderqueer people are seen as illegitimate and framed as outsiders requiring special treatment outside of standard practice.

The medical system is merely the most visible example of a way of thinking that is in many ways fundamental to our society, and which can be seen across institutions. The hostility and ignorance that many of us face when navigating the medical system is not simply the cumulative effect of bigotry or ignorance on the part of individual doctors and nurses, it's the result of a society-wide way of thinking that has gone unexamined for hundreds, if not thousands, of years.

For the majority of humans, the male/female binary system works fine. But at the same time there is a substantial group of people, increasingly visible, for whom it does not. For these people, navigating in a system that at every turn questions our existence and the validity of our identities can be exhausting, even physically harmful. It can lead to mistrust and miscommunication between patients and doctors, or an avoidance of the medical system altogether. Put briefly it puts people in danger. As interviewee CM put it:

I first went to see a counsellor in my early twenties, and didn't mention the trans thing; I didn't get good advice because I didn't tell the counsellor the truth. Twenty something years later I made the same mistake. Shame and denial about being trans meant I didn't seek the help I now realise I needed.

There are plenty of people for whom the desired outcome of a medical transition is not as clear as a binary 'swap'. When considering how best to approach the issue of nonbinary access to gender-affirming medical treatment, a number of questions are raised:

- Do all genderqueer, genderfluid or nonbinary people want to transition medically?
- What kind of treatments might a genderqueer or nonbinary person want to pursue?
- What is the ideal outcome of a nonbinary medical transition? Is there a single such outcome?
- How can clinical practice and treatment options be made more flexible and responsive to identities that are fluid, different from or more multifaceted than a simple matching up of genitalia, voice and body shape to a binary identity?
- Should separate standard practices be established for nonbinary medical transitions? How and to what extent might these practices differ from binary trans standards of practice – insofar as the latter exist at all?
- Is the answer to the previous question to create different and more specific protocols, or could a more person-centred informed consent model be the best way to make the overall trans healthcare system more inclusive and responsive to patient needs?
- What's the best way to make genderqueer patients more aware of the treatments available to them?
- What's the best way to make GPs and clinicians more aware of the subtleties of nonbinary identities, and of the treatments available?
- How do we create an environment in which genderqueer or gender-questioning people, especially younger and older people and people who don't fit the androgynous 'archetype' of a nonbinary person, are more comfortable asking for these treatments and generally exploring their identities in institutional settings?

This chapter seeks to begin to address these questions, though I can't guarantee it will come up with clear answers for all of them. The goal of this chapter is also to give an overview of the challenges nonbinary and genderqueer people who want to transition medically face specifically in obtaining gender-affirming treatment in our current system, with the intention of exploring how best medical professionals can support and accommodate them.

It is my hope that in the near future it will be a matter of course for nonbinary and genderqueer people to be connected with clinicians and practitioners who understand the treatments available and who are equipped to help them find the best treatment for them. Until then, however, we are largely on our own. I want this chapter to act as something of a guide for medical professionals such as GPs and endocrinologists who find nonbinary patients in their waiting rooms, and who want to create a safer, more supportive environment for them.

Glossary and acronyms

There are a number of terms and acronyms used in this chapter with which a layperson – or indeed a medical practitioner – may not be familiar.

AFAB/AMAB: a way to describe a trans person based on their biological sex. Assigned female at birth generally means a person with a vagina whose body naturally produces oestrogen as the primary sex hormone, and assigned male at birth generally describes a person with a penis and testes whose body naturally produces primarily testosterone. While in the vast majority of contexts it's unnecessary, inappropriate or a violation of privacy to discuss a trans person's genitalia or the gender they were assigned at birth, it can be relevant in certain medical contexts. For genderqueer or nonbinary patients, it can be a useful way of describing the gender-affirming medical treatments they may pursue, without resorting to gendered labels like trans man or trans woman.

gender-affirming medical treatment: also called gender reassignment,[119] a term which is considered outdated, inaccurate and exclusionary of nonbinary identities because it implies that a person's gender identity is being changed, when in fact it is the person's genital configuration or bodily hormones which are being changed. Surgery, or other medical treatments, designed to bring a trans person's outward appearance more in line with their inward perception of themself. For now, I'll use the term as shorthand for any medical treatment a trans or genderqueer person might undergo to make their body more closely represent their identity.

GIC: gender identity clinic. A place that provides information, counselling services and medical treatments relating to gender transition, including but not limited to surgery and hormone replacement therapy, as well as additional treatments such as speech and language therapy. There are eight (seven for adults and one for young people) NHS GICs in England and two (plus two defunct or intermittently available satellite clinics) in Scotland.[120] There are also a few privately operating clinics and physicians specialising in gender identity, such as GenderCare in London and Dr Lyndsey Myskow, who offers gender consultations through YourGP. A consultation with a private clinician generally costs between £100 and £300.

HRT: hormone replacement therapy. HRT exists in a larger context than just transition-related medical treatment, but in this context it refers to either of two types of treatment (conventionally, if problematically, called female-to-male (FtM) and male-to-female (MtF)) developed to change a person's secondary sex characteristics such as pattern of hair and fat distribution on the body, vocal pitch range (in the case of FtM) and breast size (in the case of MtF). This is achieved by treating a person with exogenous (i.e. not created by the body) hormones such as (but not limited to) testosterone or oestrogen. Further information about the specific hormones used in both types of treatment can be found in C. A. Unger's paper, 'Hormone therapy for transgender patients'.[121]

medical transition: the overarching process by which a trans person undergoes gender-affirming medical treatment. Describes not only the treatments themselves but also consultations with clinicians and any changes that those treatments make to the person's body.

puberty blockers: also called hormone blockers or puberty or hormone suppressors. These are medicines which, in a transgender context, when either injected or implanted in a prepubescent person prevent the body from being influenced by hormones, thus delaying the development of the secondary sex characteristics (changes in vocal pitch, the development of body hair or breasts) that so often cause dysphoria. This treatment is intended to give a trans or gender-questioning young person extra time to explore their gender identity.

SALT: speech and language therapy. Also called voice and communication therapy in the WPATH Standards of Care. This is a type of therapy used by some trans patients who want to bring their voices and the way they speak more in line with the gender they identify with.

top or bottom surgery: these are two types of surgery that transgender patients sometimes pursue as part of their medical transition. Top surgery generally refers to a mastectomy, or removal of the breasts, for an AFAB trans or nonbinary patient. Bottom surgery can refer to any number of procedures meant to alter a trans person's external genitalia, e.g. a phallo- or vaginoplasty.

WPATH: World Professional Association for Transgender Health. The WPATH is 'an international, multidisciplinary, professional association whose mission is to promote evidence-based care, education, research, advocacy, public policy, and respect for transgender health'.[122] The WPATH has developed a set of Standards of Care (or SOC), now in its seventh edition, that are based on cutting edge (albeit from a North American and Western European perspective) clinical research and professional expertise, and that offer guidelines for best practices in treating transgender patients. At the time of writing, the eighth version of the WPATH guidelines are being formulated, and many of the authors of this new version actually are transgender and nonbinary. Several guidelines used internationally, such as the Gender Reassignment Protocol, are based on the WPATH SOC. The SOC make several mentions of genderqueer identities, but don't specifically discuss genderqueer identities in the context of the medical treatment pathway. Please note that this version of the SOC was written in 2012, and accepted terminology may have changed since then.

My own experience and qualifications

I'm not a medical practitioner, and my experiences of navigating the medical system are primarily – though not entirely – based in the United States. Therefore this chapter will be heavily supplemented with statistics gathered by third sector organisations such as Stonewall, the Scottish Trans Alliance and UK Trans Info, as well as anecdotal evidence from a number of nonbinary, genderqueer and genderfluid people who have spoken to me about their experiences in medical institutions and with medical practitioners.

The information in this chapter is also supplemented by the advice of a interviewee, who I will call X. At the time of writing, X worked with the Scottish branch of Stonewall, the UK's largest LGBT charity, and with NHS Scotland, to develop more trans- and nonbinary-friendly policies and practices. Interviewee X spoke to me about how the NHS, GICs and GPs treat their nonbinary patients at the moment, and what they're doing to change things.

Throughout the chapter I'll also illustrate the points I make with examples from my own transition: the treatment I've undergone and what I went through to get it, and my experiences interacting with doctors as a nonbinary person in both the United States and Britain.

Summarised, I'm several years into HRT, for which I obtained a prescription while living in the United States. This prescription carried over when I moved to Scotland, and has continued to be filled by my GP and pharmacy here. This is the extent of my medical transition so far and, as my identity precludes any specific surgical outcome or an 'ideal' genital configuration, I have no real desire to pursue any other treatment at the moment. In addition, because I'm aware of how high demand for these services are at the moment, I've made a conscious decision not to use resources that could instead be accessed by someone who needs them more.

Not all nonbinary people require gender reassignment treatment

I feel it's important before we go any further to make doubly clear that medical transition is not a necessary component of nonbinary, or even of transgender, identity. A great number of genderqueer and nonbinary people do pursue gender-affirming medical treatment, which is why this chapter is here, but, just as many of us do not or cannot do so,[123] and these latter are no less genderqueer or nonbinary than those that do.

I say this emphatically now because the social pressure for trans people to pursue medical treatment in order to conform as much as possible to a binary ideal, leads many trans people, especially non-binary people, to be seen as somehow 'less trans' or less legitimate than their peers who have undergone surgery and who take hormones and so on. At the same time, because our medical system was built on a Victorian ideal of biology as fundamental and the two sexes as immutable and inextricably tied to two genders, the trans healthcare pathway is not very good at accommodating people whose genders fall outside the binary. Thus we are barred doubly from perceived authenticity.

But many nonbinary and genderqueer people have no interest in altering their bodies to more closely fit the normative idea of what a person of their gender should look like, be it male, female or otherwise:

XX2: It's not something that's vitally important to me, nor something that I plan to pursue at any point in the near future. I also don't think I'd ever go on hormones.

XX1: I am not seeking gender-affirming medical treatment since my issues are not outwardly based. I am leaning toward a demiboy identity (switching between nonbinary person and boy), gender medical treatment would probably not be beneficial. I would rather have no parts (which isn't medically possible), and I already can pass as a boy when I have short hair.

EB1: I wouldn't want to change anything. I found it a big deal to pierce my ears. I accept and enjoy being embodied. And I'm not attached to sex as a particularly gendered act, so I don't really see any need to change myself to fit any prescription of what my experience should look like.

A nonbinary person may see their gender as something separate from their body, or they may not see the point in changing anything about their body because their gender is expressed in their speech or behaviour, rather than their appearance. They may see no point in changing their body because they don't conceive of any particular body that more closely matches their identity. They may have no desire to manifest a 'gender' of any kind outside their own self-perception. They may not be comfortable altering their body under any circumstances. There are plenty of nonbinary people who don't experience gender dysphoria, and who see no reason to change their sex characteristics in order to transition socially, no matter what society might expect of them. These people may actively change their clothes, speech or behaviour, or they may simply continue existing after coming out as genderqueer as they have always done, with a new and deeper understanding of themselves and their gender.

There are also people whose gender identities by their very nature disallow them from transitioning medically. These people may have fluid identities and may relate to and express their gender in ways other than physical embodiment. For genderfluid people, such as my interviewee VK who identifies as genderflux,[124] a 'post-transition' body might be as inaccurate to their identity and dysphoria-inducing as their body is now. If a person's identity fluctuates between two or more binary, emphatic genders, a more androgynous or ambiguous body might be inappropriate. For this person, medically transitioning would be beside the point, or even counterproductive.

In addition, much of the treatment protocol, aside from being phrased in binary terms, states that patients must have a *persistent or fixed conception* of their gender. For example the WPATH SOC state that in order to qualify for gender-affirming surgery there must be a twelve-month period during which 'patients should *present consistently*, on a day-to-day basis and across all settings of life, in their desired gender role'.[125] For a genderfluid person, to present consistently as one gender or another would be to *not* live as their identity dictates.

Not all people who identify as genderqueer *can* pursue the treatment they might require. A person may feel too uncomfortable within the medical system in general, or they may find that the medical institutions and practitioners they have encountered are so hostile or inhospitable to the idea of a gender outside male or female that it is impossible for them to represent themselves accurately while seeking treatment. Many people choose to present themselves as binary in these cases but many also simply give up on pursuing treatment, considering it not worth the stress and potential trauma of misgendering themselves. They may resent anything that forces them to show a different self to the world, understandable as being openly genderqueer in public is often so costly.

What I mean to say here is that there are a range of reasons for a genderqueer person to transition medically, and just as many reasons not to. By including this chapter I'm not trying to make any claims about the importance of medical transition in and of itself, only that it is pertinent to the lives of a great number of genderqueer people and exemplary of the difficulties we face in navigating binary systems, and that therefore our experiences in the medical system should be discussed.

This is not to say, also, that the genderqueer people who don't pursue medical transition don't also experience barriers to accessing medical treatment. Nonbinary people who are visibly 'out', even without having undergone gender-affirming medical treatment, must still access medical treatment in institutions built to accommodate only two genders, and they can and do face hostility or ignorance from medical professionals when seeking *non*-transition-related medical treatment. It's commonly accepted in trans circles that often any symptom from insomnia to heart palpitations to a bad rash are attributed to being genderqueer, a phenomenon known as 'trans broken arm syndrome'.[126] In these cases doctors or other practitioners are unable to look past our identities to the person and symptoms beneath, and consequently don't look any further for a cause for the illness. My interviewee LE had this to say about their experiences in medical institutions:[127]

In general, my experiences with the medical system have ranged from uncomfortable to extremely triggering. Despite always being careful to call ahead to discuss my chosen name and pronouns, I have repeatedly been outed by the receptionist calling my birth name in the waiting room or constantly misgendering me. *This has caused me to avoiding [sic] seeking medical treatment wherever possible, even for non-transition related treatments.*

Trans broken arm syndrome can (and often does) place trans people at risk. Generally, participants in the STA report[128] on nonbinary experiences reported that they were uncomfortable being open about their gender identity when making use of general NHS health services, especially when their identity wasn't relevant to the reason they were seeking treatment, which suggests that NHS and other medical staff are generally not respectful of nonbinary gender identities.

It's my hope that giving medical practitioners, or anyone who controls access to medical treatment, a better understanding of the ways that nonbinary and genderqueer people relate to and struggle with the binary system, can make all aspects of that system much safer for us.

The treatment pathway

For a genderqueer person who does decide to pursue gender-affirming medical treatment, there is a specific pathway that they will be expected to follow.[129] There are a number of barriers and obstacles that a trans person must overcome in their pursuit of medical treatment, from confusing bureaucracy to gatekeeper hostility, and there are even more for a nonbinary person. This section will discuss the biggest issues I've observed, both nonbinary-specific and more general. I'll go through the process of medically transitioning with a hypothetical nonbinary person, from first becoming aware of the possibility of treatment, through to hormone therapy and surgeries, and discuss how they might navigate the system.[130] Some of these obstacles I have experienced myself, and some of them, that I have been lucky enough to avoid, have been experienced by nonbinary friends and acquaintances.

Nearly every step a nonbinary person takes towards medical transition is beset by obstacles stemming from the binarism and biological essentialism inherent in our medical system. We're met at every turn by hostility and scepticism, asked constantly to prove and justify ourselves.

The goal of this chapter is not to point fingers or lay blame at anyone's feet, but to give an idea of what the medical system is like from our perspective. I think most of the problems I flag up here can be addressed, and it is my hope that this chapter, and the rest of the book, will be part of a larger dialogue in the coming years towards a goal of greater nonbinary visibility and inclusion in all spheres, not just medical.

Access to information is limited

One of the first and most fundamental problems with the way our current trans healthcare system is set up is that access to accurate information about treatments, and where and how they can be acquired, is limited. This makes it difficult for prospective patients to know where to go and who to ask for information, and for practitioners to know what to tell them, and what standards of care to follow.

Health board websites often have very little information about transgender-related services, and it is often difficult to determine which clinics are seeing people from which health boards, as best practices for deciding on a clinic (which are unevenly distributed throughout the country) are not established. Even GPs are not always sure which clinic to refer a patient to; a hypothetical patient from Falkirk may be referred to either the Chalmers clinic in Edinburgh or the Sandyford clinic in Glasgow.

There are also often incongruities or gaps in services available, and overworked, understaffed clinics themselves may be inconsistent at providing information or keeping in touch with patients and prospective patients. For example, according to interviewee X, the clinician at Aberdeen's Grampian Gender Clinic retired in 2014. The clinic then privately procured the occasional services of a clinician at the Edinburgh Chalmers clinic. However, at the time of writing, they were on maternity leave, with no provisions made for patients who had been attending the Grampian clinic and who might not be able to travel to another clinic to continue their treatment.

In another example, the Sandyford clinic has been notoriously bad at sending out second appointments. A lot of people I've spoken to or heard about have had first appointments and had no follow-up scheduled, and the clinic has reportedly been evasive and inconsistent in providing information about how patients are supposed to go about obtaining follow-up appointments.

Overall the trans healthcare system is brittle and subject to all sorts of inconsistencies and gaps in service. There is often no way for people trying to access these services to know whether the information they're looking at is up to date and accurate, and often a great deal of effort can be spent on the part of a patient in trying to access a certain service, only to find out that that service or clinic or organisation is no longer available or operational. The people seeking these services on the basis of limited or outdated information are often the first to suffer when the system breaks.

Much of the information available to patients is provided by charities and other third sector organisations, such as the National Gender Identity Clinical Network for Scotland (NGICNS). Information may also be hidden on specialist sites or only accessible through several layers of links, which the average person may not know how to find. For example, the Highland Sexual Health clinic is listed on the NGICNS website as one of the places in Scotland where trans people may obtain gender-affirming medical treatment, but the Inverness clinic which serves the region is only intermittently available. In addition, the word 'transgender' is only listed once on the Highland Sexual Health clinic website; 'transsexuality and transgender issues' can be found on a page about sexual health, as part of a list of 'issues' about which a patient might find information at the clinic. There is no information anywhere on the site about whether gender-affirming medical treatment may be obtained at the Highland clinic, nor is there any information about which *specific* services might be available. To top it off, at the time of writing the website's search function was down, so if the information *was* hidden away somewhere on the Highland clinic website, it certainly wasn't anywhere I could find it.

More specific to genderqueer patients, many of the resources available to both patients and medical professionals are phrased in binary terms of male and female. Even the WPATH Standards of Care, for example, use the phrase 'male chest' when discussing the outcome of a mastectomy.¹³¹ Page eight of the WPATH Standards of Care, the overview, is phrased entirely in binary terms, describing a high level of satisfaction with the process in 'MtF' and 'FtM' patients, with no mention at all made of people whose genders are neither male nor female.

The phrase 'gender transition' is associated in the popular imagination with a skewed idea of what the process actually entails. It calls to mind dramatic tabloid articles about 'sex-swap' makeovers and surgeries gone horribly awry. Because of all this, many non-binary-identified people who wish to pursue a medical transition may never make it as far as the doctor's office. The fear, stigma and misinformation associated with so-called gender reassignment services may mean that they never ask. Even if they do decide to pursue treatment, a hypothetical genderqueer person's GP may read the WPATH Standards of Care and come away with the idea that gender-affirming medical treatment can only involve swapping a penis for a vagina or vice versa, and deny them a referral to the GIC.

A lack of accurate information is confusing, but more importantly it can also contribute to the isolation and helplessness that many trans people feel, and exacerbate feelings of depression and anxiety surrounding gender identity and transition. I have been undergoing HRT since the summer of 2014. Deciding, finally, that I wanted to pursue hormone therapy was just one step on a long and rather tortuous road that separated pre-transition me from my (even still rather nebulous) goal. Before approaching my doctor, I had to first come to the realisation that hormones, or really any kind of medical transition, was a possibility at all for someone like me. Before this realisation, in my mind the word *transition* meant mastectomy, vaginoplasty, testosterone shots, breast implants, none of which I intuitively wanted for myself. The idea of medical transition I'd got from the media, from the articles I'd read and from the medical professionals I'd spoken to – those that had actually heard of the process – was again one of moving between opposites.

This didn't actually change at any point in the process; I just learned workarounds. I can't remember where I first found out what the actual, physical results of HRT were, and the accompanying knowledge that they might be the key to a gradual, reversible process that could help me find, at long last, a body I was comfortable in. Most likely it was the internet – a blog post, a forum, an account from another nonbinary person who had already done it.

By the end of my time as an undergraduate I had managed to scrape together enough information – from trans friends, from the internet, from personal experimentation – to figure out that I was indeed nonbinary. I was seeing a therapist who, lucky for me, specialised in gender identity and dysphoria. It took only a brief conversation about my gender identity for her to write me a referral for gender-affirming medical treatment. It's difficult to describe the relief I felt at that moment. *Now*, I thought, *I'm getting somewhere.*

But it wasn't as simple as that. My general experience with medical professionals until then had been fairly conventional: I'd present with symptoms and go to the doctor, usually with my mother, and the doctor in her wisdom would diagnose and treat me, and then I'd go home. I'd never before needed treatment for something as difficult to articulate as gender dysphoria, never had symptoms I didn't know how to describe. I wasn't even sure what I should be asking for.

To this day I remember clearly the tightness I felt in my chest as I worked up the courage to say something to the effect of, 'I want to start HRT.' To which my doctor replied, 'What's HRT?'

I don't precisely remember how I responded to this, only that I left the office fairly quickly after that. I remember a crashing sense of embarrassment, of failure and of self-doubt. I had gone to the person whose job it was to make me feel better, and I had been turned away.

What could I do? Could I insist on staying in my doctor's office while she did a bit of research? I was nowhere near confident in myself enough to do that. I already felt instinctively that I had no right to be there; how was I going to assert myself to a medical professional who had just implied clearly that I didn't? I had never before gone to a doctor presenting symptoms and received no treatment at all, let alone had my state of unwellness itself denied. I was mortified, and it made me doubt myself and the legitimacy of what I was feeling. I left feeling completely and utterly alone, and it took a long time for me to recover and start the process again, and to work up the courage to do it on my own.

It's very difficult to describe just how bad this first experience was. I was faced with the prospect of undergoing a massive life change, and was in the middle of the worst period of depression I'd ever experienced. There's no doubt that the setback with my doctor made my depression worse. I left feeling that there must be something wrong with me, that I couldn't convey to my doctor what I needed and convince her to help me. I thought I must not deserve help at all.

I wish I could say that my experience was rare, or worse than average. It's not. I wish also that I could say I did everything myself from then on. I can't. The entire way through my transition I was – and still am – supported by a network of people who I came to rely upon heavily. My mother worked at that time for a health insurance company, and it was she who helped me find an endocrinologist who would accept our insurance (this was in the United States, where at the time of writing there was nothing like the NHS, and no single website or helpline to help a trans person figure out where to access care). My therapist, too, became indispensable to me, helping me through one of the worst times of my life. My trans and allied friends (I can't remember the last time I associated with someone who was *not* either trans or an ally) were essential, especially the information they shared about treatment options and their own experiences.

Many genderqueer and nonbinary people do not have the resources I had. They don't have a relative who understands how insurance works, they might not have a community to draw on (though the internet is making that easier and easier to find), they may not have a therapist, especially in the UK where most mental health services are not covered by the NHS and those that are are often not trans-specific. They may not have trans friends who they can share their experiences with. This is why more and more accessible information is so very important. Transition, especially genderqueer transition, is a distinctly DIY experience. Blogs and YouTube videos were my constant resources.

It takes a leap of faith for a nonbinary person to assert themself to a doctor, who may not understand the person's identity, who may not be receptive to the idea of a trans identity and insist on a certain course of treatment, who may even be hostile to the idea.

We're taught our whole lives that, when it comes to medicine, the doctor knows best. The idea of doing research on one's own and insisting on it to my doctor always smacked of hypochondria to me. But I, and most of the nonbinary people I've spoken to, have found that when it comes to gender-related healthcare, trans people are often forced to become expert patients, doing a great deal of research on their own before even approaching their doctors. Then when they are finally seen by a medical professional, they're often told that their own experience and expertise are not valid.

It's difficult for anyone to feel their doctor doesn't support them, or doesn't want to make an effort to do so. For someone who may not even be out as genderqueer to their friends and family, this experience can be devastating. Had more information been available, and if more official resources had explicitly acknowledged nonbinary identities, the more equipped I would have felt in asking for help, the more confident I would have been that I deserved treatment and the more willing might my doctor have been to meet me halfway.

Referral to a GIC

In the UK, after a trans or genderqueer person has realised they have dysphoria and that their dysphoria might be addressed with some kind of medical procedure, they must first acquire a referral to a gender identity clinic, where they will be assessed and prescribed the appropriate gender-affirming medical treatment. This referral can come from a number of places including a GP, a counsellor or, in rare cases,[132] a self-referral form filled out online.[133]

The actual process of obtaining a referral is almost never as straightforward as the previous paragraph suggests, however. As you might expect, the GP or counsellor deciding whether to grant a referral may not be trained in transgender cultural compentency, or well-versed in trans-umbrella identities, and may not personally accept the idea of genders outside male and female. If a patient doesn't fit the GP or counsellor's mental image of what a trans person looks like, they may deny the referral.[134] Unfortunately, referral to a GIC and gender-affirming services very often come down to the individual opinions of a single GP or counsellor, who may have very little information other than their own perceptions – which may be heavily influenced by personal bias and trans representations in popular media – to go on.

Because of this inconsistency in perception and education across institutions, the ease with which a patient obtains a referral can vary wildly. In some areas, especially more urban environments, this might relatively easy: my GP at the Edinburgh University campus health centre offered me a referral to the Edinburgh clinic on our second or third meeting, without me having to ask for it. I wasn't even seeing her for gender-related health care.[135]

My experience is not exemplary, however. I have spoken to many binary trans and genderqueer people who have been refused a referral, even by doctors at the same health centre I attend. There is a lack of standard practice for referral among medical practitioners, even within the same institution. My doctor didn't refer to any kind of document or manual before she offered me a referral, she simply asked me if I wanted one. It would have been just as easy for her, in fact easier, to simply not extend that offer. If she had not, and if I had needed the support offered at a GIC, my outlook right now would be radically different. I have heard tell of genderqueer patients taking advantage of the inconsistency and lack of standard practices by seeking a second opinion in their quest for a GIC referral, but a patient who, for example, lives in a remote area and can't afford to travel to see a different GP, would be denied this option. Situations like these contribute to inequalities in access to health care, especially along the lines of location and socioeconomic status.

At the GIC

When and if a referral to treatment is granted, our hypothetical nonbinary patient will be directed to the nearest GIC that is currently accepting new patients. If they live in a more remote area such as the Highlands of Scotland, this clinic may be hundreds of miles from where they live. Once our hypothetical nonbinary person has had their first GIC appointment scheduled – which may take several months depending on the clinic in question – they will be expected to come in for a preliminary appointment, during which they will be assessed, and treatment options, including psychotherapy, speech therapy, hormone therapy and surgery (the latter two of these requiring approval from two clinicians), will be discussed.

GICs are a big part of transitioning for many genderqueer people, despite the fact that the GIC system was built to guide patients from one binary identity to another. The GIC system was designed (and I use the word *designed* here in the loosest sense possible) at a time when the definition of a 'transsexual' person was simply someone who considered themself the opposite gender from the one they were assigned at birth, and who wanted to change their body to match.

The terminology used by and for the transgender community has changed drastically since then, and the definition of a trans person has been greatly expanded. Gender itself is now understood to be more complex than initially accepted and as such, there is still very little provision within the established institutions to support this expanded definition. The Scottish Public Health Network's (ScotPHN) Health Care Needs Assessment of Gender Identity Services points out, quite reasonably, that there is as yet no specific guidance available on diagnosing nonbinary-identified people with gender dysphoria,[136] and found that nonbinary-identified people generally had more negative experiences at GICs. For many of these people,

people who lack the funds to pursue private treatment and who don't want to run the very real risks associated with self-medicating using treatments acquired on the black market, there is no choice but to transition within a system in which they are divested of power, turned into numbers and forced to conform to a binary concept of gender.

In addition, these clinics are often unprepared and themselves lacking the funds to meet the rising demand for gender-related medical treatment. In Scotland, where I did the bulk of my research, there are two main GICs, in Glasgow and Edinburgh, and two smaller ones, Aberdeen and Inverness, which serve patients with referrals from the NHS Grampian and Highland areas, respectively. The two latter clinics are not always open or staffed, meaning that the other two clinics in Glasgow and Edinburgh, existing within 75 kilometres of each other and only about 100 kilometres north of the border, must effectively take on the burden of treating all the trans patients in Scotland. Things are, if anything, worse in other parts of the country. There is only one GIC in Northern Ireland, and all Welsh patients are referred to London Charing Cross, which as of 2016 served around 38 per cent of all UK patients. Nearly all clinics reported an increase of at least 10 per cent in the number of patients being referred for their first appointment.[137]

Wait times for and between appointments

One of the biggest difficulties associated with accessing trans health care is the massive wait times before or between appointments. Many clinic websites publish current waiting times, but according to interviewee X, and several of my acquaintances who've tried to access gender identity services, there is often little contact between clinics and individual patients regarding their appointment status or place in the queue.

GICs are also often reluctant to release demographic and wait time information, and often document their own patients in a way that is contradictory to their gender identity (such as recording and annotating them by the sex they were assigned at birth, rather than respecting their actual identities).

Most Scottish people who avail themselves of gender identity services go to the Sandyford clinic in Glasgow, which has a waiting list that averages about 12 months between referral and first appointment. The Chalmers Sexual Health clinic in Edinburgh has, over the last year or two, brought that wait time down to around three months, a vast improvement on the Sandyford wait times. It may be important to note that the Health Care Needs Assessment of Gender Identity Services document[138] posits that we may be approaching a plateau in terms of GIC referrals, as the uptick in recent years has most likely been due to more trans people feeling safe to come out than in previous years, rather than more people actually identifying as trans than in previous years.

In any case, it's clear that currently available resources are not up to the task of serving a growing trans population. Perhaps more distressingly still, while NHS England does actually specify that gender-affirming medical treatments are covered by guidelines dictating wait times between referral and treatment (abbreviated RTT for referral to treatment[139]), I was unable after an extensive internet search to find out what these wait time limits are actually supposed to be. Many of the comments on the webpages that discuss the wait time rules on gender-affirming medical treatment were from transgender people who had been waiting years for treatment, shuffled around a system which claims to be working to improve their lot. So while we may be making nominal progress towards improving these wait times, there's very little evidence to suggest these changes are actually being implemented on the ground.

Denial or withholding of treatment

The unspecificity of the existing standards of care leave a great deal of power in the hands of individual practitioners, whose judgement may be heavily dependent on their own personal biases. For example, the WPATH SOC states that any existing mental health conditions must be 'reasonably well-controlled',[140] but what this means is not specified: it's up to the clinician themself to decide, and may come down in practice to how good an individual patient is at hiding their own mental state. These guidelines generally do not offer any standard guidance or metrics by which a GP considering referral, or a clinician considering granting access to treatment, might determine whether it is the case for their patient.

Referral to a GIC, or access to trans healthcare more generally, is often denied on the grounds that the patient's mental health is not stable enough for them to undergo treatment. This happened to an acquaintance of mine at the same health centre that I currently attend; my friend was told that their mental health status was not good enough to be prescribed gender reassignment treatment.

For me, beginning hormone treatment, and ending the monumental struggle of navigating the American insurance and medical systems, correlated strongly with (dare I say *caused*?) an instant and noticeable improvement in my mental health. It marked the end of the longest and worst period of depression in my life. I can't say for certain that my acquaintance's mental health is directly dependent on their receiving treatment or if there are other complications involved, but I *can* say that pursuing this treatment is probably an essential step in improving their mental health at the moment.

The Royal College of Psychiatrists good practice guidelines state:

> Cessation or suspension of gender treatment by the treating team can only occur where there is evidence that a mental health condition is giving rise to a misdiagnosis of gender dysphoria or renders the patient untreatable until their condition is reasonably well controlled.[141]

But what precisely makes a patient untreatable? How do you tell whether a patient's dysphoria is exacerbated by an underlying mental health condition? What indicates that a patient's mental health issues are under control? How much of their own mental health status might a patient risk concealing in the pursuit of gender-affirming healthcare, and how would this deception affect their mental health outlook *apart* from the acquisition of gender-reassignment services? Do medical practitioners know that patients might be concealing their mental health status? According to the ScotPHN Health Care Needs Assessment of Gender Identity Services document, 54 per cent of participants who 'felt emotionally distressed or worried about their mental health (n=136)' weren't comfortable discussing this with their clinician, for fear that their gender-affirming treatment would be denied.[142]

Again and again we see that the decision to grant or deny access to treatment comes down to the perception of a single GP or clinician, who may not have access to all pertinent information. Gender dysphoria represents a root cause of mental illness symptoms for many trans people, so GPs prescribing antidepressants or antianxiety medication without being willing to discuss medical transition options like hormones or surgery is like putting a bandaid on a puncture wound; when a problem goes as deep as gender dysphoria, covering it up won't make it go away. But cisgender doctors, especially GPs who may be untrained in trans cultural competence and therefore unequipped to properly support their trans patients, are often reluctant to give their patients the care they request, because trans patients are generally seen as unstable, uninformed or generally incompetent to determine what treatments are in their best interests.

This is another way in which policymakers and clinicians who don't have the lived experience of being trans may inadvertently harm patients: we are very often forced to do the bulk of the research into our own care, essentially becoming expert patients. Cleaving to guidelines and protocols without listening to individual patients and operating on a basis of good faith and informed consent can and does divest trans patients of agency.

The irony of my friend's situation, which they and I both understood instinctively, was apparently lost on their GP who, being presumably cisgender, didn't have access to the experience of being trans, which would have made the necessity of treatment clear. Denial of access to mental-health-improving treatment on mental health grounds is just one manifestation of a fundamental disconnect that often occurs between a cisgender doctor's perception of trans or nonbinary identity and the nuances of its reality.

A common reason, then, for a GP to refuse to provide a referral, or for a clinician denying access to treatment, can come about from misunderstanding the complexities of a patient's gender identity, and by extension what treatments are appropriate for that patient. This is nowhere more true than with genderqueer, genderfluid and nonbinary patients.

According to interviewee X, much of the training material given to medical practitioners relating to transgender patients makes no mention of gender identities lying outside the simplistic male/female binary at all. Most GPs will have never met – or don't realise they've met – a nonbinary person. Their first point of reference will be these training materials, and potentially the visible trans people (mostly binary-identified trans women) they may have seen on television or in the news. Because most popular media outlets view 'passing' trans women and men as the only acceptable type of trans person to show on a screen (indeed, those that conform most closely to the cisgender norm are those who are considered most acceptable), the public perception of trans people will necessarily be skewed towards a very binary model. This in turn will directly affect a cisgender person's perception of what is and is not an acceptable or normal way to be gender-variant, and the cisgender – and potentially even the binary trans – people who had a hand in designing the training materials and protocols available to UK physicians will no doubt have been influenced by this lack of genderqueer visibility.

So when a GP encounters our hypothetical nonbinary person, who wants to undergo hormone treatment or have surgery or try puberty-delaying treatment like hormone blockers, the GP may interpret the patient's ambiguous or inconsistent gender presentation as an indication that they are somehow less 'committed' to their identity than a binary trans person, as indicative of a mental disorder or a 'cry for attention', rather than a genuine case of gender dysphoria. They may simply consider their patient too strange or outside their purview to even consider treating.

I've heard of trans people, especially genderqueer and nonbinary people, being denied treatment because their GP was 'uncomfortable' with the idea of administering gender identity-related treatment or granting access to it. This is all well and good for a doctor who fears legal action if their patient 'regrets' their decision (it's been estimated that medical detransition happens in about 1% of cases)[143] but the patient now finds themself back at square one.

In a meeting between a doctor and our hypothetical nonbinary person, the balance of power is vastly skewed in favour of the doctor, who acts as a gatekeeper to necessary treatment. They control the patient's access to life-improving medical care, and in this way they essentially hold the key to the patient's future. In Western society especially, we set doctors on a kind of pedestal of unassailable authority, but in truth they are as human as any of us, and are influenced by their own education, preconceptions, fears and biases. A GP's perspective of what is best for a trans person may not be what is actually best for that person, and though a denied referral is not the end of the world, it can be a massive setback for a vulnerable patient.

Nonbinary self-misrepresentation

In order for the clinician to grant the patient access to the services they need, the patient must clear several hurdles just within the clinic itself. A lack of clear clinical guidelines, and inconsistency in the criteria by which clinicians decide who does and doesn't qualify for treatment, leads to an unclear idea in patients themselves of what is expected of them. Many people, especially genderqueer and nonbinary people, feel pressure to exaggerate their gender presentation when interacting with clinicians and other gatekeepers, in order to appear 'trans enough' to qualify for treatment. Whether or not this misrepresentation is necessary, and whether or not clinicians put that much stock in presentation, the fact that this perception exists is enough to change the way patients present themselves at clinics.

Interviewee SG said:

I have never disclosed that I am non-binary or gender nonconforming, due to variously fear of it being used to invalidate my trans-ness, and the services' lack of understanding of trans issues in general (for example counsellors[sic] inability to gender my nonbinary partner correctly after repeated corrections).

The 2018 ScotPHN Health Care Needs Assessment of Gender Identity Services document says that 30 per cent of participants reported either lying to or withholding information from a clinician (n=186).[144] The 2015 US Transgender Survey reported that only 52 per cent of nonbinary participants were open about their gender identity with medical professionals or counsellors, compared to an average of 84 per cent of binary trans people. In 2015, Action for Trans Health conducted a survey[145] of 121 nonbinary-identified people in the UK, to ask them about their experiences accessing gender reassignment services. A huge proportion of the participants had negative experiences in trying to access NHS gender reassignment services – though experiences of accessing private healthcare seemed a bit better – and around half of all the participants presented as binary trans in order to access treatment. According to the 2015 Scottish Trans Alliance survey of nonbinary experiences using GICs,[146] almost 60 per cent of 221 respondents who'd accessed gender identity services in the last year said they were not comfortable being open about their nonbinary identity most of the time.

The statistics support a fear I personally hear echoed often in nonbinary circles: if your GP doesn't know or believe that nonbinary genders exist, and if all the resources available are phrased so as to exclude you, how do you convince them to treat you? Do you dress as the 'opposite' gender from the one you were assigned at birth in order to make yourself seem more convincingly trans, and then go back to your mixed or ambiguous expression the rest of the time? What happens if your clinician finds out you don't identify as binary? Today's world of social media and constant documentation have the potential to turn a nonbinary person's life into a panopticon of potential discovery. Do you then have to live full-time as a binary trans man or woman, even if doing so would make you miserable?

According to interviewee X, the actual criteria by which clinicians evaluate their patients is very informal: there's no standard set of questions for clinicians to give their trans patients, and there are not even any internationally recognised standards for who can become a gender identity clinician. Interviewee X has an intuition that the questions most clinicians ask trans patients tend to be framed in terms of binary gender, and that clinicians are generally more likely to respond to answers that are consistent with a binary identity than to answers which undermine or question the binary, or which admit to any ambiguity. Patients are asked 'What is dissonant about your identity?' and rarely, 'What about your identity aligns or is consistent with how you were assigned at birth?'

As such, and especially for genderqueer patients, access to treatment can depend heavily on both presentation and clinician perspective, with patients attempting to present in a way they perceive the clinician will approve of, with little open communication on the part of either party.

This was certainly the case during my own medical transition. My pathway was such that I was effectively passed directly from a sympathetic therapist, who specialised in treating mental illness associated with gender dysphoria, straight on to an endocrinologist (who was to provide hormones) who had little to no knowledge about transgender people. To be honest, the man seemed a bit put upon to find me in his waiting room at all; he asked me no questions about my identity or dysphoria that I can remember.

If the only information about me you had access to was my medical documentation, you might well think I was a binary trans person, because all the records (at least those I had access to) described me in terms of 'female to male'. In the interest of full disclosure (and I'm fairly sure that my treatment won't be taken away if one of my doctors reads this book), I'll say upfront that I lied in order to get treatment, even if it was a lie of omission. Even though the fact of my nonbinary identity was clearly stated in the referral letter my therapist wrote, at no point was this information acknowledged by my endocrinologist.

In this way I think I actually dodged a bullet: my endocrinologist seemed to know what he had to do (prescribe hormones, watch for side effects), and as long as the insurance was covering it and the proper forms had been signed he would do it, no questions asked.

Throughout the course of my visits, before I moved to the UK, I got the distinct impression that my doctor had no concept of a nonbinary identity. For all I know he might not have been aware that 'sex' and 'gender' were different. Maybe I'm not giving him enough credit: he clearly knew enough about trans people to know what to prescribe me, and he did allow me to start on the half dose that I'm still on to this day. He told me once or twice that my levels were not high enough but never insisted on increasing my dose (I think he had an idea that it would gradually increase until I was taking the dose recommended for a binary trans man, but I moved to the UK before he could insist).

To be honest, it was such a relief to finally get my transition started that I didn't much care if my doctor knew the ins and outs of my identity. I didn't want to make it clear to him because I had an underlying certainty that, even though I wasn't interrogated on the intake forms, to make it clear that I didn't want to 'become a man' might jeopardise everything I'd worked for. It wasn't worth the risk.

So I let my doctor think what he wanted. I asked for hormones and he gave me the prescription that has served me in good stead ever since. But the more I think about it, the more I realise that this subterfuge has left me with another legacy: an enduring feeling of illegitimacy, even guilt, whenever I interact with institutional figures of authority. Whenever I fill out a demographic form or answer a questionnaire, even if I write down my correct gender, or if my visit has nothing to do with being nonbinary, I still have a niggling feeling of insecurity because I'm used to being dishonest in an institutional setting. I'm beginning to get over this. More and more I feel comfortable with being open about my identity, both because I don't care nowadays what anyone expects of me, and because I know I won't be punished for it. Many people don't have this luxury, and so *don't* feel comfortable being open about their identities with medical professionals.

Clinicians are supposed to be gatekeepers, people who regulate access to the services we need and grant it based on certain criteria. Under our current system gatekeepers are a necessary part of the process in terms of allocating resources where they need to go. But the guidelines and safeguards that are supposed to have our best interests in mind often run counter to them, so much so that these gatekeepers have become a symbol in trans circles for a cis establishment that is in fact hostile to our community and ignorant of our needs. Because our experience with these gatekeepers is such that we have to be dishonest in order to get the treatment we need, the entire concept of gatekeeping is undermined.

Most of the time it's not a huge problem and we make do as best we can, but sometimes a person's trans status is pertinent to their medical treatment, and sometimes a miscommunication between doctor and patient can have life-threatening implications, especially when it comes to medical treatments involving hormones. In the words of one participant in the Scottish Trans Alliance's 2015 report, 'Nonbinary people's experiences in the UK':[147]

> If a form needs to know about biological sex (for medical reasons etc.), ask that separately. I don't mind stating that I'm biologically female if that is relevant, but I hate having to put my gender as female so that someone can infer my sex and thus my medical needs from that.

As long as institutions don't acknowledge that a person's sex and gender might be different, and as long as there is a gap in understanding or an assumption of bad faith between clinicians and patients, genderqueer people will not be safe or comfortable in clinical settings.

Practicalities of gender-affirming medical treatment

Nat Titman's 2014 study of nonbinary people in the UK found that 31.6 per cent of nonbinary people 'indicated that they were considering, were undergoing or had undergone some part of gender reassignment'.[148] The conventional treatment pathway does not suit the majority of genderqueer people who wish to undergo gender reassignment, because many of these treatments are conventionally only used to help a person move from one end of a binary scale to the opposite end. Medical transition will most likely look different for each individual nonbinary person, and an understanding of the treatments available and how they affect the body is necessary for both nonbinary patients and medical practitioners administering or referring to such treatment.

When asked if they thought the requirements made by clinicians of patients pursuing a medical transition were reasonable, interviewee LE said, 'for my partner at the time, they made them live as their true gender for a year without hormones before they were willing to concede that their gender identity was valid enough to transition medically'.

This practice is standard, but it places nonbinary patients in a curious double bind: aside from the trauma of ridicule and harassment that may result from a patient being forced to be out without the ability to control their presentation that hormones and surgery would facilitate, how are nonbinary patients who want to transition medically supposed to prove that they've 'lived as their affirmed gender' if the medical establishment doesn't acknowledge their gender even exists?

Myths

It occurs to me, as I search for papers and other resources to prepare to write this section, that there is a huge amount of misconception and sensationalism associated with gender-affirming medical treatment. Any google search on the topic will yield about 99 shock-value, fearmongering newspaper articles for every one scientific paper. Transgender news coverage is replete with articles full of 'graphic' photos and surgery 'disasters'; they generally give the impression that transgender people should be viewed as scientific oddities, at best medical miracles and at worst abominations, worthy of ridicule and pity, and frame gender reassignment procedures as risky, experimental and quasi-illegal. So before I go further with this section I'd like to address some of these misconceptions.[149]

Trans healthcare is often framed as experimental, unsafe and extreme, an association that contributes to the perception of trans people as socially deviant, illegitimate outsiders. Very often mainstream news articles discussing transition are doing so in order to titillate a cis audience, meaning it is the very rare cases of negative surgical outcomes, regret or detransition, rather than the vast majority of successful procedures and happy patients, that receive the spotlight. But there have been countless scientific and clinical studies that both validate the effectiveness and safety of gender-reassignment procedures, and establish a firm link between these procedures and improved quality of life for patients. The entire purpose of BAGIS (the British Association of Gender Identity Specialists), for example, is to investigate and disseminate knowledge of gender dysphoria and transgender health.

Another important thing to keep in mind, especially when treating younger trans people and people who may be unsure of what their gender identity actually is, is that there are some fully reversible treatment options,[150] such as puberty blockers, which can allow a young patient the freedom to explore alternative gender roles before puberty sets them on a development path they're not comfortable with. Even some of the effects of hormone treatments can be partially reversible as well.

In any case, most studies, as discussed in detail in the WPATH Standards of Care,[151] find that only around 2 per cent of patients express any regret after undergoing gender-affirming treatment, and that even fewer detransition – that is, go back to living and presenting as the gender they were assigned at birth. Very often the reasons for detransitioning have less to do with any kind of change or misinterpretation of the patient's gender identity, and far more to do with external social pressure and transphobic abuse that the patient might experience after transitioning.[152]

There is also a common assumption, especially when it comes to treatments for AMAB trans people, that trans healthcare is entirely cosmetic: that breast augmentation and hair removal are the beginning and end of gender reassignment. While there are some types of gender-affirming treatment that are also used by cisgender people for cosmetic purposes, it's important to keep in mind that these procedures are just as necessary, and as gender-affirming, as any kind of genital surgery, because they allow trans people to present faithfully to their genders.

The truth is that gender-affirming medical treatment is necessary, safe and effective when administered correctly. The popular perception of us as medical oddities is an artefact of our marginalisation, and the more news stories and popular accounts that present us as agents, subjects and actors instead of passive objects and victims, the more that truth will become apparent.

Nonbinary healthcare

Just as there are myriad ways for nonbinary people to present themselves and conceive of their genders, there are a wide range of treatment options that should be tailored to an individual patient's needs, provided both they and their doctor are well-informed. In this section I'll discuss the gender-affirming medical treatments most likely to be requested by genderqueer and nonbinary patients. My descriptions here are not exhaustive, but there are a number of resources available both in print and online which contain more detailed information. The most up to date and thorough of these is Ben Vincent's excellent book, *Transgender Health: A Practitioner's Guide to Binary and Non-Binary Trans Patient Care*,[153] which I highly recommend any medical practitioner treating trans patients read and absorb.

Hormone and puberty blockers

The issues surrounding the diagnosis and treatment of transgender youth is enough to fill an entire book in itself, but the main debate revolves around whether these treatments are safe, and whether it is ethical to allow patients younger than the age of majority to undergo them. But the whole point of puberty blockers is that they are a safe, reversible way to delay puberty in children for any number of reasons: in fact, these treatments have been used to treat cisgender children with precocious puberty[154] and endometriosis[155] for years.

There can be an immense feeling of pressure for a younger trans person to transition 'before it's too late', and an associated fear that any future gender-affirming treatment will be less effective because their bodies will have already been affected by naturally-occurring hormones. These treatments, then, can be used to suppress or delay the bodily changes associated with puberty, including body hair growth, change in voice quality and the development of breasts. This allows children who have expressed signs of gender dysphoria extra time in which to explore their own identities without the pressure of impending sex-characteristic development. For children who go on to identify as nonbinary or genderqueer, hormones can allow them to better control their own gender expression, which may be ambiguous or variable.

The main reason many doctors are hesitant to prescribe GnRH and other hormone blockers (aside from simple transphobia) is fear about their potential long-term effects, such as decreased bone density. As these treatments have only been used for the last few decades in any capacity, their long-term effects are still being understood. But there is evidence[156, 157] that they are generally safe, as long as they are not administered for too long a period, and as long as bone health and other development indicators, like height, are closely monitored. In the normal course of things this treatment is administered along with therapy and the child's mental health is monitored as well. Generally blockers are only administered until the child either stops experiencing dysphoria or decides to transition, at which point hormones consistent with the child's gender identity are administered, often with better effects than if puberty had been allowed to progress before administering hormones.

Puberty blockers represent a stopgap for young people who are unsure of their gender identities. The sooner we erase the stigma associated with what the popular media like to call 'child sex drugs' (don't even get me started), the sooner we can give young people the freedom to experiment, and help them get comfortable in their own bodies. The absolute best thing that parents and pediatricians can do for children who express a desire to live as a gender other than what they were assigned at birth is to take them seriously, and let them know they have options.

Hormone therapy

The majority of adult genderqueer and nonbinary people who undergo gender-affirming medical treatment will use HRT or hormone replacement therapy. This is, generally, oestrogen for AMAB patients and testosterone for AFAB patients. Everybody's body reacts differently to hormone therapy, but generally the way these treatments manifest is in changes to secondary sex characteristics. In people assigned female at birth, who undergo testosterone treatment, this means that the patient's voice will drop in pitch (often with a puberty-like stage in which the voice 'cracks'), muscle mass and body hair will increase, the structure of the face will become more angular or masculine and menstruation will cease. In some patients, especially those with a family history of male-pattern baldness, head hair will also thin. Patients who take oestrogen will experience breast growth, smoother and less oily skin, thinner body hair and a softer or 'more feminine' face shape.

In both AMAB and AFAB patients, the distribution of body fat changes (oestrogen causing it to accumulate in the breasts and hips, testosterone around the belly), and there will be changes to mood, libido and sexuality, which will stabilise as treatment continues, and a decrease in fertility, which patients may wish to discuss with their doctors before beginning treatment.

I personally have been undergoing testosterone therapy for the last four years, and have known I was nonbinary (instead of male) for about that long as well. For me, hormone therapy seemed like the most straightforward and least invasive way to achieve an 'ambiguous' or 'mixed' gender presentation, and though at no stage in the process did I know precisely what I was shooting for, so to speak, I'm happy with the way treatment has affected my body.

There was an intermediate period, soon after beginning HRT, during which I went through what the trans community calls a 'second puberty': I experienced mood swings and occasional instances of intense anger – both of which ceased after only a couple months. My face did indeed become more angular and my muscle mass seems to have increased (though I'm also a lot more active now than when I started HRT). The most dramatic effects of HRT that I've experienced were a dramatic (and sometimes frustrating) increase in my level of body hair, and a dramatic (and pleasing) deepening of my voice. Because of this treatment, and my variable presentation in terms of clothing and haircut, though I still can't avoid being gendered constantly, it's now a 50-50 chance as to *what* gender people will think I am.

So hormone replacement therapy can offer a level of control and freedom to genderqueer and nonbinary patients who wish to present more ambiguously or more variably. The biggest problem with these treatments is that, because they're most often prescribed for binary trans patients, there's a potential that too high a dose may be prescribed. I personally take half the recommended dose for a trans man, and am very pleased with the results, but the only reason I'm able to do this is because I administer my own treatment, and therefore control the dose. However, as discussed earlier in the chapter, when I was still seeing my endocrinologist in California, he expressed concern that my levels of testosterone weren't high enough (though they were ideal, for me).

The other side of this coin is the fact that many people who undergo hormone therapy do so with little physician supervision, either because they don't regularly attend a GIC or because their hormones were obtained on the black market. I pick up my prescription every two months and the rest of the time I'm on my own. It was my responsibility to discuss potential side effects with my GP, and I had to do my own research in that regard. Therefore, it's very important that both patients and physicians, especially non-clinicians like GPs who may see genderqueer patients for regular checkups, be aware of the potential side effects and long-term effects and take steps to prevent them, as with any kind of long-term medical treatment.

Surgery

Gender-reassignment surgery (sometimes called GRS) is surgery to alter the appearance of a patient's chest or genitals. This may include breast augmentation and vaginoplasty, or the construction of a vagina from phallic tissue for AMAB patients with penises, or mastectomy and phalloplasty (the construction of a penis) for AFAB patients.

There are any number of reasons for a nonbinary patient to want to undergo surgery, or conversely to *not* want to undergo hormone therapy. For example, accomplished opera singer and genderqueer activist CN Lester has said that they had a mastectomy because they were uncomfortable with the drastic and uncontrolled changes to the quality of their voice associated with HRT. For CN, hormone therapy would have destroyed their career, or at least made it necessary for them to completely retrain. Chest surgery, then, allowed them to achieve a presentation in congruence with their identity, without having to give up singing, which, as they say in their excellent book *Trans Like Me*, is as much a part of their identity and personality as is being genderqueer.

There are also some people whose bodies don't react to hormones as expected, because of some underlying medical irregularity. I've met at least one genderqueer-identified person for whom HRT had very little effect: neither their voice nor their level of body and facial hair were particularly affected, so chest surgery was their *only* option in terms of a medical transition.

Physicians may not take nonbinary patients seriously when they say they want to get surgery, or they may assume that an ambiguous or variable gender presentation means that they've not thought seriously about the ramifications of surgery, or that they're somehow 'not trans enough' for as 'drastic' a step as surgery. Nine times out of ten, though, a patient will have done extensive research on all surgical and hormone options before even approaching a doctor, and will know what's right for them when they step into the clinic. If a nonbinary person asks their doctor to let them go under the knife, chances are they're aware of the risks and ramifications.

On the other hand, surgery is often considered an implicit final stage in a patient's medical transition. Many trans people however, both binary and nonbinary, have no desire to undergo surgery, and may be pressured to undergo treatments that aren't right for them because of this assumption on the part of their clinician. In both cases the difficulty stems from the fact that nonbinary patients' own expertise and level of awareness is not acknowledged as valid.

Other 'aesthetic' and complementary treatments

There are a few other treatment options, such as the removal of facial and body hair, and speech and language therapy, available as part of the trans healthcare pathway which are sometimes considered peripheral to the process, but which can just as necessary as hormones and surgery for the alleviation of dysphoria. In addition, these therapies may also represent interim options for patients who have been denied, or are on long waiting lists for, hormones and surgery.

I haven't seen any data on nonbinary patients' use of SALT and hair removal, but there's no reason to think that these treatments are irrelevant to us, and some reason to think that we might not always be made aware of these treatments. In fact these treatments may be integral in enabling nonbinary patients to achieve a more ambiguous gender presentation, or one that can be better controlled by the patient themself on a day-to-day basis, by removing attributes that other people may use to gender them. SALT may be especially useful for giving genderfluid people the tools to better control their voice and mannerisms to more closely accord with a fluctuating identity, and clinicians may want to make genderfluid patients aware of the existence of these services.

Conclusions, recommendations and resources

Looking at the process as a whole, it is clear that there is a broad lack of standardised best practice within the trans healthcare system when it comes to genderqueer medical transition, which could even be characterised as a wholesale denial of the existence of identities outside of the gender binary. The entire system is designed, insofar as it has been designed at all, to accommodate only trans people whose identities, or more specifically whose presentations, conform to the socially accepted archetype of man and woman. As they are in society at large, genderqueer people are forced to navigate a system that at every turn tries to guide them towards one binary option or the other.

Aside from this fundamental binarism, there are also a number of interconnected problems with the trans healthcare system in this country, which must be addressed before it can adequately meet the needs of its nonbinary, genderqueer and genderfluid patients. The most notable of these are a lack of resources, a lack of mainstream and clinician understanding of nonbinary identities and a lack of patient-centred care that acknowledges patients' own expertise.

All of these issues contribute to the invisibility of nonbinary identities both within and outside of institutions.

Nonbinary invisibility leads to a perception of our identities as less legitimate or worthy of attention than binary ones, which in turn means that medical and other institutional gatekeepers are less likely to acknowledge, accept and support the nonbinary and genderqueer people they encounter. The disparity between the resources available and the number of people who require them is also connected to a lack – as discussed in Chapter 1 – of statistics on the nonbinary population, which makes it difficult for clinics and third sector organisations to justify asking for funds. At the same time, the lack of trust between trans people and institutions means that this data is very difficult to gather.

The disparity between the reality of our lived experience and the perception of it by clinicians and other medical personnel is one of the main barriers to genderqueer and nonbinary access to transition-related resources. Aside from our relative rarity, even within the greater trans population, many genderqueer people are often reluctant to be forthright with their doctors about their gender identities, which means that clinicians tend to have a skewed idea of our prevalence – in fact many clinicians seem to think that nonbinary patients simply don't make use of GICs.

The reticence on the part of nonbinary patients stems from (and feeds into) a historical mistrust of medical institutions. Because of the lack of resources geared specifically towards nonbinary people, we are often forced to go it alone when it comes to transition. This means that it's harder for clinicians to gain access to the information that would make their treatment – the questions they ask, the resources and services they grant their patients access to – more responsive to patients' actual identities. At the same time, this inability or unwillingness to take the patients' identities at face value further contributes to the patients' mistrust of institutions, creating a cycle of invisibility and invalidation.

Increasing the number of resources and educational materials created by and about genderqueer, genderfluid and nonbinary people is essential if we want to better equip cisgender medical practitioners and other gatekeepers to meet the needs of a growing population. But more than this, it's incredibly important that clinicians who want to treat trans patients get to know trans people. My interviewee TP put it eloquently when they said:

> Stop being cissexist and actually spend time with nonbinary and trans people in a trans/queer space. Just because you've read the various definitions of gender that are available now, doesn't mean you know anything. Go seek out inclusive/sensitivity training.

Interviewee SG describes how alienating navigating the medical system can be: 'I believe I am taken less seriously and all round staff tend to be less accommodating and pleasant and informative: I feel "othered" and like I'm often viewed as an irritant to be coped with politely.'

Practically speaking, there is a huge disparity within trans healthcare at the moment between the services and resources available and the number of people who need them. In the last few years the number of people getting referred to GICs has massively increased. Objectively this is a good thing: gender-affirming medical treatment can be of lifesaving import to people who need it and more and more people now feel comfortable coming forward. Unfortunately, however, services and qualified personnel available at clinics have not been increased at the same rate.

While we may not immediately be able to fix social prejudice, ignorance or alleviate a lack of funding, there are a few alternative clinic models which do show promise. For example, the single-session nurse-led model used at the Royal Children's Hospital Gender Service for gender-variant youth in Australia[158] has been proven to significantly reduce waiting times between appointments. A similar nurse-led system is being trialled at the Chalmers clinic in Edinburgh, which means there is a designated nurse who is able to refer people on to the different services they need, and offer contact between appointments. For now, the nurse won't have full license to sign off on certain procedures, though they can prescribe hormones and a few other courses of treatment. But any system that more efficiently delegates tasks and allocates resources from first contact onward is one which will improve the function of the system as a whole.

On a more fundamental level, the structure of the trans health-care system as outlined by the WPATH Standards of Care is based on a checklist of symptoms and a standardised, linear protocol which for the most part does not vary from patient to patient. This means that the system as defined on paper is brittle where it should be flexible, and unresponsive to the needs of individual patients, who increasingly do not wish to transition in conventional ways. It's been strongly suggested by various organisations, for example the Scottish Public Health Network, that the best way to make the trans health-care system more adaptable to changes in the makeup of the trans patient population, is using a *patient-centred informed consent model*.

Informed consent is not a new idea: it has been practised in various Western medical contexts for about the last hundred years, and it is uniquely suited to the trans population who by necessity often become experts in their own healthcare needs. Informed consent is a model of practice predicated on a patient's right to be informed about the treatment they are receiving.[159] Rather than more specific protocols and increasingly granular guidelines to try and account for the proliferation of diverse trans-umbrella identities, it's been posited that the best solution is to acknowledge the expertise that trans patients themselves often already have, to present each element of gender-affirming medical treatment as optional rather than obligatory and to allow fully informed patients to then choose the option that is right for them, with clinician support and guidance rather than complete clinician control. While some clinics, for example Chalmers in Edinburgh, do ostensibly allocate treatments flexibly according to individual patient needs,[160] clinicians themselves generally still have responsibility as gatekeepers, so use of the WPATH Standards of Care to specify a recommended treatment pathway is generally considered obligatory.

Under a model of informed consent, armed with full knowledge of the practicalities and risks associated with each type of treatment, nonbinary (and indeed all transgender) patients would be best equipped to determine their own treatment path. This would have positive effects on patient wellbeing, as patients could be assured that they would receive treatment tailored to their identity, and not be forced to undergo a certain course of treatment just because it was considered obligatory. This in turn would go a long way towards building trust between clinicians and patients as patients would be encouraged under this model to be open about the nuances of their identities. This in turn would allow clinicians and patients to operate on the same footing, and would make the system more efficient, safer and more effective for all trans patients.

A few clinics worldwide do operate on an informed consent model, for example the Scottish Public Health Network cites the Fenway health clinic in Boston,[61] which provides care that is 'accessible, multidisciplinary, gender affirming, and holistic, with gender affirmation seen as a part of normal primary care and not as a mental health problem'. This clinic and clinics like it have been demonstrated to improve patient outcomes and have apparently reported notable increases in patient numbers recently.

Practical suggestions for individual clinicians

On a more day-to-day operational level, improving conditions for nonbinary patients within medical institutions begins with individual clinicians and medical practitioners. Better practice with regards to respecting patients' diverse gender identities, and more support from the individuals controlling the services, would tangibly improve both the wellbeing of nonbinary patients and our trust in medical institutions.

Doctors are people we are taught from birth to trust. We're told they have our best interests at heart, and expect that if we tell them something is wrong they'll fix it or refer us to someone who can. But very often practitioners within the trans healthcare system don't actually have much experience or knowledge of transgender lived experience; interviewee LE suggests this has something to do with the training clinicians receive in medical school:

> My partner is a med student, and in the thousands of questions they have to answer about extremely rare conditions affecting less than 0.1 per cent of the population, every single one states that it's either a man or a woman seeking help. I think that if they included trans and nonbinary patients at all in the practice questions and lectures (especially if the answer to the questions was unrelated to their gender identity), the exposure would greatly help them to see us just as people like everyone else. It would also reduce the incidence of 'trans broken arm syndrome', where doctors attribute every ailment we have to our transition, even completely unrelated things like the flu or a broken limb.

Being at the doctor's office usually means a person is vulnerable, and trans people, whether we like to admit it or not, walk around in a constant state of vulnerability, which being at the doctor's only exacerbates. Clinicians themselves actually have considerable leeway when it comes to making referrals, writing prescriptions and making patients feel comfortable being honest about their identities (or even just showing up for their appointments). The power in these scenarios lies with the individual practitioners who act as gatekeepers for the services they provide, many of whom are not malicious but simply ignorant, or at worst unwilling to educate themselves. In practice, this often means nonbinary patients have limited access to the services they need to fully realise their identities, but it doesn't have to.

First of all, educate yourself. If you've read this far in this book, you're already doing better than a great many gender identity clinicians. But this book isn't a clinical guide, and my evidence is mostly anecdotal. The best way to gain an understanding of the diverse needs and experiences of nonbinary and genderqueer people is to talk to your patients and let them explain themselves without judgement. If you have intake forms or questionnaires asking about patient identities and what they want to accomplish at the clinic, allow space on these forms to discuss the complexities of their identity. Take suggestions from trans patients on what you could be doing better. Keep in mind the anxiety a nonbinary patient will likely have that treatment will be withheld if they present as less than 100 per cent male or female. If you ask questions about your patient's genitals or body, think how you would feel if you were asked about these things. Many of us feel acute dysphoria and being in medical institutions very often exacerbates these feelings by being overly concerned with bodies, rather than minds, personalities and personal goals.

When discussing treatment options, be flexible. As with any kind of medical treatment/practice, each patient has different needs, and remember that some treatments like hormones and puberty blockers are partially or completely reversible, and discuss this aspect with the patient as well. The treatment path will be less straightforward for a genderqueer patient, since their goal may not necessarily be to make their sex characteristics 'match' any particular archetype, and some experimentation may be necessary. Unlike most kinds of medical practice, trans patients are often forced to become expert patients. Keep in mind that if a patient asks for a treatment or service, they've most likely done lots of research on their own first. Be upfront with your patient about the results of these treatments, but don't try to scare them out of pursuing it. Be upfront, as well, about the inadequacies in our current system including red tape and wait times; interviewee HW suggests, 'Give people reasonable timeframes or more information on what to do while waiting.'

It takes a great deal of courage to approach a doctor about transitioning – especially if you assume the doctor won't be receptive. Be receptive. Remind yourself that your primary concern should be the wellbeing of your patient. Be practical about what that means: your idea of what's 'best' for a patient, based on your perception of their gender identity, may not quite match up to theirs, but this can be fixed by working with the patient.

My interviewees generally had very clear ideas about what clinicians, physicians and institutions could be doing better. They had this to say:

LE: I wish that they would have understood that if I went to the trouble of contacting their office ahead of time to let them know about my chosen name and pronouns, that it was because it was very important to me and not just something for them to ignore because they weren't familiar with trans people. I would ask them to trust people's truth, and not to use gendered words to discuss someone's body even if they are medical terminology. Instead they could ask their patient what words they prefer to use when discussing their own body.

SG: Understanding that the system as it stands is inadequate and routinely damages its patients health with its inadequacies, therefore treating the patients' plights with sympathy and proactive care, and seeking to counter potential for and advocate for patients at risk of harm to the best of your abilities and power.

SG (on what they've done that was helpful): Listened attentively, recognised areas where they can help without the patient having to do so and self advocate for treatment, done extra research when needed, been sympathetic and rehumanising in their approach.

XX1: My health professionals who were my exceptions admitted they do not know everything. They are not me, so they cannot know my truth. Even if they don't understand or relate to what I am going through, it is their job to help me get through it. It's not about being right or wrong or normal or crazy. It's not just about survival. It's not just about living. It's about doing more than breathing and crying.

It's about living with love for myself no matter what form or life-styles it manifests in (unless I suddenly decide to [start] maliciously harming people).

HW (on what clinicians have done that was supportive): Reassured me in feeling normal and being supportive.

CM: I think it's still very much built around a pathway for transsexual people rather than non-binary or non-conforming: I know when I initially self-referred to the GIC it was in the hope of finding an experienced counsellor, not embarking on a road to surgical transition, and I wasn't sure if the gender clinics could handle that. I'm still not sure.

I think gender stuff falls between two stools: many people with gender issues aren't necessarily headed for transition, so the gender clinics aren't really quick enough or resourced enough for those people – waiting a year or even two years for an initial psych assessment is incredibly long for people having problems with their identity; they aren't mentally ill, so community mental health services aren't appropriate either.

Resources

The Center for Excellence for Transgender Health at the University of California, San Francisco have created a useful resource for physicians with trans patients: the Guidelines for the Primary and Gender-Affirming Care of Transgender and Gender Nonbinary People. The guidelines are intended to complement rather than contradict the WPATH Standards of Care, and advocate a person-centred, informed consent approach to both gender-affirming and primary healthcare for trans people. http://transhealth.ucsf.edu/protocols

Ben Vincent, PhD, has written a wonderful book, *Transgender Health* (2018, Jessica Kingsley Publishers), which covers every aspect of trans healthcare, from using the correct terminology to helping trans patients make informed decisions about their own gender-affirming medical care pathway.

The Scottish Public Health Network Needs Assessment of Gender Identity Services document includes a detailed series of recommendations for physicians. The document can be accessed here: www.scotphn.net/wp-content/uploads/2017/04/2018_05_16-HCNA-of-Gender-Identity-Services-1.pdf

English trans and nonbinary patients can find information about locating their closes GIC here: www.nhs.uk/live-well/healthy-body/how-to-find-an-nhs-gender-identity-clinic

In Scotland, an organisation called the National Gender Identity Clinic Managed Network have done a great deal of work directly with GPs: www.ngicns.scot.nhs.uk/services/gender-identity-clinics

The Scottish Trans Alliance also provide a lot of information on gender-affirming medical services and where they can be attained: www.scottishtrans.org/trans-rights/practice/gender-reassignment/gender-specialists

At the time of writing, a Welsh Gender Team offering gender-affirming medical services in Cardiff, the first of its kind in Wales, is supposed to begin work in April of 2019. Information on the clinic and its staff can be found here: www.genderdysphoria.wales.nhs.uk/gipg-updates

Aside from the WPATH Standards of Care, they have a number of resources that contain information about gender-affirming medical treatment options, many of them from a trans perspective.

The NHS website gives a fairly straightforward overview of the kinds of treatments available, what they entail and what their results are likely to be. Please note that the phrasing of this particular webpage is outdated (transsexual) and exclusionary of nonbinary individuals. www.nhs.uk/conditions/gender-dysphoria/treatment

Darlene Tando, an American social worker and therapist, maintains a blog about gender and trans life. Her post about gender-affirming medical treatment options is very informative: https://darlenetan dogenderblog.com/2012/05/04/physical-transition-options-for-the-transgender-individual

More information on individual types of treatment can be found here:

Oestrogen therapy: https://transcare.ucsf.edu/article/informa tion-estrogen-hormone-therapy

Phalloplasty: www.savaperovic.com/ftm-srs-metoidioplasty-total-phalloplasty.htm

Chest surgery: www.ftmguide.org/chest.html

An overview of MtF surgical options can be found at: www.uptodate. com/contents/transgender-surgery-male-to-female

And in:

Heijer, M., Bakker, A. and Gooren, L. (2017). Long term hormonal treatment for transgender people. *BMJ* 2017(359), j5027.

Hembree, W. C. *et al.* (2017). Endocrine treatment of gender-dysphoric/gender-incongruent persons: An endocrine society clinical practice guideline. *The Journal of Clinical Endocrinology & Metabolism*, 102(11), 869–3903.

Exercises and discussion questions

1. Think back to the first time you encountered or heard about trans or nonbinary people, be it a trans or genderqueer friend or family member, a conversation with a friend, a depiction in a movie or a book or a news article. Was medicine an implicit or explicit part of the conversation? How (if at all) were the trans or nonbinary peoples' bodies discussed? Was the person in question's transitional status discussed? Were terms like 'pre-op' or 'the surgery' used?

2. If medicine and discussions of physical bodies was discussed (and you yourself are not trans or genderqueer), how do you think the conversation or experience might have affected someone who was trans or genderqueer? Would they have felt objectified or dehumanised by the portrayal or discussion of someone like them?

3. What are some of the specific ways that medical institutions, explicitly and implicitly, deny the existence of genders outside male and female? This could be anything from refusing to use a preferred name and pronouns to using gendered words to describe someone's genitalia. The next time you find yourself in a medical environment, try to be mindful of these aspects of policy and practice.

4. Lots of people, cis or otherwise, experience anxiety and stress within medical environments (doctors' offices, waiting rooms, contexts where forms need to be filled out, etc.) If applicable, whether you identify as nonbinary or not, what are some aspects of the medical institution that are stressful for you, and why do you think this is?

5. How does this interact with your gender identity, or how might it if your gender identity were different?

6. What specifically do you think could change about these institutions to help solve the problem? How would you go about implementing these changes if you had the chance?

CHAPTER 8

The Law

Introduction

There are two main legal questions that are currently of concern to nonbinary people, namely the legal recognition of nonbinary genders on official documentation, and the protection of nonbinary and genderqueer people from discrimination based on our gender identities. These two goals are closely interconnected, and should go hand-in-hand: the ability to specify a gender other than male or female on official documents such as IDs would allow a genderqueer person to accurately represent themself, but it would also make their genderqueer status public, opening them up to potential discrimination.

Accomplishing the twin goals of recognition and protection is not quite as simple as adding a clause here and changing a wording there; in order to achieve full protection under the law we must first ask the law to change how it conceptualises gender. There should be no question that we deserve to have our genders officially recognised and legally protected, but in trying to discover precisely how to do this we are exploring new territory.

There is very little in the law of most countries to even acknowledges the existence of genders outside of male and female. Many of the laws concerning transgender people are often phrased so as to be exclusionary of a vast proportion of the trans community. They may explicitly only extend protection to people who are undergoing transition-related medical treatment, which would exclude any trans person who doesn't feel they need to transition medically in order to live fully as their affirmed gender, a group that includes a large number of genderqueer and nonbinary people. The laws may only cover people who identify as the 'opposite' gender from that which they were assigned at birth, making anyone identifying outside the binary ineligible. If the law only covers people who live full-time as 'another' gender from how they were assigned at birth, it may not recognise presentations outside of conventional ones, or people whose gender identities are fluid, or people who aren't in a position socially to present in a way that matches their identity.

The two main UK laws that will need to be changed are the Gender Recognition Act (GRA) 2004, which covers the ability of trans people to acquire official documentation matching their identity rather than the gender they were assigned at birth, and the Equality Act 2010, which, in a context of trans identity, protects people from being discriminated against because they are undergoing a gender transition.

These laws – and pretty much any UK law you can name – were written by people who only believed in two genders. Most of these laws were written before the nonbinary population began to self-define as separate from the binary trans community. As such, loopholes and unspecific or exclusionary wording often allow people to fall through the cracks. Even if an organisation or a company doesn't set out to practise discrimination, it is still very often legal and occurs in practice at an individual level if it is not prosecutable, as a result of these loopholes.

Changing the law to acknowledge and protect nonbinary and genderqueer people would be codifying into law an acknowledgement of the limitations of the binary system; a system that is as firmly ingrained in the laws and institutions of our society as the concept of democracy or taxes. This chapter will discuss the GRA and the Equality Act and some possible or proposed changes to them. It will discuss some of the laws that exist in other countries that protect or acknowledge genders outside male and female, and which might act as models for UK lawmakers, and it will discuss some of the difficulties that present themselves in the quest for nuanced, inclusive, effective laws acknowledging nonbinary identities.

Despite the advances in official recognition and legal protection that have come about in the last decade or so, trans people are still often subject to discrimination and violence. Compared to the rest of the population, trans people are at a high risk of hate crime, harassment, sexual and domestic abuse. And despite being a relatively invisible demographic, nonbinary people are by no means immune to this abuse.

A 2017 study[162] that looked at, among other things, experiences of abuse and victimisation in trans and nonbinary youth found that nonbinary participants' experiences were similar to those of trans participants – which is to say, not very good.[163] The study found, for example, that 46 per cent of AFAB and 25 per cent of AMAB nonbinary participants had experienced abuse or violence from someone close to them in their lifetime. Eighty-three per cent of AMAB and 76 per cent of AFAB nonbinary participants had experienced verbal abuse from strangers and 47 per cent of AMAB and 28 per cent of AFAB nonbinary participants had experienced physical assault. The statistics didn't always indicate a clear, significant difference between AMAB and AFAB or between binary and nonbinary participants overall, but the numbers themselves are damning.

Thirty-one per cent of the genderqueer respondents to the 2017 Stonewall Trans Report had been the victim of a hate crime or incident in the year leading up to the survey. Thirty-five per cent of the participants in the STA survey on nonbinary experiences in the UK reported that they'd experienced sexual harassment because of their nonbinary status, 11 per cent had experienced physical assault and 13 per cent had experienced sexual assault because of their gender identity. Thirty-two per cent had experienced threats and physical intimidation. Again, the results indicate that nonbinary people are often targets of physical and sexual violence, even though a great many never pursue a medical transition that would make them 'officially' trans in the eyes of the law.

Perhaps more worryingly still, almost 80 per cent of the hate crime victims from the 2017 Stonewall Trans Report didn't report the incident to the police. The anecdotal evidence accompanying the statistics in the Stonewall report gives the impression that police personnel generally don't take crimes against trans people seriously. According to the STA report on nonbinary experiences in public services, 69 per cent of respondents said that they never felt comfortable being open about their gender identity with police personnel.[164] Stonewall survey participants report high instances of misgendering, mockery and invasive examination or questioning within public services generally.

This pattern is part of a larger problem I see cropping up distressingly often, where authority figures and other representatives of the cisgender majority, people to whom we are trained to look for guidance and support, such as doctors, counsellors and police officers, refuse to respect genderqueer and nonbinary people's identities. We are mocked, demeaned and have our privacy invaded when we are at our most vulnerable: ill, injured or traumatised.

This lack of respect for genderqueer and nonbinary identities can manifest inside the home and in close social circles as well. Even aside from specific experiences of victimisation, because of the persistent idea that genders outside of male and female simply don't exist, it is very easy for people, even family members and close friends, to invalidate and dehumanise genderqueer people.

Generational differences can have a big effect on whether someone acknowledges nonbinary genders, and as such the people who may be most likely to deny a genderqueer person's identity may be close older relatives, even parents.

The causes, and effects, of a lack of family support are intertwined with those of minority stress and discrimination. Many genderqueer people face hostility and invalidation from both outside the home and within, which can cause feelings of isolation, betrayal and help-lessness. Interviewee TP, whose family routinely simply 'forget' about their nonbinary identity, had a particularly nuanced view of their situation:

> I'm a survivor of child psychological and physical abuse, I have narcis-sistic family, and I have a lot of mental characteristics that stem from these as well as from having to live as mixed race, queer, nonbinary, and demisexual in America.

They discuss the way this history of abuse can interact with the way they relate to the world:

> I feel unsafe all the time and I feel left out. This contributes to me feeling alienated from the world around me as much as I already feel with my family. Knowing that my rights and existence are constantly debated, called into question, analyzed, ridiculed, erased, or forgot-ten...it all adds up. When the world around you and your own small world that you've created for yourself (your friends, family, coworkers, city) consistently don't understand you, and in your lifetime, they probably never will...it's easy to feel defeated and trigger depressive episodes...

Disrespect and invalidation from the people we're supposed to be able to rely upon, be they public service personnel or family members, has a direct, negative impact on our mental health. It creates an impetus for us to withdraw into our communities and rely more heavily on the support networks they represent. When we're forced to choose between the trauma of using public services and doing without them, many of us make the dangerous choice to go without.

The 2017 Stonewall Trans Report makes the following recommendations[165] for protecting trans people at home and in their daily lives:

The Home Office should:

- Improve confidence in reporting by treating hate crimes based on gender identity, sexual orientation and disability equally to those based on race and faith under the law, by making them aggravated offences.

The prosecution service and judiciary across the UK and Scotland should:

- Ensure that all prosecutors and judges are trained on transphobic hate crimes on and offline, ensure trans people's identities and privacy are respected, and provide targeted support to victims.

Police forces should:

- Improve training to all police officers and frontline staff to ensure they can identify and record transphobic hate crimes, better support victims and bring perpetrators to justice.

In the section on domestic violence, the report states:

The UK Government should:

- Consult with trans and non-binary people and organisations to ensure the Domestic Violence and Abuse programme of work and Act is inclusive of trans people's needs.

- Ensure that enough sustainable funding is available for domestic violence and homelessness support services to meet demand, including trans people affected.

The Scottish Government should:

- Ensure their domestic violence strategy is inclusive of trans and non-binary people and their needs.

Domestic violence and homelessness support services should:

- Develop and advertise services that are inclusive of trans and non-binary people drawing on best practice from other trans-inclusive services.
- Provide training for all staff on meeting the specific needs of trans service users.

Overall what is needed most in public services and policies is a combination of education, respect and inclusivity. Policies need to more explicitly protect trans people, and personnel across services must be better educated. By taking us at our word and including us in the development of policies and training materials we can start to increase genderqueer visibility and more adequately protect the people who currently fall through the gaps in existing legislation. By increasing visibility and demanding official respect, we can go a long way to tackling the culture which leads to the invalidation and abuse of genderqueer and nonbinary people.

Legal recognition and the GRA 2004

One of the first steps towards eliminating discrimination and violence towards people because of their gender identities is to increase visibility. Legal recognition of our genders is a necessary step towards this visibility. The 2015 STA survey on nonbinary and genderqueer people's experiences in the UK included a discussion of our views on legal recognition. Seventy-eight per cent of participants in the survey would change all or some of their legal documents to reflect a gender other than male or female.[166] Anecdotal evidence from this section of the survey draws a direct link between listing a nonbinary gender on official documents and nonbinary visibility.

One of the stated purposes of the STA nonbinary experiences report is specifically to provide evidence that nonbinary individuals face 'specific detriment' because of a lack of legal recognition of their genders. The report provides statistics and anecdotal evidence to demonstrate the challenges, including violence, that genderqueer people face in institutions such as social services and employment, which don't recognise their genders.

The Gender Recognition Act 2004 was the first piece of UK legislation to allow binary trans people to be legally recognised as their affirmed gender, and to represent their gender identities on official documents such as a birth certificate. It is 'An Act to make provision for and in connection with change of gender.'[167] Because of the way various parts of the GRA are written, and because of the criteria by which the Gender Recognition Certificate (GRC), which legally 'proves' a trans person has the right to these gender-affirming documents, is granted, the GRA somewhat ironically represents an obstacle to full *nonbinary* equality within the UK.

The first and foremost issue that emerges when looking at the GRA 2004 from a genderqueer perspective is the fact that the GRA, as it is, does not even allow for the possibility of a gender option outside male and female. Before even entering the system, nonbinary people are excluded.

The difficulty here comes from the fact that the GRA is designed as a mechanism by which a trans person can acquire documentation that resembles in every way a document which would be used by a cisgender member of their affirmed gender. But the only gender options available are those that already exist in the UK, that is to say, binary male and female. Part of the problem here is because of the diverging purposes or goals for which binary and nonbinary trans people need the documents. For a binary trans person, in our society that is so concerned that trans people pass as a cisgender example of the gender they identify with, there is immense pressure for binary trans people to *hide* their transgender status in any way possible. Certainly not every binary trans person wants or is able to pass as cisgender, and the reasons for a binary trans person to want a GRC and altered documents are as numerous as there are binary trans people, but what a GRC does in essence is to hide a person's 'transgender history'.

For a genderqueer person to officially declare their identity on a passport or new birth certificate, then, is for them to publicly declare their trans status. Further, if we were to change the GRA to make it of use to genderqueer people, it wouldn't be enough to just allow the applicant to change to the other option; we would have to *create a new way of representing gender*.

The question then becomes, if nonbinary and genderqueer people are to represent themselves accurately on official documentation, what is the best way to do this? Should there be a different marker for each gender identity? Should there be a single 'X' marker for anything not male or female? Should there simply be passports and birth certificates that don't list gender at all?

It's fairly obvious that, for a community that is still settling on standard terminology, it's not practical to allow a different marker for every single gender identity. There's no standard abbreviation for 'nonbinary', 'genderfluid' or 'genderqueer', and the only reason that 'M' and 'F' are so easy to interpret is because for the majority of the population this binary is understood to be the default.

On the other hand, allowing gender to simply not be listed on official documents seems a little beside the point to me. The 'prefer not to say' option, available on some demographic forms, is something I only personally use if the only other options are 'male' and 'female'. While removing gender entirely from an ID or passport might work for, say, an agender person who rejects the idea of gender completely, someone who *does* identify with a gender, even if it's not male or female, may not be comfortable with this option.

To remove gender entirely seems to me to be like saying that people who don't identify as male or female simply don't deserve to have gender at all. Further, for much the same reason that some people prefer 'genderqueer' to 'nonbinary', the 'gender of F/M vs no gender at all' scenario in some ways simply creates a new binary, between those who have gender (the mainstream, the default, binary-identified people), and those who do not (the *other*, nonbinary-identified people).

I think the best option, and the option most likely to be adopted by lawmakers, is to allow an 'X' or other marker to indicate a status of 'neither male nor female'. Even though the genderqueer and nonbinary community is by no means monolithic, I believe that under the system we have this is the best option. It would allow a genderqueer person to declare that they have a gender, and that it is not binary, and I believe that including *neither*, an X, as a third and equal option alongside female and male would go a long way towards eroding its 'other' status.

So despite it being a landmark piece of legislation, and the best we could do in 2004, the GRA is now widely understood to be outdated and generally unfit for purpose, and not only because it makes no allowance for genders outside male and female. Many of the requirements that the Gender Recognition Panel (or GRP, the body that grants a gender recognition certificate) makes of applicants are unreasonable, and the way it is administered involves lots of bureaucratic red tape, to the detriment of all applicants, binary or not.

Applying for a GRC is a laborious process: in order to qualify for a certificate applicants are required to provide doctors' or psychiatrists' notes and other medical documentation of their trans status, evidence of dysphoria and of a commitment to 'living full-time as your acquired gender'. Much of this documentation, for many trans people, is very difficult to obtain. First and foremost, the wait times and expenses associated with gender-affirming medical treatment such as hormones and surgery – necessary if one is to prove that they are sufficiently 'committed' to transition – mean that a great many people, especially those who are poorer, younger or who live in remote areas or for whatever reason don't have access to a GIC, are simply excluded from the start.

Requiring applicants to provide 'proof' of their gender identities generally means they must occupy an extremely limited space of gender presentation. Trans people with more 'middle of the road' or inconsistent presentations are often advised to present in a more categorical, binary way at their GIC appointments to prove that they're 'really trans'. To 'fake it' for the sake of acquiring legal documentation requires a person to misrepresent themself and may contribute to a lack of trust and assumptions of bad faith between clinicians and nonbinary people. Considering how difficult it is for us to live congruously with our identities, many trans people are simply not willing to put themselves in this position.

There's also the matter of the £140 fee associated with the application. Trans people are statistically one of the poorest demographics, and for many of us this cost is prohibitive. There are workarounds: in England, low-income applicants can fill in yet more paperwork and endure further delays to try for a fee waiver. At the time of writing I personally made, working full-time for minimum wage, £1 more than the maximum monthly income to be eligible for fee assistance (though I live in Scotland, where the fee waiver eligibility requirements are different and even more complicated).

Aside from the confusion of navigating the legal and bureaucratic system, trying to convey something as sensitive and personal as gender identity to a faceless panel of judges can be both invasive and humiliating. The level of detail often required by the GRP with regards to, for example, sexual conduct or plans for genital surgery, generally requires the applicant to be categorical and unequivocal about an aspect of themself that is often fluid and difficult to define. This dehumanisation, I think, is the primary reason why many transgender people don't bother with the process: why should I grovel for the approval of a system that barely sees me as human, especially if my application may not even be successful?

More specifically to nonbinary people, there are many ways in which the GRA and its mechanisms are actively exclusionary of genders outside male and female, and fixing this is more complex than a simple change of wording. The very first line of the Act,[168] for example, defines a potential applicant for gender recognition as living as 'the other gender'. Already we can see the underlying model which is explicitly binary: *the other* implies of the crossing from one discrete option to the other, with no room for gradation or nuance.

The GRA allows for the legal recognition of a person's (provided they are aged 18 or older) affirmed gender under two circumstances: if they can prove to the GRP's satisfaction that they've been living as that affirmed gender for a period of two years, or they can prove they are legally recognised as their affirmed gender in a country outside the UK.

For people who have no foreign proof of their gender identity, in order for the GRC to be issued, the panel must be satisfied that several stringent criteria have been met:

- the applicant has or has had gender dysphoria
- the applicant has lived as their affirmed gender for a full two years before making their application
- the applicant intends to continue living as this gender until death
- the applicant has compiled and presented to the gender recognition panel a collection of official documentation including medical diagnoses of gender dysphoria and treatment plans.

I'm sure you can already see how each of these points might be inherently exclusionary of nonbinary people. For one thing, as discussed in the chapters on medicine and mental health, not every genderqueer person experiences gender dysphoria. Not even all *binary* trans people experience dysphoria, and these people too are at risk of being excluded from having their genders legally recognised. Applicants who choose not to medically transition for any number of reasons, as is the case for many genderqueer people, are also ineligible, as they won't be able to provide treatment plans for surgery and hormones.

The two-year 'life experience' requirement is by definition exclusionary of people whose genders fluctuate over time, of people whose clinicians aren't convinced by their ambiguous or inconsistent presentation and of people whose circumstances prohibit them from being 'out' in all contexts. Most of the qualifying documents required for this criteria to be met don't allow an identification outside male and female. According to Stonewall's report from 2017, half of all nonbinary respondents have hidden or disguised their nonbinary status at work for fear of discrimination. Half of nonbinary people change the way they dress in public for the same reason. A quarter of genderqueer people are not open about their gender identity with their families. For many people, the 'living as your gender' requirement is simply not an option.

The fact that the panel requires applicants to declare an intention to live as their affirmed gender *until death*, too, is problematic in that it automatically excludes people whose gender identities shift or change over their lifetime. Gender is a tricky, intensely personal thing and it's not at all inconceivable that a person's gender identity could change based on their environment, relationship status or any number of other internal factors. Genderfluid people are an important but understudied group within the larger trans community, and this mentality of gender as monolithic and static contributes directly to their erasure and invalidation.

In July 2018, the UK government released a document,[169] on the advice of the Minister for Women and Equalities, with concerns and recommendations for the reform of the GRA in England and Wales.[170] There is a specific section in this document relating to nonbinary gender identities, which points out that there are a number of areas, for example the state pension age or single-gender hospital wards, in which a person's gender (either male or female) allows them different legal entitlements or places them in different environments. The binary format of gender in many nationwide IT systems will be affected if nonbinary people are granted full legal recognition.

As part of the UK government's LGBT Action Plan, it was announced in July 2018 that they would put out a 'call for evidence', requesting feedback from nonbinary and genderqueer people, in order to better understand their needs and experiences. The 2018 consultation document acknowledges that nonbinary people seem statistically less likely to make use of treatments and services for gender dysphoria, such as those available at the GIC, and that acquiring documentation for the 'lived experience' requirement would be difficult for us.

The document also acknowledges that many areas of the law make specific provisions for people depending on their sex assigned at birth, especially relating to marriage and civil partnerships, and pregnancy and maternity. A number of participants in the 2015 STA nonbinary survey reported trepidation with regards to nonbinary gender on official documentation if it meant that, in relevant medical contexts, sex assigned at birth was hidden from physicians. The fact that our laws do not acknowledge a difference between sex and gender means that many of the people for whom these two attributes are different are sometimes put in danger. I believe that introducing this distinction into law might represent a way forward for trans and genderqueer equality, but that it will require a lot of effort, experimentation and feedback from the community in order to come up with a workable solution to the question of alternative gender recognition.

The 2017 Stonewall Trans Report makes several recommendations for the UK and Scottish governments for reforming the GRA, including the following:

- reform the GRA 2004 so that obtaining legal gender recognition does *not require medical evidence* and is replaced with a *simple administrative process* based on *self-declaration*

- ensure that the reformed Gender Recognition Act makes specific provision for *recognising non-binary identities.*

Self-declaration here is an important idea for the nonbinary community: if a nonbinary gender is acknowledged by a new version of the GRA, self-declaration would be infinitely preferable to attempting to adapt myriad legal and medical requirements to include nonbinary genders. In the same way that the trans healthcare system could be made more inclusive by allowing patients, who are experts in their own lived experience, to pursue treatments based on a model of informed consent, self-declaration may be the key to creating gender recognition laws which are responsive to the needs of the entire trans community, including nonbinary and genderqueer people.

Removing the medical diagnosis requirement, too, would allow for people with a more diverse range of identities to qualify for a GRC. Unlinking the processes of medical and legal transition from each other would combat medicalisation by legitimising non-normative gender identities regardless of medical transition status, and drastically lower the level of stress associated with the process.

Legal protections and the Equality Act 2010

A number of respondents to the 2015 STA nonbinary experiences report expressed concern that, if nonbinary people were *required* to declare their nonbinary status on official documents, they would be more open to discrimination, especially within institutions. In light of this, any move towards increased visibility for and legal recognition of nonbinary people ought to be accompanied by a corresponding increase in legal protection. At present, the only law which explicitly protects trans people from discrimination and harassment in the UK is the Equality Act 2010:[171]

(1) A person has the protected characteristic of *gender reassignment* if the person is proposing to undergo, is undergoing or has undergone

a process (or part of a process) for the purpose of reassigning the person's sex by changing physiological or other attributes of sex.

The Act is long and very complex and defines discrimination in a variety of ways. Generally speaking it only makes reference to trans people (with the outdated term 'transsexuals') within a context of *gender reassignment*. So as we saw with the GRA, the difficulty here is in the wording of the legislation. The Equality Act protects people who are, or more aptly who are *perceived* as, undergoing a medical gender transition. It should be fairly obvious by now why this presents a problem for genderqueer and nonbinary people.

The law itself was written, even less than a decade ago, in a time when transition, specifically medical transition, was in mainstream thought the be-all, end-all of transness, and the main criteria for *identifying* a person as trans. The nonbinary community was in very early stages of development, at least as a cohesive demographic, and as such we remained largely invisible, which of course entailed its own hardships. The trans people who were experiencing the most visible discrimination were those who were attempting to pass, or who couldn't or didn't pass, as cisgender. Because the act was written largely before genderqueer people as a demographic were widely acknowledged to even exist, it would have been very difficult to convince legislators that we deserved protection as a specific group, and that we were being discriminated against based on a criteria that was separate from our gender-reassignment status.

Nowadays, however, popular understanding of gender is both more nuanced and more inclusive. The act of transition is no longer seen as a prerequisite for, or the ultimate goal of, being trans, and it's generally understood that many of us face discrimination in various forms because of our gender, not necessarily because of our *transitional* status. This means that, like the GRA, the section of the Equality Act that lays out protections for trans people is no longer fit for purpose.

According to Nat Titman of Practical Androgyny,[172] '12% of people who qualify for Equality Act 2010 "Gender Reassignment" protected characteristic identify outside of the binary and that more than 65% of nonbinary people do not fall under the Equality Act's protections for gender minorities.'

Under the Equality Act in its current form, people whose gender presentations are unconventional, ambiguous or inconsistent, or people who are trans but are medically or socially unable to transition in the eyes of the law, have no legal protection. In any case, there is no acknowledgment or explicit protection of any genders outside man and woman under the Act. A nonbinary-identified person could only be protected if they experience discrimination or harassment because they are perceived by their attacker as binary trans, or because they are perceived as undergoing or considering undergoing a transition from male to female or vice versa.

International laws on nonbinary gender

A number of countries around the world do legally recognise the existence of genders outside of male and female, though the legal and social realities for genderqueer people in these countries – and indeed the way people in these countries conceptualise gender – may still be very different. Nonetheless these countries offer practical models and examples that might be used by UK lawmakers, and offer evidence that neutral options on official documents, alternative model schooling and explicit protection for trans people regardless of transitional status are workable, realistic possibilities.

In 2012, Argentina, a country with a transgender population estimated at 12,000, passed a gender identity law that, among other rights, granted transgender people the ability to declare their gender on official documents without requiring them to provide proof of a medical or psychiatric diagnosis. Denmark and Malta have also passed laws that allow for self-determination. While Argentina's *Ley de Identidad de Género* and laws like it are a boon to trans people who can't or don't want to transition medically, a group that widely intersects with the genderqueer and nonbinary community, many of the countries where the medical requirement has been waived still only allow people seeking to change their gender on official documents to the option of either 'male' or 'female'.

Denmark's transgender law also grants trans people a document that allows them to change all their official documents to reflect a neutral, 'X' gender. Canada, Nepal, Pakistan, India, Australia, New Zealand and certain US states all also allow an alternative gender marker, usually 'X' but also sometimes 'O', on a passport or other identity document.

None of these laws are perfect, and none of them yet seem to be a perfect model for full nonbinary equality and recognition. Denmark's transgender law, for example, requires applicants to go through a rather patronising six-month 'reflection period' before their documents may be updated. Many of the laws concerning trans people throughout the world are based on criteria that don't apply to all of us.

But what these laws do represent, however, is strong evidence that allowing for full recognition of gender identities outside male and female can be accomplished without the administrative disruption that naysayers love to cite. These laws prove that working on a model of informed consent and self-declaration is not only the best way to streamline the process of making these laws more inclusive, but also to create environments that are not inherently binaristic.

In 2009 the UK's Office for National Statistics produced a 'position paper' on transgender equality,[173] the result of an extensive data review. The goal of this paper was to determine methodological issues limiting or otherwise affecting transgender equality, with a view to derive new methodologies and creative approaches to gathering data on the transgender population and combating the ingrained mistrust of authority within the trans community. The resulting paper is only one of many such works making recommendations and suggestions by which government bodies can be more supportive of the trans population. Papers like these, very often nowadays conducted in partnership with LGBT and transgender organisations, are integral to the movement towards full transgender equality. Unfortunately, the recommendations made by these bodies are just that: recommendations. There is still massive leeway for discrimination to continue and it is very difficult to take suggestions further if lawmakers are not then willing to meet us halfway.

There have been multiple attempts by various third sector organisations and government bodies to reform both the GRA and the Equality Act, some of which have gotten as far as nationwide consultations on what precise form these changes should take. But in many of these instances the lack of visibility of the nonbinary and genderqueer population means that the general reader might not know or care about changing a law that doesn't affect them.

The road to full equality is a complex cycle of increased visibility, activism, lobbying and public engagement. In times of political upheaval regression is possible – indeed it is often a fact of life. Increased trans and nonbinary visibility has done great things for the community: without increased genderqueer visibility there would be little impetus for the law to be extended to cover people whose transition experiences don't fall into the traditional 'sex change' narrative. Without progress in one area, progress in any other is meaningless. It's only by working on all points, from increasing visibility in media and the arts, to demanding wider legal protections and legal recognition, that we can move forward.

Exercises and discussion questions

Legislating for something as institutionalised and entrenched as gender is tricky. Looking at two or three of the various laws existing throughout the world that acknowledge and extend rights to a gender other than male or female, consider the specific ways they are written.

1. What specific rights or protections are extended to those covered by these laws?

2. Who, precisely, is covered? What are the legal, written criteria a person must meet to qualify for these rights or protections? Is there bureaucratic red tape involved in the process?

3. What are some of the potential pitfalls, exclusions and loopholes to these laws that might mean that some people fall through the cracks?

4. What are some potential ways to fix these problems? What would you change about the wording to make the the laws both more specific and more inclusive?

5. Consider the people and institutions which created these laws. What social attitudes, prejudices or changing perceptions are implicit in the way the laws are worded? If a law was written more than five or so years ago, would you say it is up to date and still capable of protecting and extending rights to the people to whom it is relevant?

6. If the law does seem to be out of date, how would you go about deciding what to change, and how might you implement these changes?

CHAPTER 9

Looking Ahead

As genderqueer people, as a community, begin publicly pushing the boundaries of gender expression, old categories and conventions are being questioned, broken down and recreated. Definitions of masculinity, femininity and even gender itself are in a state of flux, for cis and trans people alike. The existence of genderqueer people proves, in a way, that much of what we've been taught to see as discrete, binary, rigid and clear-cut is actually fluid, granular and blurry. The proliferation of gender identities has come hand in hand with intellectual movements like poststructuralism and intersectionality, and with unprecedented public acceptance of difference and diversity of experience. All people, cis or trans, likewise have unprecedented access to the lived experience of others, and it is now largely accepted as a matter of course that we educate ourselves. We take classes, watch videos, read books, work and make friends with people different from ourselves. We're more globalised, informed and interconnected than ever before.

This book is just a small part of what I hope will become a much larger conversation. My voice is just one of many nonbinary and genderqueer people writing, blogging, vlogging and speaking publicly about their experiences right now. The more visible we become, the more the diversity of our community will emerge.

What's next for the nonbinary and genderqueer community? Part of what's so exciting is that uncertainty. Everything about our community is growing and changing daily, and with this change comes the possibility of public acceptance, legal recognition, protection from discrimination and representation in literature, academic writing and popular media. We're only just starting to explore the idea of living openly outside of the binary, of complete equality – whatever that might mean. Equality and openness are dreams that have seemed impossible, and then proven attainable, for minority after minority since the beginning of human history. Now it's our turn.

CHAPTER 10

Resources and References

These are the main surveys and studies I refer to throughout the book. What I discuss is just a fraction of the data now available, and I highly recommend browsing the executive summaries of each of these studies:

Valentine, V. (2015b). Non-binary people's experiences in the UK. *Scottish Trans Alliance*. www.scottishtrans.org/wp-content/uploads/2016/08/Report-final.pdf

Bachmann, C. L. and Gooch, B. (2017). LGBT in Britain – Trans report. *Stonewall*. www.stonewall.org.uk/sites/default/files/lgbt-in-britain-trans.pdf

Thomson, R., Baker, J. and Arnot, J. (2018). Health care needs assessment of gender identity services. *Scottish Public Health Network*. ScotPHN. www.scotphn.net/wp-content/uploads/2017/04/2018_05_16-HCNA-of-Gender-Identity-Services-1.pdf

James, S. E., Herman, J. L., Rankin, S., Keisling, M., Mottet, L. and Anafi, M. (2016). The report of the 2015 U.S. Transgender Survey. Washington, DC: National Center for Transgender Equality. www.transequality.org/sites/default/files/docs/USTS-Full-Report-FINAL.PDF

Grant, J. M., Mottet, L. A., Tanis, J., Harrison, J., Herman, J. L. and Keisling, M. (2011). Injustice at every turn: A report of the National Transgender Discrimination Survey. Washington: National Center for Transgender Equality and National Gay and Lesbian Task Force. www.thetaskforce.org/injustice-every-turn-report-national-transgender-discrimination-survey

Resources for trans, genderqueer and nonbinary people

Lambda Legal, 'a national organization committed to achieving full recognition of the civil rights of lesbians, gay men, bisexuals, transgender people and everyone living with HIV' have numerous resources on trans legal rights. In their trans toolkit 'readers will find answers to many questions that transgender people and their advocates may ask as they navigate through life': www.lambdalegal. org/publications/trans-toolkit

The Terrence Higgins Trust (THT) is 'the UK's leading HIV and sexual health charity'. The THT maintains a page on sexual health specifically geared towards trans men (www.tht.org.uk/hiv-and-sexual-health/sexual-health/improving-your-sexual-health/sex-trans-man) and trans women (www.tht.org.uk/hiv-and-sexual-health/sexual-health/improving-your-sexual-health/sex-trans-woman). Note that the information is generally organised based on sex assigned at birth, and there's no information specifically for nonbinary-identified people, though it does acknowledge that the information might be useful to nonbinary people.

Mind Out are a third sector organisation which provide LGBT-specific mental health services, more information can be found here: www.mindout.org.uk

LGBT Health and Wellbeing Scotland offer a range of online resources for LGBT people dealing with mental illness, as well as a range of films, helplines and resources for service providers and organisations who work with LGBT people. These can be accessed at: www.lgbthealth.org.uk/online-resources

CliniQ is an alternative sexual health and wellbeing clinic specifically for transgender and other gender-nonconforming people. CliniQ run a weekly clinic for trans people in London. https://cliniq.org.uk/about

Nonbinary-created resources for the general reader

I highly recommend taking a look at the work of Meg-John Barker, CN Lester, Dean Spade and Jack/Judith Halberstram.

Ash Mardell is a queer YouTuber and author whose channel talks about their own experiences of gender and queerness. They've written a book called *The ABCs of LGBT+ (Miami, FL; Mango Media)*, 'for questioning teens, teachers or parents looking for advice, or anyone who wants to learn how to talk about gender identity and sexual identity'. ISBN 9781633534094

My Genderation is a YouTube channel and film series created by trans artists and filmmakers, including popular duo Fox and Owl, who both identify as nonbinary. The My Genderation channel can be accessed here: www.youtube.com/user/MyGenderation

Beyond the Binary UK is an excellent online magazine that publishes articles about a range of topics from a nonbinary perspective. They can be accessed here: http://beyondthebinary.co.uk

Practical Androgyny, edited by Nat Titman, whose research I relied so heavily upon in the introductory chapter, is a resource 'devoted to the practicalities of ambiguous gender presentation within a binary-gendered society'. Practical Androgyny can be accessed here: https://practicalandrogyny.com

Apart from being a prolific academic and theorist Meg-John Barker has created a range of accessible resources, many of them free, that explore gender, queerness, sexuality and the diversity of nonbinary experience. Their website can be found at www.rewriting-the-rules.com

Savage, S. and Fisher, F. (2015). *Are You a Boy or Are You a Girl?* London: Jessica Kingsley Publishers. This is a great book for discussing nonbinary gender and gender diversity with very young children.

Sojwal, S. (2015). What does 'agender' mean? 6 things to know about people with non-binary identities. *Bustle.* www.bustle.com/articles/109255-what-does-agender-mean-6-things-to-know-about-people-with-non-binary-identities

Girshick, L. B. (2008). *Transgender Voices: Beyond Women and Men.* Hanover: University Press of New England.

Scout, Ph.D. (2013). (A) Male, (B) Female, (C) Both, (D) Neither. *The Huffington Post.* www.huffingtonpost.com/scout-phd/a-male-b-female-c-both-d-neither_b_2887462.html

Parsons, V. (2018). I am non-binary. And this is how mental-health services are failing people like me. *The Pool.* www.the-pool.com/health/mind/2018/20/vic-parsons-how-mental-health-cuts-are-affecting-the-LGBTQ-community

Mamone, T. (2018). We need to talk about how non-binary invisibility affects mental health. *Ravishly.* https://ravishly.com/non-binary-invisibility-affects-mental-health

The All About Trans Non-Binary Gender Factsheet expresses some of the fears and anxieties nonbinary and genderqueer people face on a daily basis, and includes some quotes from nonbinary people about their experiences. The factsheet is accessible at www.allabouttrans.org.uk/wp-content/uploads/2014/05/non-binary-gender-factsheet.pdf

In addition, page two of the All About Trans Non-Binary Gender Factsheet references the following books and articles, which I haven't personally used for this book but which may be useful for academic, institutional or general readers:

Richards, C., Bouman, W. and Barker, M. J. (eds.) (2016). *Genderqueer and Non-Binary Genders*. Basingstoke: Palgrave Macmillan.

Barker, M. J. and Richards, C. (2015). Further genders. In C. Richards and M. J. Barker (eds.) *Handbook of the Psychology of Sexuality and Gender*. pp.166–182. Basingstoke: Palgrave Macmillan.

Harrison, J., Grant, J. and Herman, J. L. (2012). A gender not listed here: Genderqueers, gender rebels, and otherwise in the National Transgender Discrimination Survey. Los Angeles, CA: eScholarship, University of California.

Joel, D., Tarrasch, R., Berman, Z., Mukamel, M. and Ziv, E. (2013). Queering gender: Studying gender identity in 'normative' individuals. *Psychology & Sexuality*, 5(4), 291–321.

Richards, C., Bouman, W. P., Seal, L., Barker, M. J., Nieder, T. O. and T'Sjoen, G. (2016). Non-binary or genderqueer genders. *International Review of Psychiatry*, 28(1), 95–102.

Trans Media Watch. (2014). Understanding non-binary people: A guide for the media. www.transmediawatch.org/Documents/non_binary.pdf

Resources for employers, service providers, academics and physicians

Lev, A. I. (2004). *Transgender Emergence: Therapeutic Guidelines for Working With Gender-Variant People and Their Families*. Philadelphia, PA: Haworth Press.

Chang, S. C., Singh, A. A. and dickey, l. m. (2019). *A Clinician's Guide to Gender-Affirming Care: Working with Transgender and Gender-Nonconforming Clients*. Oakland, CA: New Harbinger Publications.

Valentine, V. (2015a). Including non-binary people: guidance for service providers and employers. Scottish Trans Alliance. www.scottishtrans. org/wp-content/uploads/2016/11/Non-binary-guidance.pdf

Vincent, B. (2018). *Transgender Health: A Practitioner's Guide to Binary and Non-Binary Trans Patient Care*. London: Jessica Kingsley Publishers.

East Sussex County Council. (2014). Trans* inclusion schools toolkit. Mermaids UK. www.mermaidsuk.org.uk/assets/media/East%20 Sussex%20schools%20transgender%20toolkit.pdf

Gender Identity Research and Education Society. (2010). Guidance on combating transphobic bullying in schools. GIRES. www.gires.org.uk/ wp-content/uploads/2017/04/TransphobicBullying-print.pdf

Gay, Lesbian & Straight Education Network. (2017). How to support non-binary students. GLSEN. www.youtube.com/ watch?v=KQUQIoBrKnA

World Professional Association for Transgender Health. (2012). Standards of Care, 7th Version. www.wpath.org/publications/soc

The UCSF CFE for transgender health primary care guidelines for trans patients: http://transhealth.ucsf.edu/protocols

All references used in this book

Abby Jean. (2009). Ableist word profile: Hysterical. Disabled Feminists. http://disabledfeminists.com/2009/10/13/ableist-word-profile-hysterical

ATH Team. (2015). Non binary survey: Preliminary results. *Action for Trans Health*. http://actionfortranshealth.org.uk/2015/02/22/non-binary-survey-preliminary-results

ADDitude Editors. Dexedrine: ADHD medication FAQ. *ADDitude*. www.additudemag.com/dexedrine-adhd-medication-faq

American Psychiatric Association. (2013). *Diagnostic and Statistical Manual of Mental Disorders, 5th Edition*. Washington, DC: APA.

Amherst, M. (2018). *Go the Way Your Blood Beats*. London: Repeater Press.

Bachmann, C. L. and Gooch, B. (2017). LGBT in Britain – Trans report. *Stonewall*. www.stonewall.org.uk/sites/default/files/lgbt-in-britain-trans.pdf

Barker, M. J. (2016). Gender Continuum. www.rewriting-the-rules.com/gender-continuum

Baron, D. (1981). The epicene pronoun: The word that failed. *American Speech, 56*(2), 83–97.

Beecher, D. (2005). Concerning sex changes: The cultural significance of a renaissance medical polemic. *The Sixteenth Century Journal, 36*(4), 991–1016.

Berenbaum, S. A. and Beltz, A. M. (2016). How early hormones shape gender development. *Current Opinion in Behavioral Sciences, 7*, 53–60.

Byne, W., Bradley, S.J., Coleman, E. *et al.* (2012). Report of the American Psychiatric Association task force on treatment of gender identity disorder. *Archives of Sexual Behaviour, 41,* 759–796.

Center for Young Women's Health. (2016). Health guides. Endometriosis: Hormonal treatment overview. https://youngwomens health.org/2014/08/01/endometriosis-hormonal-treatment-overview

Chak, A. (2015). Beyond 'he' and 'she': The rise of non-binary pronouns. *BBC.* https://www.bbc.co.uk/news/magazine-34901704

Clark, T., Lucassen, M., Bullen, P., Denny, S., Fleming, T., Robinson, E. and Rossen, F. (2014). The health and well-being of transgender high school students: Results from the New Zealand Adolescent Health Survey (Youth'12). *Journal of Adolescent Health, 55*(1), 93–99.

Colizzi, M., Costa, R. and Todarello, O. (2014). Transsexual patients' psychiatric comorbidity and positive effect of cross-sex hormonal treatment on mental health: Results from a longitudinal study. Department of Medical Basic Sciences, Neuroscience and Sense Organs, University of Bari.

Connolly, M. D., Zervos, M. J., Barone, C. J., Johnson, C. C. and Joseph, C. L. (2016). The mental health of transgender youth: Advances in understanding. *Journal of Adolescent Health, 59*(5), 489–495.

Crouch, E. (2017). What happens if you're genderqueer – but your native language is gendered? *Medium.* https://medium.com/the-establishment/what-happens-if-youre-genderqueer-but-your-native-language-is-gendered-d1c009dc5fcb

Davies, S. G. (2006). *Challenging Gender Norms: Five Genders Among Bugis in Indonesia (Case Studies in Cultural Anthropology).* Belmont, CA: Cengage Learning.

Davies, S. G. (2002). Sex, gender, and priests in South Sulawesi, Indonesia. *International Institute for Asian Studies. IIAS Newsletter 29*, 27.

Drescher, J. (2015). Out of DSM: Depathologizing homosexuality. *Behavioral Sciences, 5*(4), 565–575.

Van der Drift, M., Lall, N. and Raha, N. Radical Transfeminism Zine. https://radicaltransfeminismzine.tumblr.com

Drydakis, N. (2017). Trans employees, transitioning, and job satisfaction. *Journal of Vocational Behavior, 98*, 1–16.

Eade, D. M., Telfer, M. M. and Tollit M. A. (2018). Implementing a single-session nurse-led assessment clinic into a gender service. *Transgender Health, 3*(1), 43–46.

Eagly, A. H. and Wood, W. (1999). The origins of sex differences in human behavior: Evolved dispositions versus social roles. *American Psychologist, 54*(6), 408–423.

East Sussex County Council. (2014). Trans* inclusion schools toolkit. *Mermaids UK.* www.mermaidsuk.org.uk/assets/media/East%20 Sussex%20schools%20transgender%20toolkit.pdf

Effrig, J. C., Bieschke, K. J. and Locke, B. D. (2011). Examining victimization and psychological distress in transgender college students. *Journal of College Counseling, 14*, 143–157.

Ehrhardt, A. and Meyer-Bahlburg, H. F. (1981). Effects of prenatal sex hormones on gender-related behavior. *Science, 211*(4488), 1312–1318.

Eliana. (2014). Definitions of bisexuality, pansexuality and polysexuality. *Beyond the 'Talk'.* http://beyondthetalk.ca/ definitions-bisexuality-pansexuality-polysexuality-eliana

Elliott, I. (2016). *Poverty and Mental Health: A Review to Inform the Joseph Rowntree Foundation's Anti-Poverty Strategy*. London: Mental Health Foundation.

Emory Health Sciences. (2014). Having a Y chromosome doesn't affect women's response to sexual images, brain study shows. *Science Daily*. www.sciencedaily.com/releases/2014/11/141105165209.htm

Equality Act. (2010). C. 15. www.legislation.gov.uk/ukpga/2010/15/pdfs/ukpga_20100015_en.pdf

Fang, J. (2015). Indo-European languages originated 6,000 years ago in Russian grasslands. *IFL Science*. www.iflscience.com/plants-and-animals/indo-european-languages-may-have-originated-6000-years-ago-russian-grasslands

Gay, Lesbian & Straight Education Network. (2017). How to support non-binary students. *GLSEN*. www.youtube.com/watch?v=KQUQIoBrKnA

Gender Identity Research and Education Society. (2010). Guidance on combating transphobic bullying in schools. *GIRES*. www.gires.org.uk/wp-content/uploads/2017/04/TransphobicBullying-print.pdf

Gender Recognition Act. (2004). C. 7. www.legislation.gov.uk/ukpga/2004/7/pdfs/ukpga_20040007_en.pdf

Gender Wiki – 'boi'. http://gender.wikia.com/wiki/Boi

GLAAD. (n.d.) GLAAD media reference guide: Glossary of terms – Transgender. www.glaad.org/reference/transgender

Grant, J. M., Mottet, L. A., Tanis, J., Harrison, J., Herman, J. L. and Keisling, M. (2011). Injustice at Every Turn: A Report of the National Transgender Discrimination Survey. Washington: National Center for Transgender Equality and National Gay and Lesbian Task Force.

Hall, D. E., Prochazka A. V. and Fink A. S. (2012). Informed consent for clinical treatment. *Canadian Medical Association Journal*, 184(5), 533–540.

Heijer, M., Bakker, A. and Gooren, L. (2017). Long term hormonal treatment for transgender people. *BMJ*, 2017(359), j5027.

Hembree, W. C. *et al.* (2017). Endocrine treatment of gender-dysphoric/gender-incongruent persons: An endocrine society clinical practice guideline. *The Journal of Clinical Endocrinology & Metabolism*, 102(11), 869–3903.

Herdt, G. (1993). *Third Sex, Third Gender: Beyond Sexual Dimorphism in Culture and History*. New York: Zone Books.

Herman, J. L. (2013). Gendered restrooms and minority stress: The public regulation of gender and its impact on transgender people's lives. *Journal of Public Management and Social Policy*, Spring, 65–80.

Hiller, V. and Baudin, T. (2016). Cultural transmission and the evolution of gender roles. *Mathematical Social Sciences*, 84(C), 8–23.

Hines, M. (2011). Prenatal endocrine influences on sexual orientation and on sexually differentiated childhood behavior. *Frontiers in Neuroendocrinology*, 32(2), 170–182.

Intersex Society of North America. How common is intersex? Rohnert Park, CA: ISNA. www.isna.org/faq/frequency

Intersex Society of North America. What is intersex? Rohnert Park, CA: *ISNA*. www.isna.org/faq/what_is_intersex

James, S. E., Herman, J. L., Rankin, S., Keisling, M., Mottet, L., and Anafi, M. (2016). The report of the 2015 U.S. Transgender Survey. Washington, DC: National Center for Transgender Equality.

Jeffreys, S. (1997). Transgender activism. *Journal of Lesbian Studies, 1*(3–4), 55–74.

Jellestad, L. *et al.* (2018). Quality of life in transitioned trans persons: A retrospective cross-sectional cohort study. *BioMed Research International, 2018*(3), 1–10.

Jin, Z. W., Jin, Y., Li, X. W., Murakami, G., Rodríguez-Vázquez, J. F. and Wilting, J. (2016). Perineal raphe with special reference to its extension to the anus: a histological study using human fetuses. *Anatomy & Cell Biology, 49*(2), 116–124.

Kagan, R. L. and Dyer, A. (2004). *Inquisitorial inquiries: Brief lives of secret Jews and other heretics.* Baltimore, MD: Johns Hopkins University Press. Cited by Rolker, C. (2016) at https://intersex.hypotheses.org/2720

Keuroghlian, A. S., Reisner, S. L., White, J. M. and Weiss, R. D. (2015). Substance use and treatment of substance use disorders in a community sample of transgender adults. *Drug and Alcohol Dependence, 152*, 139–146.

Kibirige, H. (2018). Creating a trans-inclusive school environment – response to Transgender Trend. *Stonewall*. https://www.stonewall.org.uk/our-work/blog/education-youth/creating-trans-inclusive-school-environment-response-transgender-trend

Kim, E. Y. (2015). Long-term effects of gonadotropin-releasing hormone analogs in girls with central precocious puberty. *Korean Journal of Pediatrics, 58*(1), 1–7.

Krege, S., Bex, A., Lümmen, G. and Rübben, H. (2001). Male-to-female transsexualism: A technique, results and long-term follow-up in 66 patients. *BJU International, 88*(4), 396–402.

Lamb, K. (2015). Indonesia's transgender priests face uncertain future. *AlJazeera America.* http://america.aljazeera.com/articles/2015/5/12/indonesias-transgender-priests-face-uncertain-future.html

Laquer, T. (1990). *Making Sex: Body and Gender from the Greeks to Freud.* Cambridge, MA: Harvard University Press.

Lehavot, K. and Simoni, J. M. (2011). The impact of minority stress on mental health and substance use among sexual minority women. *Journal of Consulting and Clinical Psychology, 79*(2), 159–170.

MacLellan, L. (2017). Sweden's gender-neutral preschools produce kids who are more likely to succeed. *QZ.* https://qz.com/1006928/swedens-gender-neutral-preschools-produce-kids-who-are-more-likely-to-succeed

McNeil, J., Bailey, L., Ellis, S., Morton, J. and Regan, M. (2012). Trans mental health study 2012. *Scottish Transgender Alliance.*

Marshall, W. (1789). Provincialisms of the Vale of Gloucester. *Gloucestershire Notes and Queries.*

Mayo Clinic Staff. (2017). Precocious puberty: Diagnosis and treatment. *Mayo Clinic.* www.mayoclinic.org/diseases-conditions/precocious-puberty/diagnosis-treatment/drc-20351817

Mesoudi, A. (2011). *Cultural Evolution: How Darwinian theory can explain human culture and synthesize the social sciences.* Chicago, IL: University of Chicago Press.

Meyer, I. H. (1995). Minority stress and mental health in gay men. *Journal of Health and Social Behavior 36*(1), 38–56.

Meyer, I. H. (2003). Prejudice, social stress, and mental health in lesbian, gay, and bisexual populations: Conceptual issues and research evidence. *Psychological Bulletin, 129*(5), 674–697.

Morales, E. (2018). Why I embrace the term Latinx. *The Guardian.* www.theguardian.com/commentisfree/2018/jan/08/why-i-embrace-the-term-latinx

Mordaunt, P. (2018). *Reform of the Gender Recognition Act – Government Consultation.* Ministry for Women and Equalities. https://assets.publishing.service.gov.uk/government/uploads/system/uploads/attachment_data/file/721725/GRA-Consultation-document.pdf

Murad, M. H., Elamin, M. B., Garcia, M. Z., Mullan, R. J., Murad, A., Erwin, P. J. and Montori, V. M. (2010). Hormonal therapy and sex reassignment: A systematic review and meta-analysis of quality of life and psychosocial outcomes. *Clinical Endocrinology, 72*(2), 214–231.

Newfield, E., Hart, S., Dibble, S. and Kohler, L. (2006). Female-to-male transgender quality of life. *Quality of Life Research, 15*(9), 1447–1457.

NHS England. (2015). Recording and reporting referral to treatment (RTT) waiting times for consultant-led elective care: Frequently Asked Questions. www.england.nhs.uk/statistics/wp-content/uploads/sites/2/2013/04/Accompanying-FAQs-v7.2.pdf

O'Hara, M. E. (2015). 'Trans Broken Arm Syndrome' and the way our healthcare system fails trans people. *The Daily Dot.* www.dailydot.com/irl/trans-broken-arm-syndrome-healthcare

Office for National Statistics. (2009). Trans data position paper. *ONS.* www.ons.gov.uk/ons/guide-method/measuring-equality/equality/equality-data-review/trans-data-position-paper.pdf

Olson, J., Schrager, S., Belzer, M., Simons, L. and Clark, L. (2015). Baseline physiologic and psychosocial characteristics of transgender youth seeking care for gender dysphoria. *Journal of Adolescent Health, 57*(4), 374–380.

Padilla, Y. (2016). What does 'Latinx' mean? A look at the term that's challenging gender norms. *Complex.* www.complex.com/life/2016/04/latinx/rise-latinx

Payton, N. (2015). Feature: The dangers of trans broken arm syndrome. *Pink News.* www.pinknews.co.uk/2015/07/09/feature-the-dangers-of-trans-broken-arm-syndrome

Pfafflin, F. (1993). Regrets After Sex Reassignment Surgery. *Journal of Psychology & Human Sexuality, 5*(4), 69–85.

Psychology Today. (2018). Paraphilias. www.psychologytoday.com/us/conditions/paraphilias

Rehman, J., Lazer, S., Benet, A.E. *et al.* (1999) The Reported Sex and Surgery Satisfactions of 28 Postoperative Male-to-Female Transsexual Patients. *Archives of Sexual Behavior, 28*(1), 71–89.

Rimes, K. A., Goodship, N., Ussher, G., Baker, D. and West, E. (2017). Non-binary and binary transgender youth: Comparison of mental health, self-harm, suicidality, substance use and victimization experiences. *International Journal of Transgenderism*, 18 September, 1–11.

Roberts, A. (2015). Dispelling the myths around trans people detransitioning. *VICE*. www.vice.com/en_uk/article/kwxkwz/dispelling-the-myths-around-detransitioning

Rolker, C. (2016). I am and have been a hermaphrodite: Elena/Eleno de Céspedes and the Spanish Inquisition. Männlich-weiblich-zwischen. https://intersex.hypotheses.org/2720

Royal College of Psychiatrists. (2013). Good practice guidelines for the assessment and treatment of adults with gender dysphoria. *RCPsych*. www.teni.ie/attachments/14767e01-a8de-4b90-9a19-8c2c50edf4e1.PDF

Rude, M. (2014). Time for people to stop using the social construct of 'biological sex' to defend their transmisogyny. *Autostraddle*. www.autostraddle.com/its-time-for-people-to-stop-using-the-social-construct-of-biological-sex-to-defend-their-transmisogyny-240284

Saner, E. (2014). RBS: the bank that likes to say Mx. *The Guardian*. www.theguardian.com/world/shortcuts/2014/nov/17/rbs-bank-that-likes-to-say-mx

Savic, I., Garcia-Falgueras, A. and Swaab, D. F. (2010). Sexual differentiation of the human brain in relation to gender identity and sexual orientation. *Progress in Brain Research, 186*, 41–62.

Sayers, W. (2005). The Etymology of Queer. *ANQ: A Quarterly Journal of Short Articles, Notes and Reviews, 18*(2), 17–19.

Scott, G. Gender differences in modern Japanese. *Lingualift*. www.lingualift.com/blog/gender-differences-in-japanese

Scottish Government. (2012). Gender Reassignment Protocol. www.sehd.scot.nhs.uk/mels/CEL2012_26.pdf

Seelman, K. L. (2016). Transgender Adults' Access to college bathrooms and housing and the relationship to suicidality. *Journal of Homosexuality, 63*(10), 1378–1399.

Segal, C. (2014). OkCupid expands gender and sexuality options. *PBS NewsHour.* www.pbs.org/newshour/nation/ okcupid-expands-gender-sexuality-options

Senden, M. G., Back, E. A. and Lindqvist, E. (2015). Introducing a gender-neutral pronoun in a natural gender language: The influence of time on attitudes and behavior. *Frontiers in Psychology, 6,* 893.

Smith, S. E. (2010). Psychiatrisation: A Great Way To Silence Troublesome Women. *Meloukhia.* http://meloukhia.net/ 2010/08/psychiatrisation_a_great_way_to_silence_troublesome_ women.html

Smith, S. E. (2011). We're all mad here: Race, gender, and mental illness in pop culture. *Bitch Media.* www.bitchmedia.org/post /were-all-mad-here-race-gender-and-mental-illness-in- pop-culture

Spack, N. P., Edwards-Leeper, L. and Feldman, H. A. (2012). Children and adolescents with gender identity disorder referred to a pediatric medical center. *Pediatrics, 129*(3), 418–425.

Surrey, E. S. and Hornstein, M. D. (2002). Prolonged GnRH agonist and add-back therapy for symptomatic endometriosis: Long-term follow- up. *Obstetrics and Gynecology, 99*(5), 709–719.

Thaler, C. Putting transgender health care myths on trial. *Lambda Legal.* www.lambdalegal.org/publications/ putting-transgender-health-care-myths-on-trial

Thomson, R., Baker, J. and Arnot, J. (2018). Health care needs assessment of gender identity services. *Scottish Public Health Network*. ScotPHN. www.scotphn.net/wp-content/uploads/2017/04/2018_05_16-HCNA-of-Gender-Identity-Services-1.pdf

Titman, N. (2014). How many people in the United Kingdom are nonbinary? *Practical Androgyny*. https://practicalandrogyny.com/2014/12/16/how-many-people-in-the-uk-are-nonbinary

Tyrer, P. (2014). A comparison of DSM and ICD classifications of mental disorder. *Advances in Psychiatric Treatment, 20*(4), 280–285.

Unger, C. A. (2016). Hormone therapy for transgender patients. *Translational Andrology and Urology, 5*(6), 877–884.

Valentine, V. (2015a). Including non-binary people: Guidance for service providers and employers. *Scottish Trans Alliance*. www.scottishtrans.org/wp-content/uploads/2016/11/Non-binary-guidance.pdf

Valentine, V. (2015b). Non-binary people's experiences in the UK. *Scottish Trans Alliance*. www.scottishtrans.org/wp-content/uploads/2016/08/Report-final.pdf

Valentine, V. (2015c). Non-binary people's experiences of using UK gender identity clinics. *Scottish Trans Alliance*. www.scottishtrans.org/wp-content/uploads/2016/11/Non-binary-GIC-mini-report.pdf

Veale, J. F., Watson, R. J., Peter, T. and Saewyc, E. M. (2017). Mental health disparities among Canadian transgender youth. *Journal of Adolescent Health, 60*(1), 44–49.

Vincent, B. (2018). *Transgender Health: A Practitioner's Guide to Binary and Non-Binary Trans Patient Care*. London: Jessica Kingsley Publishers.

Wade, N. (2012). Family tree of languages has roots in Anatolia, biologists say. *The New York Times*. www.nytimes.com/2012/08/24/ science/indo-european-languages-originated-in-anatolia-analysis-suggests.html

Waters, E. (2016). Lesbian, gay, bisexual, transgender, queer, and HIV-affected hate violence in 2016. New York: National Coalition of Anti-Violence Programs (NCAVP).

Williams, C. (2016). Radical inclusion: Recounting the trans inclusive history of radical feminism. *Transgender Studies Quarterly* 3(1–2), 254–258.

Wong, C. F., Schrager, S. M., Holloway, I. W., Meyer, I. H. and Kipke, M. D. (2014). Minority stress experiences and psychological well-being: The impact of support from and connection to social networks within the Los Angeles House and Ball communities. *Prevention Science*, 15(1), 44–55.

Wood, W. and Eagly, A. H. (2012). Biosocial construction of sex differences and similarities in behavior. *Advances in Experimental Social Psychology*, 46, 55–123.

World Professional Association for Transgender Health. (2012). *Standards of Care*, 7th Version. www.wpath.org/publications/soc

Wyndzen, M. H. (2008) DSM – IV. All Mixed Up. www.genderpsychology.org/transsexual/dsm_iv.html

Endnotes

1   I'll use the word 'queer' in a number of different contexts throughout this book, and I understand that some readers may only be familiar with the derogatory use of this word. When I describe myself as queer, for example, I use it in the reclamative sense, a sense which encompasses all that is subversive and ambiguous about it. My gender and the way I experience attraction cannot easily be defined using words like 'man', 'woman', 'gay' and 'straight', and I use 'queer' as a kind of shorthand to signify both membership in the larger LGBT community and a nuanced identity outside the mainstream.

2   Herman, J. L. (2013). Gendered restrooms and minority stress: The public regulation of gender and its impact on transgender people's lives. *Journal of Public Management and Social Policy*, Spring, 65–80.

3   For further discussion of the issues surrounding intersex conditions and nonconsensual sex-assignment, see the Intersex Society of North America's page, 'What is intersex?'.

4   A good example of gender conceptualised as different diametrically opposed characteristics is Dr Meg-John Barker's Gender Continuum, which can be found on their website.

5   For a more detailed explanation of cultural evolution, see Mesoudi, A. (2011). *Cultural Evolution: How Darwinian theory can explain human culture and synthesize the social sciences*. Chicago, IL: University of Chicago Press. Alex Mesoudi's website, alexmesoudi.com/research, has some excellent visual and interactive resources as well.

6   Hiller, V. and Baudin, T. (2016). Cultural transmission and the evolution of gender roles. *Mathematical Social Sciences*, 84(C), 8–23.

7   For further information see: Eagly, A. H. and Wood, W. (1999). The origins of sex differences in human behavior: Evolved dispositions versus social roles. *American Psychologist*, 54(6), 408–423.; Wood, W. and Eagly, A. H. (2012). Biosocial construction of sex differences and similarities in behavior. *Advances in Experimental Social Psychology*, 46, 55–123.

8   Savic, I., Garcia-Falgueras, A. and Swaab, D. F. (2010). Sexual differentiation of the human brain in relation to gender identity and sexual orientation. *Progress in Brain Research*, 186, 41–62.

9   Hines, M. (2011). Prenatal endocrine influences on sexual orientation and on sexually differentiated childhood behavior. *Frontiers in Neuroendocrinology*, 32(2), 170–182.

10   For an explanation of why the term biological female is problematic, refer to Mey Rude's article, 'It's time for people to stop using the social construct of "biological sex" to defend their transmisogyny' on autostraddle.com.

11   Waters, E. (2016). *Lesbian, gay, bisexual, transgender, queer, and HIV-affected hate violence in 2016*. New York: National Coalition of Anti-Violence Programs (NCAVP).

12   Sayers, W. (2005). The Etymology of Queer. *ANQ: A Quarterly Journal of Short Articles, Notes and Reviews*, 18(2), 17–19.

13   Linguistic phenomena whereby a word's meaning becomes more specific and more negative, respectively.

14   James, S. E., Herman, J. L., Rankin, S., Keisling, M., Mottet, L. and Anafi, M. (2016). *The Report of the 2015 U.S. Transgender Survey*. Washington, DC: National Center for Transgender Equality.A summary of the results can be read, or watched in video form, here: www.ustranssurvey.org

15   Grant, J. M., Mottet, L. A., Tanis, J., Harrison, J., Herman, J. L. and Keisling, M. (2011). *Injustice at Every Turn: A Report of the National Transgender Discrimination Survey*. Washington, DC: National Center for Transgender Equality and National Gay and Lesbian Task Force.

16   Titman, N. (2014). How many people in the United Kingdom are nonbinary? *Practical Androgyny*.

17   McNeil, J., Bailey, L., Ellis, S., Morton, J. and Regan, M. (2012). Trans mental health study 2012. *Scottish Transgender Alliance*. 13.

18   Clinics where trans people go to receive gender-affirming medical treatments will be discussed in more detail in Chapter 7.

19   Bachmann, C. L. and Gooch, B. (2017). LGBT in Britain – Trans report. *Stonewall*.

20   Note that in the context of language I don't distinguish between gender and sex.

21   Though there is some debate surrounding this conclusion. For more information see Janet Fang's article, 'Indo-European languages originated 6,000 years ago in Russian grasslands', on iflscience.com, and Nicholas Wade's article, 'Family tree of languages has roots in Anatolia, biologists say', on nytimes.com.

22   This is a relatively controversial theory, however, and difficult to prove. For more information see the Cyril Babaev Linguistic Studies archive: http://babaev.tripod.com/archive/article11.html

23   For a more in-depth discussion of gendered conventions in spoken Japanese and how they've evolved (also a good example of language change!) see Greg Scott's article, 'Gender differences in modern Japanese', on lingualift.com

24   The majority of discussions I've seen about the use of neutral pronouns and suffixes in Spanish has been in a context of cisgender native speakers calling the alternative uses improper and ridiculous. However, I have managed to find an interesting discussion here, by some nonbinary-identified Spanish speakers on Reddit: www.reddit.com/r/genderqueer/comments/4sv30p/how_do_i_talk_about_myself_in_spanish

25   For a discussion of the origins and meaning of Latinx and the related term Chicanx, see Ed Morales's article in *The Guardian*, 'Why I embrace the term Latinx' and Yesenia Padilla's article, 'What does "Latinx" mean? A look at the term that's challenging gender norms', for Complex.

26   There's an excellent article by Erin Crouch on Medium.com, 'What happens if you're genderqueer – but your native language is gendered?', which has some discussion on gendered and genderqueer pronoun usage in various languages, including Finnish and Estonian as well as Russian.

27   The study is discussed in Lila MacLellan's article, 'Sweden's gender-neutral preschools produce kids who are more likely to succeed' on qz.com. Note that the studies that have been conducted generally have small sample sizes: more evidence should be collected before we can know whether the results hold true, and 'more likely to succeed' is a pretty vague concept in any case.

28   Senden, M. G., Back, E. A. and Lindqvist, E. (2015). Introducing a gender-neutral pronoun in a natural gender language: The influence of time on attitudes and behavior. *Frontiers in Psychology*, 6, 893.

29   In linguistics this is called a synchronic perspective, meaning a view of a language or languages as spoken at a single point in time, as opposed to a diachronic perspective which refers to a single language as it has changed through time.

30   Spoken roughly during the Elizabethan and Jacobean periods.

31   Indeed the use of these pronouns has been strongly connected to social context and notions of politeness, and in some areas, such as Quaker communities, thee and thou are still used in different contexts.

32   Note that there are other versions of this passage that use the masculine-as-default 'he' in place of 'they'; it's difficult to tell which would have been used in the original work, but both versions are considered legitimate and may vary due to variations in the region and dialect of the editor. Nonetheless there were writers working in Chaucer's day who considered a gender-neutral third person singular 'they' to be perfectly acceptable usage.

33   For more information about these pronouns see 'The Words that Failed', an article by Dennis Baron, originally published in Baron, D. (1981). The epicene pronoun: The word that failed. *American Speech* 56, 83–97, and updated at www.english.illinois.edu/-people-/faculty/debaron/essays/epicene.htm

34   Marshall, W. (1789). Provincialisms of the Vale of Gloucester. *Gloucestershire Notes and Queries.*

35   Spivak pronouns, best known for their use by mathematician Michael Spivak, are generally formed by removing or combining the part of the pronoun which determines its gender (i.e. sh/h, ers/is, etc.). They've been invented spontaneously at various points since the late nineteenth century and are probably the best established inclusive pronoun outside of they/them/their.

36   Chak, A. (2015). Beyond 'he' and 'she': The rise of non-binary pronouns. BBC. www.bbc.co.uk/news/Magazine-34901704. This article also includes a useful expanded 'pronoun card' with conjugations included.

37   Though not necessarily completely true: a number of scholars have challenged Laqueur's one-sex/two-sex model, advocating a more heterogeneous one tied to different social contexts. When dealing with historical sources and making guesses about the way ancient people understood something as nebulous, essential, changeable and controversial as gender, there is bound to be some level of uncertainty.

38   Laquer, T. (1990). *Making Sex: Body and Gender from the Greeks to Freud.* Cambridge, MA: Harvard University Press.

39   Herdt, G. (1993). *Third Sex, Third Gender: Beyond Sexual Dimorphism in Culture and History.* New York: Zone Books.

40   Beecher, D. (2005). Concerning sex changes: The cultural significance of a Renaissance medical polemic. *The Sixteenth Century Journal,* 36(4), 991–1016.

41   p.127.

42   Intersex Society of North America. *How common is intersex?* Rohnert Park, CA: ISNA.

43   Jin, Z. W., Jin, Y., Li, X. W., Murakami, G., Rodríguez-Vázquez, J. F. and Wilting, J. (2016). Perineal raphe with special reference to its extension to the anus: A histological study using human fetuses. *Anatomy & Cell Biology,* 49(2), 116–124.

44   Emory Health Sciences (2014). Having a Y chromosome doesn't affect women's response to sexual images, brain study shows. *Science Daily.*

45   For more information, see Rolker, C. (2016). I am and have been a hermaphrodite: Elena/Eleno de Céspedes and the Spanish Inquisition. Männlich-weiblich-zwischen.

46   A term bandied about a lot but now generally considered offensive by the intersex and LGBT communities.

47 It's worth pointing out here that the historical figures discussed above are merely the most accessible recorded examples available to us today, and mostly lived in a Western context. Most of these people are recorded in Western sources, and the relative visibility of these particular figures could be due to any number of factors, especially the early and widespread practice of writing in Indo-European culture.

48 Kagan, R. L. and Dyer, A. (2004). *Inquisitorial Inquiries: Brief Lives of Secret Jews and Other Heretics.* Baltimore, MD: Johns Hopkins University Press. Cited by Rolker, C. (2016) at https://intersex.hypotheses.org/2720

49 Included in Herdt, G. (1993). *Third Sex, Third Gender: Beyond Sexual Dimorphism in Culture and History.* New York: Zone Books. pp.213–239.

50 Included in Herdt (1993). pp.85–109.

51 Herdt (1993). p.92.

52 van der Meer, T. (1993). Sodomy and the Pursuit of the Third Sex in the Early Modern Period. Included in Herdt, G. *Third Sex, Third Gender: Beyond Sexual Dimorphism in Culture and History.* New York: Zone Books. pp.137–212.

53 As such, the language of any culture in which two-spirit exists will have its own name for the phenomenon.

54 Though this perception may be a result of Western observer bias.

55 Included in Herdt, G. (1993). *Third Sex, Third Gender: Beyond Sexual Dimorphism in Culture and History.* New York: Zone Books. pp.329–372.

56 Though 'shared' culture doesn't mean that all instances of gender liminality have been borrowed or taken from a single original source, or even necessarily that they're descended from the same original tradition.

57 Besnier, N. (1993). Polynesian gender liminality through time and space. In Herdt, G. *Third Sex, Third Gender: Beyond Sexual Dimorphism in Culture and History.* New York: Zone Books. pp.285–328.

58 Liminality is an academic term loosely defined as a state of being between two other states, and characterised by that betweenness.

59 Though all Polynesian cultures that have had any sustained contact with the West are likely to also have or be aware of trans women as well, whose identities aren't necessarily the same as gender liminal identities.

60 It's important to note here that despite their adhering to the social roles of the opposite gender from that which they were assigned at birth, the personal identities of *calalai* and *calabai* are not the same as Western trans men and women. For more information, please see Sharyn Graham Davies' book, *Challenging Gender Norms: Five Genders Among Bugis in Indonesia.*

61 Davies, S. G. (2002). Sex, gender, and priests in South Sulawesi, Indonesia. *International Institute for Asian Studies Newsletter, 29,* 27.

62 Lamb, K. (2015). Indonesia's transgender priests face uncertain future. *AlJazeera America.*

63   Valentine, V. (2015b). *Non-binary people's experiences in the UK.* Scottish Trans Alliance.

64   Gender Wiki – 'boi'.

65   Bachmann, C. L. and Gooch, B. (2017). *LGBT in Britain – Trans report.* Stonewall. p.13.

66   Bachmann, C. L. and Gooch, B. (2017). *LGBT in Britain – Trans report.* Stonewall. p.15.

67   For a more in-depth discussion of bisexuality and sexual fluidity I recommend Michael Amherst's excellent book, *Go the Way Your Blood Beats* (2018, Repeater Press).

68   James, S. E., Herman, J. L., Rankin, S., Keisling, M., Mottet, L. and Anafi, M. (2016). *The Report of the 2015 U.S. Transgender Survey.* Washington, DC: National Center for Transgender Equality. p.40.

69   Valentine, V. (2015b). *Non-binary people's experiences in the UK.* Scottish Trans Alliance.

70   Jeffreys, S. (1997). Transgender activism. *Journal of Lesbian Studies,* 1(3–4), 55–74.

71   For more information on the ways that radical feminism can be trans-inclusive, see Williams, C. (2016). Radical inclusion: Recounting the trans inclusive history of radical feminism. *Transgender Studies Quarterly,* 3(1–2), 254–258.

72   For example, see Mijke van der Drift, Natasha Lall and Nat Raha's Radical Transfeminism Zine at https://radicaltransfeminismzine.tumblr.com

73   Bachmann, C. L. and Gooch, B. (2017). *LGBT in Britain – Trans report.* Stonewall. p.15.

74   Bachmann, C. L. and Gooch, B. (2017). *LGBT in Britain – Trans report.* Stonewall. p.15.

75   Segal, C. (2014). OkCupid expands gender and sexuality options. *PBS NewsHour.*

76   A sexuality characterised, like bisexuality, by attraction to more than one gender, but not necessarily all genders. For more information see Eliana (2014). Definitions of bisexuality, pansexuality and polysexuality. *Beyond the 'Talk'.*

77   Valentine, V. (2015b). *Non-binary people's experiences in the UK.* Scottish Trans Alliance. pp.55–67.

78   Valentine, V. (2015a). *Including non-binary people: Guidance for service providers and employers.* Scottish Trans Alliance.

79   Valentine, V. (2015a). *Including non-binary people: Guidance for service providers and employers.* Scottish Trans Alliance. p.10.

80   Valentine, V. (2015b). *Non-binary people's experiences in the UK.* Scottish Trans Alliance. Beginning p.41.

81   Saner, E. (2014). RBS: the bank that likes to say Mx. *The Guardian.*

82   p.17 of the 2015 STA guidance for service users and employers document (Valentine 2015a) contains a useful list of gender-neutral language.

83   East Sussex County Council. (2014). Trans* inclusion schools toolkit. Mermaids UK.

84   Gender Identity Research and Education Society. (2010). Guidance on combating transphobic bullying in schools.

85   Gay, Lesbian & Straight Education Network (2017). How to support non-binary students. *GLSEN YouTube channel.*

86   Kibirige, H. (2018). *Creating a trans-inclusive school environment – response to Transgender Trend.* Stonewall.

87   Though still in use by some organisations, usually in a clinical context, the term 'transsexual' is now considered obsolete by many of the trans and genderqueer community. For a more thorough explanation of why, see the GLAAD media reference guide: Glossary of terms – Transgender.

88   Berenbaum, S. A. and Beltz, A. M. (2016). How early hormones shape gender development. *Current Opinion in Behavioral Sciences, 7,* 53–60.; Ehrhardt, A. and Meyer-Bahlburg, H. F. (1981). Effects of prenatal sex hormones on gender-related behavior. *Science, 211*(4488), 1312–1318.

89   Most up-to-date version: American Psychiatric Association. (2013). Diagnostic and Statistical Manual of Mental Disorders, 5th Edition. APA.

90   Tyrer, P. (2014). A comparison of DSM and ICD classifications of mental disorder. *Advances in Psychiatric Treatment, 20*(4), 280–285.

91   Rimes, K. A., Goodship, N., Ussher, G., Baker, D. and West, E. (2017). Non-binary and binary transgender youth: Comparison of mental health, self-harm, suicidality, substance use and victimization experiences. *International Journal of Transgenderism,* 18 September, 1–11.

92   Veale, J. F., Watson, R. J., Peter, T. and Saewyc, E. M. (2017). Mental health disparities among Canadian transgender youth. *Journal of Adolescent Health,* 60(1), 44–49.

93   Keuroghlian, A. S., Reisner, S. L., White, J. M. and Weiss, R. D. (2015). Substance use and treatment of substance use disorders in a community sample of transgender adults. *Drug and Alcohol Dependence, 152,* 139–146.

94   For a result to be statistically significant, the likelihood it occurred by chance (derived from a test called Statistical Hypothesis Testing) must be below a certain threshold, generally 5 per cent. Any result that is more than 5 per cent likely to have occurred by chance is generally disregarded or not taken as a firm basis on which to build a conclusion.

95   Elliott, I. (2016). *Poverty and Mental Health: A Review to Inform the Joseph Rowntree Foundation's Anti-Poverty Strategy.* London: Mental Health Foundation.

96   Meyer, I. H. (1995). Minority stress and mental health in gay men. *Journal of Health and Social Behavior, 36*(1), 38–56.

97 Lehavot, K. and Simoni, J. M. (2011). The impact of minority stress on mental health and substance use among sexual minority women. *Journal of Consulting and Clinical Psychology*, 79(2), 159–170.

98 Wong, C. F., Schrager, S. M., Holloway, I. W., Meyer, I. H. and Kipke, M. D. (2014). Minority stress experiences and psychological well-being: The impact of support from and connection to social networks within the Los Angeles House and Ball communities. *Prevention Science*, 15(1), 44–55.

99 Attitude Editors. Dexedrine: ADHD medication FAQ. *ADDitude*.

100 James, S. E., Herman, J. L., Rankin, S., Keisling, M., Mottet, L. and Anafi, M. (2016). *The Report of the 2015 U.S. Transgender Survey*. Washington, DC: National Center for Transgender Equality. p.103.

101 Connolly, M. D., Zervos, M. J., Barone, C. J., Johnson, C. C. and Joseph, C. L. (2016). The mental health of transgender youth: Advances in understanding. *Journal of Adolescent Health*, 59(5), 489–495.; Clark, T., Lucassen, M., Bullen, P., Denny, S., Fleming, T., Robinson, E. and Rossen, F. (2014). The health and well-being of transgender high school students: Results from the New Zealand Adolescent Health Survey (Youth'12). *Journal of Adolescent Health*, 55(1), 93–99.; Olson, J., Schrager, S., Belzer, M., Simons, L. and Clark, L. (2015). Baseline physiologic and psychosocial characteristics of transgender youth seeking care for gender dysphoria. *Journal of Adolescent Health*, 57(4), 374–380.

102 Effrig, J. C., Bieschke, K. J. and Locke, B. D. (2011). Examining victimization and psychological distress in transgender college students. *Journal of College Counseling*, 14, 143–157.

103 Seelman, K.L. (2016). Transgender adults' access to college bathrooms and housing and the relationship to suicidality. *Journal of Homosexuality*, 63(10), 1378–1399.

104 A mild mood disorder characterised by short periods of alternating mild depression and mania.

105 Royal College of Psychiatrists. (2013). Good practice guidelines for the assessment and treatment of adults with gender dysphoria. *RCPsych*. p.19.

106 Spack, N. P., Edwards-Leeper, L. and Feldman, H. A. (2012). Children and adolescents with gender identity disorder referred to a pediatric medical center. *Pediatrics* 129(3), 418–425. Also note that all the young people who were seen in the Boston service were reported to be in counselling, and the authors reference several studies to show that those 'who do not receive counselling have a higher risk of behavioural and emotional problems and psychiatric diagnoses' (p.422).

107 Drescher, J. (2015). Out of DSM: Depathologizing homosexuality. *Behavioral Sciences*, 5(4), 565–575.

108 Abby Jean. (2009). Ableist word profile: Hysterical. *Disabled Feminists.*; Smith, S. E. (2011). We're all mad here: Race, gender, and mental illness in pop culture. *Bitch Media.*; Smith, S. E. (2010). Psychiatrisation: A great way to silence troublesome women. *Meloukhia.*

109   Included in Herdt, G. (1993). *Third Sex, Third Gender: Beyond Sexual Dimorphism in Culture and History*. New York: Zone Books. pp.213–239.

110   The most up-to-date version is the DSM-5.

111   *Psychology Today*. (2018). Paraphilias. Italics mine.

112   For more information see this reproduction of the 'Gender Identity Disorder' section of the DSM-IV reproduced by Madeline Wyndzen on her website, All Mixed Up.

113   At www.nhs.uk/conditions/gender-dysphoria

114   Jellestad, L. *et al.* (2018). Quality of life in transitioned trans persons: A retrospective cross-sectional cohort study. *BioMed Research International*, 2018(3), 1–10; Murad, M. H., Elamin, M. B., Garcia, M. Z., Mullan, R. J., Murad, A., Erwin, P. J. and Montori, V. M. (2010). Hormonal therapy and sex reassignment: A systematic review and meta-analysis of quality of life and psychosocial outcomes. *Clinical Endocrinology, 72*, 214–231.; Drydakis, N. (2017). Trans employees, transitioning, and job satisfaction. *Journal of Vocational Behavior, 98*, 2017, 1–16.; Colizzi, M., Costa, R. and Todarello, O. (2014). Transsexual patients' psychiatric comorbidity and positive effect of cross-sex hormonal treatment on mental health: Results from a longitudinal study. Department of Medical Basic Sciences, Neuroscience and Sense Organs, University of Bari.; Newfield, E.; Hart, S., Dibble, S. and Kohler, L. (2006). Female-to-male transgender quality of life. *Quality of Life Research, 15(9)*, 1447–1457.

115   Meyer, I. H. (2003). Prejudice, social stress, and mental health in lesbian, gay, and bisexual populations: Conceptual issues and research evidence. *Psychological Bulletin, 129*, 674–697.

116   Byne, W., Bradley, S. J., Coleman, E. *et al.* (2012). Report of the American Psychiatric Association task force on treatment of gender identity disorder. *Archives of Sexual Behavior, 41*, 759.

117   Though, of course, not all of these people will identify specifically as transgender.

118   This is a document created by the Scottish Government as a guideline for medical practitioners with trans and genderqueer patients. Scottish Government (2012) Gender Reassignment Protocol. http://www.sehd.scot.nhs.uk/mels/CEL2012_26.pdf

119   I also occasionally encounter the term 'gender realignment', which is sometimes used by cisgender people to describe gender-affirming medical treatment. This term has never been standard within the trans community, and is inaccurate because the person's gender is not what is being 'realigned'.

120   More information on locating a GIC can be found at the end of this chapter.

121   Unger, C. A. (2016). Hormone therapy for transgender patients. *Translational Andrology and Urology, 5(6)*, 877–884.

122   World Professional Association for Transgender Health. (2012). *Standards of Care*, 7th Version. p.1.

123 As yet there are no reliable statistics as to what percentage of the nonbinary community pursues, or wants to pursue, a medical transition.

124 An identity that fluctuates between two points on a scale, as discussed in Chapter 4.

125 World Professional Association for Transgender Health. (2012). *Standards of Care*, 7th Version. p.64. Italics mine.

126 For a fuller explanation of this problem, see: O'Hara, M. E. (2015). 'Trans Broken Arm Syndrome' and the way our healthcare system fails trans people. *The Daily Dot*.: Payton, N. (2015). Feature: The dangers of trans broken arm syndrome. *Pink News*.

127 Italics mine.

128 Valentine, V. (2015b). *Non-binary people's experiences in the UK*. Scottish Trans Alliance. p.35.

129 For an excellent flowchart of the standard UK treatment path, from first contact with GP (or self-referral for Scottish patients specifically) to post-surgical ongoing hormone treatment, see p.2 of the Scottish Gender Reassignment Protocol, which can be accessed on the NHS Scotland website. Please note that this edition of the GRP was drawn up in 2012 and that some of the terminology, such as use of the word 'transsexual', is commonly considered out of date.

130 Policies, practices and institutions often differ between the United Kingdom and other countries, and I'll flag up some instances of this, especially when discussing my own early transition, but I have consciously chosen to focus on the situation in the UK for this edition.

131 World Professional Association for Transgender Health (2012). *Standards of Care*, 7th Version. p.57.

132 Specifically in Scotland at the Sandyford clinic in Glasgow.

133 In the US a referral usually comes from a doctor or a psychiatric professional who has determined that the patient experiences dysphoria and therefore qualifies for gender-affirming medical treatment. My therapist wrote me a letter that I showed to both my doctor, who did nothing, and an endo-crinologist who accepted my insurance, and who eventually started me on HRT. If my insurance company had refused to cover my treatment, as often happens – especially since most insurance companies in the States are privately run and operate to varying standards – I would have had to pay out of pocket. Indeed, while I was waiting for my claim to be processed I did just that, paying for one or two rounds of treatment of over $100 each out of my own meager part-time wages. Transgender people are notoriously one of the poorest demographics: for many a cost of even $100 per month may be prohibitive.

134 My interviewee, X, reckons that many genderqueer people who can do so may default to self-referral, assuming that their GP will not refer them, a decision that would severely limit the clinics they may be seen at.

135 Since I've already got a recurring prescription for hormones, prescribed by my GP in the US (obtaining this was a fraught process in and of itself), and since I'm aware of the high volume of patients and long wait times, I turned down the offer. I would have liked to have seen someone but could not in good conscience take an appointment away from another person who really needed it.

136 Thomson, R., Baker, J. and Arnot, J. (2018). *Health Care Needs Assessment of Gender Identity Services.* Scottish Public Health Network. ScotPHN. p.33.

137 p.90.

138 p.11.

139 NHS England. (2015). Recording and reporting referral to treatment (RTT) waiting times for consultant-led elective care: Frequently Asked Questions. p.13.

140 World Professional Association for Transgender Health. (2012). *Standards of Care*, 7th Version. p.34.

141 Royal College of Psychiatrists. (2013). *Good practice guidelines for the assessment and treatment of adults with gender dysphoria.* RCPsych. p.23.

142 Thomson, R., Baker, J. and Arnot, J. (2018). Health Care Needs Assessment of Gender Identity Services. *Scottish Public Health Network.* ScotPHN. p.80.

143 World Professional Association for Transgender Health (2012). *Standards of Care*, 7th Version. p.8.

144 Thomson, R., Baker, J. and Arnot, J. (2018). Health Care Needs Assessment of Gender Identity Services. *Scottish Public Health Network.* ScotPHN. p.79.

145 ATH Team (2015). Non binary survey: Preliminary results. *Action for Trans Health.* It's important to keep in mind that, though these results are shocking, the sample size of the survey is fairly low, and participants who have had negative experiences may have been slightly more likely to want to participate.

146 Valentine, V. (2015c). Non-binary people's experiences of using UK gender identity clinics. *Scottish Trans Alliance.* p.8.

147 Valentine, V. (2015b). Non-binary people's experiences in the UK. *Scottish Trans Alliance.* p.42.

148 Titman, N. (2014). How many people in the United Kingdom are nonbinary? *Practical Androgyny.*

149 For a more exhaustive discussion of the misconceptions surrounding trans healthcare, see Lambda Legal's page entitled 'Putting Transgender Health Care Myths on Trial' by Cole Thaler.

150 World Professional Association for Transgender Health. (2012). *Standards of Care*, 7th Version. pp.18, 19.

151 For example Pfafflin, F. (1993). Regrets After Sex Reassignment Surgery. *Journal of Psychology & Human Sexuality*, 5(4), 69–85.; Rehman, J., Lazer, S., Benet, A.E. *et al.* (1999) *Archives of Sexual Behavior*, 28(1), 71–89; Krege, S., Bex, A., Lümmen, G. and Rübben, H. (2001). Male-to-female transsexualism: A technique, results and long-term follow-up in 66 patients. *BJU International*, 88(4), 396–402.

152 The VICE article by Amber Roberts entitled 'Dispelling the myths around trans people detransitioning' includes some discussion of individual people's reasons for detransitioning.

153 Vincent, B. (2018). *Transgender Health: A Practitioner's Guide to Binary and Non-Binary Trans Patient Care*. London: Jessica Kingsley Publishers.

154 Mayo Clinic Staff. (2017). Precocious puberty: Diagnosis and treatment. *Mayo Clinic*.

155 Center for Young Women's Health. (2016). Health Guides. Endometriosis: Hormonal treatment overview.

156 Kim, E. Y. (2015). Long-term effects of gonadotropin-releasing hormone analogs in girls with central precocious puberty. *Korean Journal of Pediatrics*, 58(1), 1–7.

157 Surrey, E. S. and Hornstein, M. D. (2002). Prolonged GnRH agonist and add-back therapy for symptomatic endometriosis: Long-term follow-up. *Obstetrics and Gynecology*, 99(5), 709–719.

158 Eade, D. M., Telfer, M. M. and Tollit, M. A. (2018). Implementing a single-session nurse-led assessment clinic into a gender service. *Transgender Health*, 3(1), 43–46.

159 For a more detailed explanation of the origins, meaning and different contexts in which an informed consent model is used, see Hall, D. E., Prochazka, A. V. and Fink, A. S. (2012). Informed consent for clinical treatment. *Canadian Medical Association Journal*, 184(5), 533-540.

160 http://lothiansexualhealth.scot.nhs.uk/Services/GIC/FrequentlyAsked-Questions/Pages/default.aspx

161 Thomson, R., Baker, J. and Arnot, J. (2018). Health Care Needs Assessment of Gender Identity Services. *Scottish Public Health Network*. ScotPHN. p.31.

162 Rimes, K. A., Goodship, N., Ussher, G., Baker, D. and West, E. (2017). Non-binary and binary transgender youth: Comparison of mental health, self-harm, suicidality, substance use and victimization experiences. *International Journal of Transgenderism*, 18 September, 1–11.

163 Statistics focussing exclusively on genderqueer people are relatively hard to come by; this section will make use of statistics on both genderqueer and nonbinary people, and on trans people as a whole. I'll distinguish in the text in each case.

164 Bachmann, C. L. and Gooch, B. (2017). LGBT in Britain – Trans report. *Stonewall.* p.27.

165 Bachmann, C. L. and Gooch, B. (2017). LGBT in Britain – Trans report. *Stonewall.* Beginning p.9.

166 Valentine, V. (2015b). Non-binary people's experiences in the UK. *Scottish Trans Alliance.* p.68.

167 Gender Recognition Act. (2004). c. 7, original print PDF, p.3.

168 Gender Recognition Act. (2004). c. 7, p.1.

169 Mordaunt, P. (2018). Reform of the Gender Recognition Act – Government Consultation. *Ministry for Women and Equalities.*

170 Scotland has held a similar consultation, the results of which are still in the process of being analysed.

171 Equality Act. (2010). c. 15, Original print PDF, p.5. Italics mine.

172 Titman, N. (2014). How many people in the United Kingdom are nonbinary? *Practical Androgyny.*

173 Office for National Statistics. (2009). Trans data position paper. *ONS.*

Index

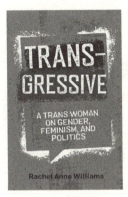

Transgressive
A Trans Woman on Gender, Feminism, and Politics
Rachel Anne Williams

272pp
Paperback
ISBN: 978 1 78592 647 1
eISBN: 978 1 78592 648 8

How do I know I am trans? Is trans feminism real feminism? What is there to say about trans women's male privilege?

This collection of insightful, pithy and passionately argued think pieces from a trans-feminist perspective explores issues surrounding gender, feminism and philosophy and challenges misconceptions about trans identities. The book confronts contentious debates in gender studies to alleviate ongoing tension between feminism and trans women. Split into six sections, this collection covers wider issues, as well as autobiographical experiences, designed to stimulate the reader and encourage them to actively participate.

Life Isn't Binary
On Being Both, Beyond, and In-Between
Meg-John Barker and Alex Iantaffi
Foreword by CN Lester

240pp
Paperback
ISBN: 978 1 78592 479 8
eISBN: 978 1 78450 864 7

'Barker and Iantaffi have written the book we all need for this moment in time.' – CN *Lester*

Much of society's thinking operates in a highly rigid and binary manner; something is good or bad, right or wrong, a success or a failure and so on. Challenging this limited way of thinking, this ground-breaking book looks at how non-binary methods of thought can be applied to all aspects of life, and offers new and greater ways of understanding ourselves and how we relate to others.

Using bisexual and non-binary gender experiences as a starting point, this book addresses the key issues with binary thinking regarding our relationships, bodies, emotions, wellbeing and our sense of identity and sets out a range of practices that may help us to think in more non-binary, both/and, or uncertain ways.

A truly original and insightful piece, this guide encourages reflection on how we view and understand the world we live in and how we all bend, blur or break society's binary codes.

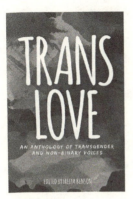

Trans Love
An Anthology of Transgender and Non-Binary Voices
Edited by Freiya Benson

296pp
Paperback
ISBN: 978 1 78592 432 3
eISBN: 978 1 78450 804 3

Selected as a 2019 LGBT Book of the Year by Dazed and Ms. Magazine

A ground-breaking anthology of writing on the topic of love, written by trans and non-binary people who share their thoughts, feelings and experiences of love in all its guises. The collection spans familial, romantic, spiritual and self-love as well as friendships and ally love, to provide a broad and honest understanding of how trans people navigate love and relationships, and what love means to them.

Reclaiming what love means to trans people, this book provokes conversations that are not reflected in what is presently written, moving the narrative around trans identities away from sensationalism. At once intimate and radical, and both humorous and poignant, this book is for anyone who has loved, who is in love, and who is looking for love.

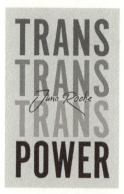

Trans Power
Own Your Gender
Juno Roche

256pp
Paperback
ISBN: 978 1 78775 019 7
eISBN: 978 1 78775 020 3

'All those layers of expectation that are thrust upon us; boy, masculine, femme, transgender, sexual, woman, real, are such a weight to carry round. I feel transgressive. I feel hybrid. I feel trans.'

In this radical and emotionally raw book, Juno Roche pushes the boundaries of trans representation by redefining 'trans' as an identity with its own power and strength, that goes beyond the gender binary.

Through intimate conversations with leading and influential figures in the trans community, such as Kate Bornstein, Travis Alabanza, Josephine Jones, Glamrou and E-J Scott, this book highlights the diversity of trans identities and experiences with regard to love, bodies, sex, race and class, and urges trans people – and the world at large – to embrace a 'trans' identity as something that offers empowerment and autonomy.

Powerfully written, and with humour and advice throughout, this book is essential reading for anyone interested in the future of gender and how we identify ourselves.